PELICAN BOOKS

A642

THE LIFE OF SHAKESPEARE

F. E. Halliday, was educated at
Giggleswick School and King's College, Cambridge.
He taught for many years at Cheltenham College,
where he was head of the English department. Soon
after the war he moved to St Ives in Cornwall to
devote his time to writing. He is married and has
one son and two grandchildren. He has published,
among other things, *Five Arts* (an essay in aesthet-
ics), *The Legend of the Rood*, *A History of Cornwall*,
Indifferent Honest (an autobiography), and a volume
of poems, *Meditation at Bolerium*. However, he is
best known for his books on Shakespeare. Apart
from *The Life of Shakespeare*, these include *Shakespeare and His Critics*, *The Poetry of Shakespeare's
Plays*, *The Cult of Shakespeare*, and *A Shakespeare
Companion*.

*Cover design by Romek Marber, incorporating a
C.O.I. photograph of Shakespeare's gravestone*

THE LIFE OF
SHAKESPEARE

F. E. HALLIDAY

PENGUIN BOOKS
BALTIMORE · MARYLAND

Penguin Books Ltd, Harmondsworth, Middlesex
U.S.A.: Penguin Books Inc., 3300 Clipper Mill Road, Baltimore 11 Md
AUSTRALIA: Penguin Books Pty Ltd, 762 Whitehorse Road,
Mitcham, Victoria

—

First published by Gerald Duckworth 1961
Published in Pelican Books 1963

—

Copyright © F. E. Halliday, 1961

—

Made and printed in Great Britain
by Cox and Wyman Ltd,
London, Reading, and Fakenham
Set in Monotype Garamond

TO

Phyllis and Ernan Forbes Dennis

MARVELLOUS

GOOD NEIGHBOURS

CONTENTS

PREFACE

*

ANY new Life of Shakespeare should begin with an apology, for after all the theme can scarcely be claimed as one yet unattempted, and any addition to the vast literature of Shakespeare needs some justification. My main defence, however, is that I was asked to write a Life of Shakespeare, and that this coincided with my wish to write one, to expand the short account I had already given in my *Shakespeare: A Pictorial Biography*,* the value of which, as the title suggests, is primarily dependent on its illustrations. Yet it is ten years since the last full-scale Life was written, and quite a lot of new biographical material has been unearthed in that time, thanks mainly to the inspired researches of Dr Leslie Hotson, my indebtedness to whom I here gratefully acknowledge. And again, I know of no Life that sets out to do quite what I have attempted.

The book is not a critical study: I have said comparatively little about Shakespeare's art, as I have written elsewhere about the plays and their poetry; nor is it a romance, a fanciful reconstruction of Shakespeare's 'lost years', or of events of which we can never hope to have more than a shadowy knowledge, or of amorous adventures with a certain dark lady celebrated in the *Sonnets*. Yet it is something more than a bare record of facts. Of these we have a fair number, strung like beads along the fifty years of his life, very thinly along the first half, but closer together after his arrival in London, the publication of his first works and his joining the company of players for which he was to write for the rest of his career. By using these clues, bibliographic and theatrical, as well as our knowledge of Elizabethan grammar-school education recently revealed by Professor

* Thames & Hudson, 1956.

T. W. Baldwin, by taking hints from the early traditions and from the plays and poems themselves, I have tried to fill in the gaps between the beads of biographical fact with as great a degree of probability as possible, yet without resorting to any extravagance of speculation.

It seems to me that too much emphasis has been placed on Shakespeare as an actor. Although he probably began his London career as a player, although nobody knew more about acting and stagecraft than he, by the time he was a full adventurer with the Chamberlain's with half a dozen plays to his credit, his fellows must have realized that he was far too valuable an asset to be wasted on the memorizing of long parts and unprofitable travel in the provinces; it would be only common sense, therefore, to reduce his acting to the playing of minor parts, and to leave him free to write plays for them while they went on their summer tours. 'He was wont to goe to his native Country once a yeare,' wrote Aubrey, and there can be little doubt, I think, that he normally spent a month or two every year in Stratford with his family, and after 1597, when he bought New Place, his visits would become more frequent and his summer sojourns even longer. Of course he would visit friends and stay at other houses in other parts of the country, but the normal rhythm of his life would be winter and spring in London, summer and autumn in Stratford. This would account for the fact that he never, as far as we know, had a residence in London and brought his family to live there. It is therefore possible, I think, to trace his movements with some degree of certainty during the most important years of his life.

A list of a few of the books to which any modern biographer must be indebted is given on pages 288–9. I am also grateful to Sir John Summerson for information from the Accounts of the Office of Works concerning preparation for plays at Court.

St Ives, Cornwall   F. E. H.
August 1960

INTRODUCTION

*

In January 1612, when Shakespeare was living in retirement at Stratford, Sir Thomas Bodley wrote to the curator of his recently founded library at Oxford:

I would yow had foreborne to catalogue our London bookes till I had bin priuie to your purpose. There are many idle bookes, & riffe raffes among them, which shall neuer com into the Librarie, & I feare me that litle, which yow haue done alreadie, will raise a scandal vpon it, when it shall be giuen out, by suche as would disgrace it, that I haue made vp a number, with Almanackes, plaies & proclamacions: of which I will haue none, but such as are singular.

Such 'idle bookes and riffe raffes' as plays were no material for a gentleman's library and, though the Folio of 1623 was too imposing a volume to be excluded, it was almost forty years before a Shakespeare quarto, the fifth edition of *Hamlet*, was considered 'singular' enough for the shelves of the Bodleian.

When, therefore, not long after Bodley's peevish letter, a retired actor and dramatist died in a remote provincial town, his passing was scarcely noticed. There were no obituaries and, though a monument was erected in the parish church giving his age and the date of his death, though commendatory verses were prefixed to the first collected edition of his plays, most of the contemporary allusions were to his work and not to the man. And even his work was rapidly declining in popularity, for the sophisticated Jacobean romances of Beaumont and Fletcher were more to the liking of the age than the comedies, histories, and tragedies of the Elizabethan. Then, when the Civil War broke out and the Puritans had their way, when the theatres were closed and remained closed for nearly two decades, not only the man but his work was almost forgotten. There was, however, one man who remembered, passionately remembered.

This was William Davenant, son of John and Jane Davenant of the Crown Tavern, Oxford, where Shakespeare was said to have lodged on his journeys between London and Stratford, and to have become so friendly with the couple that he agreed to stand godfather to their child. That was in 1606, when he was writing *King Lear* or *Macbeth*. Davenant, like the other William, was also a poet and dramatist, and when in 1637 he succeeded Ben Jonson as Poet Laureate he celebrated the occasion by writing an ode 'In Remembrance of Master William Shakespeare':

> Beware (delighted Poets!) when you sing
> To welcome Nature in the early Spring;
>   Your num'rous Feet not tread
> The Banks of Avon; for each Flowre
> (As it nere knew a Sunne or Showre)
>   Hangs there, the pensive head.

It was only when the theatres reopened, however, at the Restoration in 1660, that Davenant was able to achieve his ambition of producing his godfather's plays on the stage, and introducing them – in refined and polished versions, of course, as befitted the new enlightened age – to audiences, most of whose members had never before seen a play. As nearly all the old actors were dead, he had to train a new company, and was more than fortunate in finding a young man, Thomas Betterton, whom he infected with his own enthusiasm. Davenant died in 1668, but Betterton continued his work and such was 'his veneration for the memory of Shakespeare' that forty years later he 'made a journey into Warwickshire, on purpose to gather up what remains he could of a name for which he had so great a value'.

He did not find very much. Shakespeare had lain in Stratford church for almost a century; his daughters, his only grandchild, and his last surviving nephew had long been dead, and little remained but old wives' tales and tradition. And until scholars of the late eighteenth century began a serious search of the records in Stratford and London, gossip and tradition were to be the essence of all attempts at biography. It is of course impossible to say how far this early material is to be trusted; no doubt there is an element of truth in some of it, an element of fancy in most of it, and no doubt much of it is mere romance, the later the legend the more likely to be fable.

It is perhaps significant that the first sketch of Shakespeare's life appeared after the Restoration when Thomas Fuller's *Worthies of England* was published in 1662, for one cannot help wondering whether Fuller would have thought Shakespeare worthy of inclusion if it had not been for Davenant's revival of his plays on the London stage:

William Shakespeare was born at Stratford on Avon. . . . He was an eminent instance of the truth of that Rule, *Poeta non fit, sed nascitur,* one is not *made,* but *born* a Poet. Indeed his Learning was very little . . . so *nature* itself was all the *art* which was used upon him.

Many were the wit-combates betwixt him and Ben Johnson, which two I behold like a Spanish great Gallion and an English Man of War; Master Johnson (like the former) was built far higher in Learning; Solid but Slow in his performances. Shakespear, with the English-man of War, lesser in bulk, but lighter in sailing, could turn with all tides, tack about and take advantage of all winds, by the quickness of his Wit and Invention. He died *Anno Domini* 16 . . . and was buried at Stratford upon Avon, the Town of his Nativity.

This of course tells us nothing, being merely an elaboration of Jonson's line, 'And though thou hadst small Latin and less Greek', and his remark to Drummond of Hawthornden that 'Shakespeare wanted art', comments that were to bedevil Shakespearean criticism and biography until quite recent times.

Much more interesting is the memorandum made by the new vicar of Stratford, John Ward, in 1661–2: 'A letter to my brother, to see Mrs Queeny.' Judith Quiney, Shakespeare's younger daughter, was still alive, an old lady of seventy-seven. No wonder Ward added, 'Remember to peruse Shakespear's plays, and bee versd in them, that I may not be ignorant in that matter.' He is an admirable example of the educated man who knew nothing about Shakespeare at the time of the Restoration. Yet he seems to have picked up a little information from Judith before she died in 1662, and perhaps from Shakespeare's nephew, Thomas Hart, who, though he was only eleven when his uncle died, may still have been living at the Birthplace:

Shakespear had but 2 daughters, one whereof M. Hall, the physitian, married, and by her had one daughter, to wit, the Lady Bernard of Abbingdon. . . .

I have heard that Mr Shakespeare was a natural wit, without any art at all; he frequented the plays all his younger time, but in his elder days lived at Stratford: and supplied the stage with 2 plays every year, and for that had an allowance so large, that hee spent at the Rate of a 1,000*l* a year, as I have heard.

Shakespear, Drayton and Ben Johnson, had a merry meeting, and itt seems drank too hard, for Shakespear died of a feavour there contracted.

Twenty years later John Aubrey, the antiquary, tapped another source of information when he interviewed William Beeston, an old actor and the son of Christopher Beeston, who had acted with Shakespeare in the first production of Jonson's *Every Man in his Humour* as far back as 1598. Although Anthony Wood, for whom Aubrey worked, accused him of being so 'magotie-headed and exceedingly credulous' that he would stuff his letters with follies and misinformation, there is probably something more than this in his account:

Mr William Shakespear was borne at Stratford vpon Avon, in the County of Warwick; his father was a Butcher, & I have been told heretofore by some of the neighbours, that when he was a boy he exercised his father's Trade, but when he kill'd a Calfe, he would doe it in a *high style*, & make a Speech. There was at that time another Butcher's son in this Towne, that was held not at all inferior to him for a naturall witt, his acquaintance & coetanean, but dyed young. This Wm. being inclined naturally to Poetry and acting, came to London I guesse about 18 and was an Actor at one of the Play-houses and did exceedingly well: now B. Johnson was never a good Actor, but an excellent Instructor. He began early to make essayes at

Dramatique Poetry, which at that time was very lowe; and his Playes tooke well: He was a handsome well shap't man: very good company, and of a very readie and pleasant smooth Witt. The Humour of —the Constable in a Midsomernight's Dreame, he happened to take at Grendon in Bucks which is the roade from London to Stratford.... Ben Johnson and he did gather Humours of men dayly where ever they came. One time as he was at the Tavern at Stratford super Avon, one Combes an old rich Usurer was to be buryed, he makes there this extemporary Epitaph

> Ten in the Hundred the Devill allowes
> But *Combes* will have twelve, he sweares & vowes:
> If any one askes who lies in the Tombe:
> Hoh! quoth the Devill, 'Tis my John o' Combe.

He was wont to goe to his native Country once a yeare. I thinke I have been told that he left 2 or 300*li* per annum there and therabout: to a sister. I have heard Sr Wm. Davenant and Mr Thomas Shadwell ... say, that he had a most prodigious Witt, and did admire his naturall parts beyond all other Dramaticall writers ... Though as Ben: Johnson sayes of him, that he had but little Latine and lesse Greek, He understood Latine pretty well: for he had been in his younger yeares a Schoolmaster in the Countrey. He was not a company keeper, lived in Shoreditch, wouldnt be debauched, & if invited to writ; he was in paine.

Aubrey had a delicate ear for scandal, and appears to have been the first to record the story that William Davenant was something more than the mere godson of William Shakespeare:

Sr William Davenant Knight Poet Laureate was born in — street in the City of Oxford, at the Crowne Taverne. His father was John Davenant a Vintner there, a very grave and discreet Citizen: his mother was a very beautifull woman, & of a very good witt and of conversation extremely agreable ... Mr William Shakespeare was wont to go into Warwickshire once a yeare, and did commonly in his journey lye at this house in Oxon: where he was exceedingly respected. I have heard parson Robert Davenant say that Mr W Shakespeare here gave him a hundred kisses. Now Sr. Wm would sometimes when he was pleasant over a glasse of wine with his most intimate friends ... say, that it seemed to him that he writt with the very spirit that Shakespeare, and was seemed contentended enough to be thought his Son: he would tell them the story as above.

In the spring of 1693 a Mr Dowdall wrote an account of his visit to Stratford. After quoting the epitaph on Shakespeare's grave, 'made by himselfe', he added:

the clarke that shew'd me this Church is aboue 80 yrs old; he says that this Shakespear was formerly in this Towne bound apprentice to a butcher; but that he Run from his master to London, and there was Recd Into the Playhouse as a servicure, and by this meanes had an oppertunity to be what he afterwards prov'd.

The clerk was William Castle, sexton of Stratford, whose age and insubordination made him something of a problem to the local authorities. He had been born in 1614, two years before Shakespeare's death, and on the strength of this intimacy appointed himself the poet's official biographer. No doubt Aubrey got the earlier form of the butcher story from him, and we seem to hear the old man's grisly fancy in Charles Gildon's anecdote, that he had been 'assured' that Shakespeare wrote the ghost scene in *Hamlet* 'in a Charnel House in the midst of the Night', presumably the charnel house attached to the church, which Castle delighted to show his victims.

The first account of the deer-stealing episode, and the only reference to Shakepeare's religion, are in a manuscript note made by Richard Davies in about 1700, when he was rector of the Cotswold village of Sapperton, near Cirencester:

William Shakespeare. much given to all unluckinesse in stealing venison & Rabbits particularly from Sr Lucy who had him oft whipt & sometimes Imprisoned & at last made Him fly his Native Country to his great Advancemt. but His reveng was so great that he is his Justice Clodpate and calls him a great man & yt in allusion to his name bore three lowses rampant for his Arms . . . He dyed a papist.

It was now that Betterton made his celebrated 'journey into Warwickshire', much to the satisfaction of the dramatist Nicholas Rowe, then engaged in editing the plays of Shakes-

speare, which he published in 1709. To these he prefixed the
first real Life, compounded of the fragments of seventeenth-
century tradition and the information brought home by Betterton, which he acknowledged to be 'the most considerable part
of the Passages relating to his Life'. They did not amount to
much, though apparently Betterton had done some genuine
research and consulted the Stratford parish register, for here is
the first mention of John Shakespeare and his family (though
Betterton bungled their number, and the sex and precedence of
William's children), of the Quineys and the Hathaways. The
Southampton story, however, was an old one, which he remembered Davenant telling him some forty years before. Rowe's
Life remained the standard biography of the eighteenth century,
popularizing and perpetuating the traditions, and the biographical prefaces of the editors of the age, of Pope, Johnson,
Steevens, are little more than reprints or variations on the
theme of Rowe.

He was the son of Mr John Shakespear, and was Born at Stratford
upon Avon, in Warwickshire, in April 1564. His Family, as appears
by the Register and Publick Writings relating to that Town, were of
good Figure and Fashion there, and are mention'd as Gentlemen.
His Father, who was a considerable Dealer in Wool, had so large a
Family, ten Children in all, that tho' he was his eldest Son, he could
give him no better Education than his own Employment. He had
bred him, 'tis true, for some time at a Free-school, where 'tis probable
he acquir'd that little Latin he was Master of: But the narrowness of
his Circumstances, and the want of his assistance at Home, forc'd his
Father to withdraw him from thence, and unhappily prevented his
further Proficiency in that Language. . . .
Upon his leaving School, he seems to have given intirely into
that way of Living which his Father propos'd to him; and in order to
settle in the World after a Family manner, he thought fit to marry
while he was yet very young. His Wife was the daughter of one
Hathaway, said to have been a substantial Yeoman in the Neighbourhood of Stratford. In this kind of Settlement he continu'd for some
time, 'till an Extravagance that he was guilty of, forc'd him both out of
his Country and that way of Living which he had taken up; and tho'
it seem'd at first to be a Blemish upon his good Manners, and a

Misfortune to him, yet it afterwards happily prov'd the occasion of exerting one of the greatest Genius's that ever was known to Dramatick Poetry. He had, by a Misfortune common enough to young Fellows, fallen into ill Company; and amongst them, some that made a frequent practice of Deerstealing, engag'd him with them more than once in robbing a Park that belong'd to Sir Thomas Lucy of Cherlecot, near Stratford. For this he was prosecuted by that Gentleman, as he thought, somewhat too severely; and in order to revenge that ill Usage, he made a Ballad upon him. And tho' this, probably the first Essay of his Poetry, be lost, yet it is said to have been so very bitter, that it redoubled the Prosecution against him to that degree, that he was oblig'd to leave his Business and Family in Warwickshire, for some time, and shelter himself in London.

It is at this Time, and upon this Accident, that he is said to have made his first Acquaintance with the Play-house. He was receiv'd into the Company then in being, at first in a very mean Rank; but his admirable Wit, and the natural Turn of it to the Stage, soon distinguish'd him, if not as an extraordinary Actor, yet as an excellent Writer. His Name is Printed, as the Custom was in those Times, amongst those of the other Players, before some old Plays, but without any particular Account of what sort of Parts he used to play; and tho' I have inquir'd, I could never meet with any further Account of him this way, than that the top of his Performance was the Ghost in his own *Hamlet*. . . .

Besides the advantages of his Wit, he was in himself a goodnatur'd Man, of great sweetness in his Manners, and a most agreeable Companion; so that it is no wonder if with so many good Qualities he made himself acquainted with the best Conversations of those Times. Queen Elizabeth had several of his Plays Acted before her, and without doubt gave him many gracious Marks of her Favour. . . . She was so well pleas'd with that admirable Character of Falstaff, in the two Parts of Henry the Fourth, that she commanded him to continue it for one Play more, and to show him in Love. This is said to be the Occasion of his Writing *The Merry Wives of Windsor*. . . .

What Grace soever the Queen confer'd upon him, it was not to her only he ow'd the Fortune which the Reputation of his Wit made. He had the honour to meet with many great and uncommon Marks of Favour and Friendship from the Earl of Southampton, famous in the Histories of that Time for his Friendship to the unfortunate Earl of Essex. It was to that Noble Lord that he Dedicated his *Venus* and

Adonis, the only Piece of his Poetry which he ever publish'd himself, tho' many of his Plays were surrepticiously and lamely Printed in his Life-time. There is one instance so singular in the Magnificence of this Patron of Shakespear's, that if I had not been assur'd that the story was handed down by Sir William D'Avenant, who was probably very well acquainted with his Affairs, I should not have ventur'd to have inserted, that my Lord Southampton, at one time, gave him a thousand Pounds, to enable him to go through with a Purchase which he heard he had a mind to. A Bounty very great, and very rare at any time.

What particular Habitude or Friendships he contracted with private Men, I have not been able to learn, more than that every one who had a true Taste of Merit, and could distinguish Men, had generally a just Value and Esteem for him. His exceeding Candour and good Nature must certainly have inclin'd all the gentler Part of the World to love him, as the power of his Wit oblig'd the Men of the most delicate Knowledge and polite Learning to admire him. . . .

His Acquaintance with Ben Johnson began with a remarkable piece of Humanity and good Nature; Mr Johnson, who was at that Time altogether unknown to the World, had offer'd one of his Plays to the Players, in order to have it Acted; and the Persons into whose hands it was put, after having turn'd it carelessly and superciliously over, were just upon returning it to him with an ill-natur'd Answer, that it would be of no service to their Company, when Shakespear luckily cast his Eye upon it, and found something so well in it as to recommend Mr Johnson and his Writings to the Publick. After this they were profess'd Friends; tho' I don't know whether the other ever made him an equal return of Gentleness and Sincerity. . . .

Falstaff is allow'd by every body to be a Master-piece: the Character is always well-sustain'd, tho' drawn out into the length of three Plays. . . . Amongst other Extravagances, in *The Merry Wives of Windsor,* he has made him a Deer-stealer, that he might at the same time remember his Warwickshire Prosecutor, under the Name of Justice Shallow; he has given him very near the same Coat of Arms which Dugdale, in his Antiquities of that County, describes for a Family there, and makes the Welsh Parson descant very pleasantly upon 'em. . . .

The latter Part of his Life was spent, as all Men of good Sense will wish theirs may be, in Ease, Retirement, and the Conversation of his Friends. He had the good Fortune to gather an Estate equal to his Occasion, and, in that, to his Wish; and is said to have spent some

Years before his Death at his native Stratford. His pleasurable Wit, and good Nature, engag'd him in the Acquaintance, and entitled him to the Friendship of the Gentlemen of the Neighbourhood. Amongst them, it is a Story almost still remember'd in that Country, that he had a particular Intimacy with Mr Combe, an old Gentleman noted thereabouts for his Wealth and Usury. ....

He Dy'd in the 53rd Year of his Age, and was bury'd on the North side of the Chancel, in the Great Church at Stratford, where a Monument is plac'd in the Wall. ...

He had three Daughters, of which two liv'd to be marry'd; Judith, the Elder, to one Mr Thomas Quiney, by whom she had three Sons, who all dy'd without Children; and Susannah, who was his Favourite, to Dr John Hall, a Physician of good Reputation in that Country. She left one Child only, a Daughter, who was marry'd first to Thomas Nash, Esq; and afterwards to Sir John Bernard of Abington, but dy'd likewise without Issue.

This is what I could learn of any Note, either relating to himself or Family: The Character of the man is best seen in his Writings.

The Shakespeare legend was now fairly launched, the success story of a scarcely educated boy who got into a scrape and ran away to London, where he made a fortune before retiring to his native town, 'the Homer', as Dryden put it, 'or father of our dramatic poets'. The story had the fascination of a fairy tale, a character with whom most people could identify themselves, and before long pilgrims began to arrive in Stratford to see the house where he was born, the house where he died, the church where he was buried, and to pick up any further crumbs of biographical information. It was astonishing how much there was to be found, despite the criminal negligence of the Warwick baker who, according to one authority, lost two large chests of the Great Man's papers in the disastrous conflagration of 1694. Yet it was scarcely surprising that another epitaph on a member of the Combe family should turn up in Stratford, and it was only to be expected that the bitter ballad on Sir Thomas Lucy would be discovered; it proved to be in a chest of drawers in Shottery. Then it was remembered that one of Shakespeare's younger brothers, as a very old man, used to delight in telling how he once went to London to see Will play the part of Adam in *As You Like It*. And again there was the story of how the poet had been forced to spend the night under a crab tree in a hedge after a drinking bout with the topers of Bidford. Even Dr Johnson was able to add an anecdote to the *Life* of Rowe, which he reprinted in his edition of Shakespeare:

When Shakespear fled to London from the terror of a criminal prosecution, his first expedient was to wait at the door of the playhouse, and hold the horses of those that had no servants, that they might be ready again after the performance. In this office he became so conspicuous for his care and readiness, that in a short time every man as he alighted called for Will Shakespear, and scarcely any other waiter was trusted with a horse while Will Shakespear could be had. This was the first dawn of better fortune. Shakespear, finding more horses put into his hand than he could hold, hired boys to wait under his inspection, who when Will Shakespear was summoned, were immediately to present themselves, *I am Shakespear's boy, Sir*. In time Shakespear found higher employment, but as long as the practice of riding to the play-house continued, the waiters that held the horses retained the appellation of *Shakespear's Boys*.

It was said to be a story that Davenant told Betterton, who told Rowe, who told Pope, who told Dr Newton, who told a gentleman, who told Johnson's secretary, who told the Great Lexicographer himself.

The demand for anecdotes rose to boom proportions after the Shakespeare Jubilee organized by Garrick at Stratford in 1769, and fortunately there was no falling off in supply, thanks largely to William Castle's successor, John Jordan, a wheelwright with a passion for poetry and antiquity. It was Jordan who acted as guide to the artist Samuel Ireland and his son William-Henry in 1793, and saw to it that they returned to London with a fund of stories and an adequate supply of relics: knick-knacks made from the mulberry tree that the poet had planted, a sliver from the crab tree under which he had slept, the purse that he had given to Anne Hathaway, and the very chair on which he had courted her. But young William-Henry Ireland improved on Jordan. In London he found the long-lost Shakespeare papers, a letter to John Heminge, another to the

Earl of Southampton, another to Anna Hatherrewaye, the manuscript of *King Lear*, and finally a play that the scholars had never heard of, the tragedy of *Vortigern*.

The Ireland forgeries were the inevitable culmination of the frenzied demand for romantic biography, and if William-Henry had not found the Shakespeare papers it would not have been long before someone else did. The fraud was exposed by the Irish barrister, Edmond Malone, and with him a new age of Shakespeare scholarship began, an age of austere research instead of picturesque gossip, of record instead of hearsay. Rowe's *Life* had been a matter of some twenty or thirty pages. Malone's, based on his knowledge of Elizabethan theatrical records, was more than ten times as long, and though he added little new strictly biographical material he did at least disentangle fact from fiction. His work was continued in the nineteenth century by J. O. Halliwell-Phillipps, who published the Stratford records and extant legal documents relating to Shakespeare, and before he died in 1889 his *Outlines of the Life of Shakespeare* had grown into a volume of almost a thousand pages. Unfortunately he perpetuated the romantic concept of the uneducated peasant:

Removed prematurely from school [he wrote], residing with illiterate relatives in a bookless neighbourhood, thrown into the midst of occupations adverse to scholastic progress, it is difficult to believe that when he first left Stratford he was not all but destitute of polished accomplishments.

It was certainly difficult to reconcile this Shakespeare with the man who was, according to the adulatory criticism of the age, as great a philosopher and scholar as dramatist and poet, and the result was the fantasies of those who found the real author of the plays in Francis Bacon, Viscount St Albans, or the Earl of Oxford, or the Earl of Derby, or any other peer who took their fancy. The disciples of these quaint creeds still base their arguments on the antiquated scholarship of the Victorians, but there is no reason to suppose that Shakespeare was ill-educated, though he was certainly not the omniscient sage or profound and original thinker that they would have had him be. Much has been discovered since their day, and with the help of these more recent revelations it is now possible to sketch something more than an outline of the half century of Shakespeare's life.

CHAPTER I

1564–80

THE SCHOOLBOY

*

In the middle of the sixteenth century, towards the end of the reign of Henry VIII, Robert Arden, a gentleman farmer, was living at Wilmcote, a hamlet three miles north-west of Stratford. He was a kinsman, possibly the cousin, of Thomas Arden, the head of an old and distinguished Warwickshire family, who lived at Park Hall near the little town of Birmingham. Robert Arden's home may have been the long, half-timbered, sixteenth-century farmhouse, now called 'Mary Arden's House', with a high-pitched roof and dormer windows, the back of which opened on to a yard flanked by barns, byres, and a great stone dovecote. In this pleasant and modest house he brought up his family of eight daughters, and after the death of his first wife married Agnes Hill, a widow with children of her own, and sister of Alexander Webbe of the neighbouring village of Bearley. That was in 1548, by which time most of his daughters were married, and only Joyce, Alice, and the youngest, Mary, still merely a child, remained at home.

In addition to his property at Wilmcote, Robert owned two other estates at Snitterfield, close to the highroad between Stratford and Warwick. The tenant of one of these was Richard Shakespeare, who farmed the land with the help of his two young sons, John and Henry. Robert Arden and his tenant were neighbours of long standing, well known to each other, and as there were only three miles of easy road between their houses young John Shakespeare must often have gone over to Wilmcote on his father's business, where he would meet the members of the Arden household. But John was ambitious, Stratford and trade were more attractive than Snitterfield and the plough, and so, leaving his father and younger brother to

25

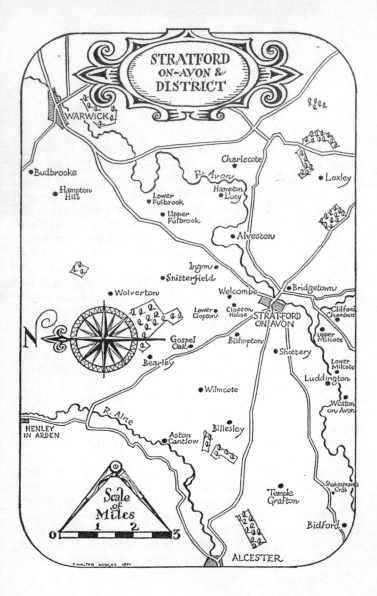

STRATFORD
ON~AVON &
DISTRICT

WARWICK

Budbrooke

Hampton
Hill

Charlecote

R. Avon

Hampton
Lucy

Loxley

Lower
Fulbrook

Upper
Fulbrook

Alveston

Ingon

Snitterfield

Welcombe

Bridgetown

Wolverton

Lower
Clopton

Clopton
House

STRATFORD
ON AVON

Clifford
Chambers

Gospel
Oak

Bishopton

Shottery

Upper
Milcote

Lower
Milcote

Bearley

Luddington

Wilmcote

Weston
on Avon

R. Alne

Billesley

HENLEY
IN ARDEN

Aston
Cantlow

Scale
of
Miles

0   1   2   3

Temple
Grafton

Shakespeare's
Crab

Bidford

E WALTER HODGES 1951

ALCESTER

manage the farm, he found a master glover who would take him as an apprentice, and moved into the town. The period of his apprenticeship was to coincide with important events in its history.

Stratford was a compact medieval market town of some two thousand inhabitants, who lived in rows of half-timbered houses, fronted by broad streets and backed by orchards and gardens. Its eastern side bordered the River Avon, across which, some sixty years before, Sir Hugh Clopton had built the splendid many-arched bridge that carried the highway from London and Oxford towards Alcester and Henley-in-Arden. It was a vital link, for before this time there was only a frail wooden bridge and no firm passage across the marshy meadows at the approach to the town, so that people refused to go to Stratford when the Avon was up, as so often it was. Now, however, the traveller who crossed the bridge rode safely along a stone causeway, to the left of which was the Bankcroft, a common pasture for cattle, sheep, and pigs, with a strip, the Butt Close, where the townsmen practised their archery. The causeway ran into Bridge Street, at the entrance to which, strategically placed to catch the traveller, were the two chief inns, the Bear on one side, the Swan on the other. Bridge Street was so broad that down the middle was a row of houses that stretched as far as the High Cross, a wattle and plaster hut supported by four wooden pillars and topped by a turret with a clock. It was here that the glovers had their stalls on market day, and here was the whipping-post for rogues, sturdy beggars, and prostitutes, a sight to be recalled by Shakespeare when writing *The Taming of the Shrew*: 'I had as lief be whipped,' says Gremio, 'at the High Cross every morning.' From this important centre of the town's activities Henley Street forked right towards Henley-in-Arden, while the Alcester road ran straight on through Wood Street, encumbered with piles of timber, to Rother Market, where cattle and hides were sold and salt-wains unloaded, and so into the open country.

The other main street cut through the town from north to south, running parallel to the river from the High Cross to New

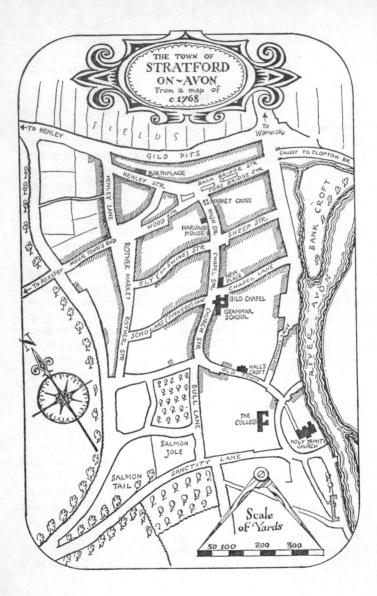

THE TOWN OF
STRATFORD
ON~AVON
From a map of
c.1768

← TO HENLEY

FIELDS

TO Warwick →

GILD PITS

CAUSEY TO CLOPTON BR.

HENLEY STR.

BIRTHPLACE

BACK BRIDGE STR.

FORE BRIDGE STR.

MARKET CROSS

BANK CROFT

HENLEY LANE

WOOD STR.

HARVARD HOUSE

HIGH STR.

SHEEP STR.

MOOR TOWN'S END

ROTHER MARKET

ELY (or SWINE) STR.

CHAPEL STR.

NEW PLACE

CHAPEL LANE

← To Alcester

CHAPEL LANE

ROTHER STR.

SCHOLARS (TINKERS) LANE

CHURCH STR.

GILD CHAPEL

GRAMMAR SCHOOL

RIVER AVON

SOUTHERN'S LANE

HALL'S CROFT

OLD TOWN

THE COLLEGE

BULL LANE

SALMON JOLE

SANCTITY LANE

SALMON TAIL

HOLY TRINITY CHURCH

Scale
of Yards

50 100   200   300

Place, the fine house erected by Sir Hugh Clopton, who also rebuilt, in the airy, late Perpendicular style, the Gild Chapel just across the way. When John Leland visited Stratford in 1540 he called New Place 'a praty house of bricke and timbre', but a few years later the Cloptons let it and John Shakespeare saw it falling sadly into disrepair, for in 1549 it was described as being 'in great ruyne and decay'. Adjoining the Gild Chapel was the Gild Hall, a long, half-timbered building, and the school, beyond which the road bent past the College that housed the chantry priests towards the Avon, on the banks of which stood the great grey church of the Holy Trinity, its tower (there was no spire in Shakespeare's day) mirrored in the river. With its orchards and gardens, willows, ashes, and elms, Stratford must have been one of the most beautiful towns of Tudor England.

Since Saxon times the lords of the manor of Stratford had been the bishops of Worcester, though for almost four centuries the townsmen had enjoyed some measure of self-government, and the charitable religious Gild of the Holy Cross, founded in the thirteenth century, had become an additional organ of government, caring for the poor and maintaining an almshouse as well as a free school. But when in 1547 the boy Edward VI succeeded his father as king, all this was changed, for one of the first acts of the fanatically Protestant government was to suppress religious gilds and appropriate their funds. The Stratford Gild and popish College of chantry priests were dissolved, and the bishops of Worcester deprived of their manor of Stratford, which remained a possession of the Crown until 1562, when Elizabeth granted it to one of her favourites, Ambrose Dudley, Earl of Warwick. As compensation the burgesses were given a charter of incorporation: there was to be a bailiff, fourteen aldermen, and fourteen capital burgesses, the bailiff and one alderman acting as justices of the peace, and the bailiff presiding over the Court of Record with jurisdiction in civil cases up to £30. Some at least of the Gild property was transferred to the Corporation, though out of it they had to maintain the almshouses and pay the schoolmaster and vicar, appointed by the

lord of the manor, who might also object to the bailiff elected
by the Council, for the bailiff, unlike a mayor, was in theory the
servant of the lord of the manor. Finally, the town was licensed
to hold a weekly market and two annual fairs, valuable sources
of income, since all outsiders had to pay for the privilege of
setting up their stalls. Although the Catholics bitterly resented
this high-handed dissolution of their institutions, the Protestants were more than satisfied, for they had the best of both
worlds, or at least of this world; not only was the money that
would have gone to pay priests to pray for the souls of the dead
diverted to more immediately profitable and mundane ends,
but they were now masters of their own affairs.

By the time this phase of the Protestant revolution was over
John Shakespeare was out of his apprenticeship. What he
thought about it we do not know, but as he was a pushing
young man and the future seemed to lie with Protestantism, the
creed of those who wanted to get on in this world, of those
whom Henry VIII had bribed by allowing them to share on
easy terms in the plunder of the Church, it is probable that he
approved, particularly as the new town charter offered him another means of advancement; for if he prospered in business
there was no reason why he should not become one of the fourteen aldermen, even in course of time rise to the rank of bailiff,
principal burgess of the town. The first thing was to make a
success of his business. As a glover he was a freeman of the
Mystery of Glovers, Whittawers and Collarmakers, one of the
principal trade gilds in Stratford, and seems to have combined
the crafts of glovemaker and whittawer, one who cured and
whitened the skins, with dealing in other local products, including timber and wool. His house and shop were in Henley Street,
and in the spring of 1552 he and his neighbour, Adrian Quiney,
were fined a shilling each for making a rubbish dump in that
thoroughfare, a convenient way of disposing of refuse, but in-
convenient to traffic and clean contrary to regulations, for even
in those days rubbish was recognized as a source of the almost
annual scourge of plague, and there was an official dump on the
outskirts of the town.

His business proved so prosperous that four years later, having money to invest, he bought two houses, one in Greenhill Street, the other in Henley Street, probably the one in which he was living as tenant, the eastern half of the block that came to be known as the 'Birthplace'. He was now a man of property, assumed to be able and discreet, as no doubt he was, and because of his substance, ability, and discretion he was elected one of the two tasters of the borough, inspectors of bread and ale, responsible for seeing that bakers and brewers did not contravene the regulations about quality and price. He had his feet on the first rung of civic promotion.

Hard as he worked, however, all his time was not given up to business and borough affairs. Wilmcote was only three miles from Stratford, and he must have spent much of his leisure in walking or riding up the Henley road to Gospel Oak and the track that forked left to the hamlet where Mary Arden lived. Her father had no objection to the wooing of his youngest daughter by the rising young glover whom he had known since he was born, some twenty-five years before, and apparently settled part of his Wilmcote property upon her, and when he made his will in November 1556 left her all his land 'in Willmecote cawlidc Asbyes, and the crop apone the grounde sowne and tyllide as hitt is, and vj*li.* xiij*s.* iiij*d.* of money', with a share in a reversionary interest of his Snitterfield estate. He had every confidence in Mary, and appointed her joint executrix with his other unmarried daughter, Alice, charging her to keep the peace between her sister and stepmother, who were to share, 'quyetlye to ynyoye', his house at Wilmcote. Evidently Mary Arden was a capable young woman.

Robert Arden died soon after making his will, and in the following year John Shakespeare married Mary, presumably in the church at Aston Cantlow, within which parish Wilmcote lay, and carried her back to Henley Street. It was a good match for the young man, for not only was Mary a member of the family that had been lords of Warwick before the Conquest, and an heiress in a small way, but she was a wife who would be able to help and advise an energetic and ambitious husband. Their first child, Joan, was born in September 1558, but died young, possibly soon after her christening. This was the month in which John was elected one of the four constables of Stratford, in command of the watch and responsible for the peace of the borough, an office that would often keep him out in the streets at night. It was the second rung of the municipal ladder. Two months later the Catholic Queen Mary died and was succeeded by her half-sister, Elizabeth, a woman of twenty-six.

It was a formidable task that confronted the young Queen after the excesses of her father Henry VIII, of the Protestant government of her half-brother Edward VI and the Catholic reaction under Mary. The country was bewildered by the changes and divided against itself, half Catholic, half Protestant, the treasury was on the verge of bankruptcy, while the collapse of the medieval social structure had produced the new phenomena of widespread unemployment, destitution, and vagrancy. However, to her Tudor courage and tenacity Elizabeth added a formidably masculine intelligence, an altogether feminine intuition and a genius for picking the right men to carry out her policy. As the Secretary of her Privy Council and virtual Prime Minister she chose William Cecil, later Lord Burghley, a man of immense ability and absolutely devoted to the mistress whom he was to help to guide through the labyrinthine intricacies of her perilous and splendid reign. As her Archbishop of Canterbury she selected the moderate Protestant Matthew Parker, who carried through a religious settlement acceptable to all but extremists, fanatical Catholics on the one hand, fanatical Puritans on the other. As her financial adviser she took Sir Thomas Gresham, who restored the debased currency, doubled the value of English money on the foreign exchange and in the course of the next twenty years prepared the country's finances for the almost inevitable war with Spain. Within a few years Elizabeth was on the way to becoming almost a legendary figure, Gloriana, the symbol of England, ruling a people already dimly conscious of their destiny and united as never before. It was just as well, for her Catholic enemies abroad maintained that she was an illegitimate child, and that the rightful heir to the English throne was her young cousin Mary Stuart, Queen of Scotland. And the Catholic Mary was indeed incontestably her heir if Elizabeth were to die childless. It was more than important, therefore, that she should marry, but though she flirted with Robert Dudley, gave him Kenilworth Castle, and created him Earl of Leicester, she still remained dangerously and distressingly a virgin queen.

These changes had their effect on Stratford. The Catholic vicar was removed and replaced by the Protestant John Bretchgirdle, who reintroduced the Prayer Book of Edward VI and reorganized the services according to the rules laid down by Elizabeth. No doubt there were many Catholics who easily accommodated themselves to the new dispensation, but there were zealots like the Cloptons, Reynoldses, and Lanes who refused to attend church and preferred to pay the monthly fine for their recusancy. They were in a minority, however, for Stratford was becoming increasingly Protestant, and John Shakespeare's progress suggests that he supported the new order.

In 1559 he was an affecror, or assessor of fines, and in 1561 one of the two chamberlains in charge of the Corporation's property and finances of the borough, an office that he held for four years. Although he was not directly responsible, it was during his tenure that the medieval wall paintings in the Gild Chapel were defaced, some of them mutilated, others merely whitewashed: the Last Judgement, the murder of Becket, and the Invention of the Cross. Meanwhile, in the winter of 1560, his father had died, leaving an estate of almost £40, equal to some £1,200 today, for early Elizabethan money was worth almost thirty times as much as ours. He administered the estate, in the legal documents of which he is called *agricola*, or husbandman, of Snitterfield, so perhaps he still had an interest in his father's farm. Two years later a second child was born, again a daughter, Margaret, but she lived little longer than her sister, and was buried, aged five months, at the end of April 1563.

Exactly a year later, on 26 April 1564, John Bretchgirdle christened their third child, this time a boy, William, and his baptism was entered in the parish register: 'Gulielmus filius Johannes Shakspere'. Tradition has it that he was born on Sunday, the 23rd, St George's Day, and no day could have been more appropriate for the birth of England's greatest poet than that of England's patron saint. It may have been so, a happy coincidence, though it is perhaps significant that his granddaughter was to choose 22 April, not the 23rd, as the day of her wedding. The previous year, 1563, had been one of severe plague, and it is possible that the baby Margaret had been one of the victims. If so, John and Mary Shakespeare would look forward to the plague-breeding summer with misgiving. Their fears were justified. On 11 July Bretchgirdle buried Oliver Gunn, a weaver's apprentice, and after the entry in the register wrote the ominous words, '*hic incipit pestis*', 'here begins the plague'. In the first half of the year there had been twenty-two burials, in the second half there were to be two hundred and thirty-seven. Whole families perished: Christopher Smith the glover, his three daughters and maidservant; William Perrott, his wife, son, and four daughters; and in Henley Street, close to the Shakespeares, Roger Greene the miller lost his two sons. It would have been folly for Mary not to take her baby into the country, at least as far as Wilmcote, but John stayed at his post, and in the following year was elected an alderman. He was now 'Master Shakespeare', with a special seat in church, where he wore, as on all official occasions, a sober gown of black cloth trimmed with fur; there were no scarlet gowns in Stratford – the colour was too suggestive of 'the Papistry'.

It may well have been in the next year that the little boy caught his first glimpse of the Queen. It was Elizabeth's custom every summer to take a holiday in the form of a progress, when, preceded by scores of carts bearing her baggage, attended by members of her Household and followed by another train of carts with the royal furnishings, she rode on horseback or in her coach to visit those great houses of her subjects which lay within reach of her capital. By the middle of August 1566 she was at Coventry, where the gildsmen gave a special performance of their miracle plays, and on the 19th she reached Kenilworth.

There she spent two days with her favourite, the Earl of Leicester, before moving on to visit his brother, Ambrose Dudley, Earl of Warwick, and so to Charlecote to stay with Thomas Lucy, a young man of thirty-three, her own age, whom she knighted. Charlecote is only four miles from Stratford, and the road must have been thronged with its people, among them, we may imagine, John Shakespeare with his two-year-old son on his shoulders, to welcome the Queen or to cheer her as, early on that August morning, she left the park gates on her way to Banbury and Oxford.

Mary Shakespeare would not be there, as another baby was due in a few weeks' time, and at the beginning of October she gave birth to a second son, Gilbert. Bretchgirdle had died, worn out perhaps by the labours of the plague year, and it was his successor, William Smart, who christened the boy, whose god-father was probably Gilbert Bradley, a glover like John Shakespeare, and his neighbour in Henley Street.

Another two years, and John Shakespeare was elected bailiff. He had achieved his youthful ambition. William was now four and a half, old enough to understand the honour and to appreciate the attendant ceremonial: the buff-uniformed sergeants with their maces, who accompanied his father when he inspected the market on Thursdays, the fair on fair-days, and escorted him to and from church on Sundays. There he would sit with his parents in the front pew on the north side of the nave, and perhaps even sit on his father's knee when a play was given in the Gild Hall. For it was in the summer of 1569, while John Shakespeare was still bailiff, that a company of travelling players arrived in Stratford.

Of course there were local dramatic entertainments in Stratford as in any other town, mainly traditional folk plays and buffoonery celebrating the principal festivals of the year. On Ascension Day there was the pageant of *St George and the Dragon*, when the armoured saint, followed by warriors and the jesting Vice, rode through the streets leading the vanquished monster, and there would be similar festivities at Easter and Whitsuntide, morris dancers and perhaps a play of Robin Hood.

Farther afield at Coventry, the gildsmen still occasionally performed their medieval miracle plays, and then there were troupes of professional entertainers who wandered about the country, performing in town halls, inn yards, or any convenient place in the open air. Although they were mostly musicians, clowns, tumblers, and jugglers, some of them were capable of putting on a dramatic performance of a kind, a knockabout farce, or even a morality play or an interlude. The morality was a late-medieval derivative of the miracle play, in which, instead of a dramatized version of a Bible story, a moral was enforced by personifications of qualities such as Wisdom and Wealth, as in *The Castle of Perseverance*, where the World, the Flesh, and the Devil struggle for the soul of Man. Moralities were very serious and very dull, not much, therefore, to popular taste, and inevitably developed into interludes, in which the moral and didactic element was leavened by the addition of farce from the miracles and folk plays, while real characters, no longer biblical, began to oust the colourless personifications and abstractions. When Shakespeare was a small boy, then, although there were the beginnings of a crude and vigorous native drama, it was quite formless, and there were no plays, in our sense of the word, to be seen in the provinces, and there were no public theatres, even in London.

There were, however, private theatres of a sort. In schools and the universities the new learning of the Renaissance led naturally to the study of Latin plays, the comedies of Plautus and Terence, and the Latin versions of Greek tragedy written by Seneca, who 'improved' the great Greek tragedians much as Davenant, Dryden, and others were to reform and refine Shakespeare. It was a short step from the reading to the acting, and by the middle of Henry VIII's reign the boys of St Paul's, Eton, and Westminster were performing the plays of Plautus and Terence as part of their curriculum. The writing of Latin plays at the universities followed as a matter of course, and soon schoolmasters and dons were beginning to write English plays based on classical models. The first of these 'regular' English plays was *Ralph Roister Doister*, written in rhyming doggerel about 1550 by the headmaster of Eton, Nicholas Udall; regular in the sense that it was constructed according to classical 'rules', though most of the incidents and some of the characters came out of the native interlude. The sprawling English drama had been given a coherent classical form. Soon afterwards, a similar though broader comedy, *Gammer Gurton's Needle*, was acted at Christ's College, Cambridge, and in 1561, three years before Shakespeare's birth, the first regular English tragedy was written by two law students of the Inner Temple, where it was performed. It was a monumentally dull affair 'climbing to the height of Seneca his style', which meant that nothing happened on the stage, all the bloody slaughter, and there was little else, being reported by messengers in speeches of a hundred lines or more. And their speech was equally wearisome, and yet it was epoch-making, for *Gorboduc* was the first play to be written in blank verse, stumping, rigid, wooden blank verse it is true, but the medium that was to be transformed by Shakespeare into the poetry of *Antony and Cleopatra* and *The Tempest*.

All these plays were acted by amateurs, schoolboys and masters, undergraduates and dons, law students and benchers, in the dining-halls of their schools, colleges, and inns of court, which became private theatres for the occasion. Thus, when Queen Elizabeth left Charlecote to go to Oxford, it was to see a series of plays, Latin and English, presented on a stage set up in Christ Church hall.

The halls of the great houses of the nobility and of the royal palaces in and about London were also used as private theatres, though here the players were generally professionals, simple men lacking the learning of the amateurs, innocent of Latin and brought up in the tradition of the moralities and interludes. The Earls of Essex and Oxford had companies of interluders in the reign of Henry VII, who formed the first royal company of four men, doubled in numbers by Henry VIII. As the services of these retainers were normally required only for winter entertainment, they were free for the rest of the year to tour the provinces, where they competed with the irregular troupes of permanent wanderers, varying their interludes with mere horseplay and 'feats of activity', which were their real speciality.

Elizabeth inherited her father's ageing interluders, but their crude antics and old-fashioned ways had no attraction for the fastidious Queen who spoke Latin almost as well as English, and though she kept them on her establishment she turned elsewhere for her entertainment, to the new company of players that Leicester formed for her delight, and to the choir boys of St Paul's and the Chapel Royal, who could play women's parts, sing like angels, and speak Plautus and Terence like young Romans. The Queen's Interluders performed at Whitehall in the first winter of her reign, but 'the plaers plad shuche matter that they wher commondyd to leyff off'. That was positively their last appearance at Court, they disappeared into the obscurity of the provinces, and these were the actors who arrived in Stratford in August 1569 to play before the bailiff, John Shakespeare, and other worthies of the town.

They were compelled by law to give their first performance to the mayor or bailiff, who, if he found their matter satisfactory, neither politically nor theologically controversial, would reward and license them to give public performances in the town. The play would be presented on a stage erected in the long chamber of the Gild Hall, where there was a side-entrance from the Council Chamber, which made an admirable dressing-room, or tiring-house, for the little troupe of actors, who had to be prepared to play any number of parts, women as well as men. If, as is most probable, five-year-old William Shakespeare saw the play, it may well have been *The Cradle of Security* seen at about the same time by another small boy called Willis, who was taken by his father to the mayor's play at Gloucester. It was a very moral morality, in which a king was seduced from his graver counsellors and preachers of sermons by three beautiful young ladies who persuaded him to lie down in a cradle in which they rocked and sang him asleep 'that he snorted again'. Circe-like they changed their royal victim into a swine by fixing a mask on his face under cover of the clothes by which he was concealed, an operation that the audience was not supposed to notice, any more than the three thin wires of the mask which the singing ladies held in their hands. When they displayed the transformed prince to the marvelling spectators two old men, one with a mace, the other with a sword, stole out of the tiring-house and struck a fearful blow upon the cradle, whereat 'all' the courtiers, the singing ladies and the vizard vanished, after which the desolate and bare-faced king was carried off by wicked spirits. 'The prince did personate in the moral, the wicked of the world; the three ladies, Pride, Covetousness and Luxury; the two old men, the End of the World and the Last Judgement'. It was scarcely matter to entangle the fancy of Elizabeth, but it served well enough in Gloucester and Stratford; no mayor could find fault with such a moral, though how the mayor of Gloucester rewarded the players we do not know. But John Shakespeare gave them four shillings and licensed them to give public performances in the town, perhaps in the yard of the Bear or Swan.

By this time there was <u>another baby in</u> the Shakespeare house in Henley Street, <u>another Joan, born in April 1569</u>, destined to be the only daughter who survived, and to outlive her four brothers by thirty years. Gilbert was three, and William, two years older, was beginning his elementary education. One does not think of his father as a bookish man, but rather as a shrewd man of affairs, whose reading and writing were devoted mainly to business and civic matters. It is true that we do not know that he could write, and that instead of signing his name he made his mark, but then so did other men, his friend Adrian Quiney for example, who certainly could sign his name when he wished to, and it is scarcely likely that the people of Stratford would entrust their accounts to an illiterate affeeror and elect him into the office of bailiff. But John Shakespeare would be too busy to teach his children, and it would be their mother who first taught them their letters and told them stories full of the wonder of local folklore. Mary Shakespeare must have been an uncommon mother, and we can imagine the joy that she felt in teaching her quick, eager, and imaginative eldest son, and her pride in his progress.

There were, however, men and women who eked out their

livings by teaching young children to read and write, thus preparing them for entry to the free grammar school at the age of seven. Shakespeare's own children would be taught by Thomas Parker and his seamstress wife, who kept a little school later in the century, and he himself may have learned from William Gilbert, or 'Sir Willy' as he was affectionately known, curate, scrivener, and keeper of the two town clocks. His first book was a hornbook, so called from the piece of transparent horn that protected from grubby and destructive little fingers the piece of paper on which was printed the alphabet and a few elementary aids to spelling: 'ab, eb, ib, ob, ub; ba . . .' – the *ba* of Moth and Holofernes in *Love's Labour's Lost*. The next stage was the Absey book, or *ABC with the Catechism*, a twelve-page pamphlet containing the alphabet, simple spelling exercises, the catechism, the ten commandments, the Lord's Prayer, graces, and a page of admonition on the duties of subjects, essential reading for a young Elizabethan, for the object of this early teaching was to make good Anglicans who were satisfied with their station in life.

When Shakespeare came to write he would have to supply himself with paper, ink, pen, ruler, desk, a penknife to cut his quill, and a dustbox to mop up his blots. It must have been an anxious and messy business for the teacher controlling the apparatus of a score or more six-year-olds. Fortunately a copybook was published at this time, the first in English, and from this the infant Shakespeare learned to form his letters, not however in the new and fashionable Italian hand, the 'sweet Roman hand' of Olivia, but in the old-fashioned secretary hand which, if we may judge from his signatures, he always employed. It is doubtful if the boy was his teacher's pride, for even by Elizabethan standards he seems always to have been an original and imaginative speller.

While still struggling with his letters, William was too young to understand or care about the momentous goings-on in the great world when his father was bailiff, though he must have experienced some of the attendant excitement. It meant nothing to him that Mary Queen of Scots had been made to abdicate in favour of her infant son James, one day to become his king, and that by the summer of 1568 she had fled to England where she was held a prisoner by Elizabeth; that in November she was in Coventry, only twenty miles from Stratford, while the Catholic earls of the north had risen to place her on the throne; that his kinsman Simon Arden, a stout Protestant, had been made sheriff of Warwickshire, whence a hastily raised force was marching north to crush the rebellion. Fortunately they were not needed, for the rising collapsed, though the cause was taken up by the Pope, who in 1570 excommunicated Elizabeth, declared her illegitimate, and so released her Catholic subjects from their allegiance. Philip of Spain also began a covert offensive, and from this time there was always the danger of invasion from his base in the Spanish Netherlands where, however, his Protestant subjects were in revolt.

The Catholics in Stratford, as elsewhere, were now suspect, and it would not be easy for them to gain civic promotion, but John Shakespeare continued his prosperous career, and in September 1571 was elected chief alderman and deputy to the new bailiff, his old friend Adrian Quiney. A few weeks later he took his daughter Anne to be christened by the recently appointed vicar, Henry Haycroft, who had succeeded William Butcher, deprived of his living because of his Catholic sympathies. It is probable that at about the same time he took the seven-year-old William to the grammar school and introduced him to the master, Walter Roche, the successor of John Acton, another man who had lost his job after the northern rebellion.

As there are no school records of the period, we do not know that Shakespeare went to the grammar school, but the only early mention of his education, that of Rowe, presumably on the authority of Betterton, states that he went to 'a free school'. But there is no need of such authority; of course he must have gone there. It is inconceivable that one of Stratford's leading townsmen should not send his son to the local grammar school, a particularly good one, which for the children of burgesses was free.

We can therefore imagine John Shakespeare, early one morning in 1571, reassuring his reluctant though excited son as they walked along Henley Street to the High Cross, and then down High Street, past the Quiney house on the right, past New Place on the left, to the Gild Chapel, on the south side of which was the school. The original schoolhouse was in the quadrangle, but after the dissolution of the Gild the boys had been moved into the long room over the Gild Hall. They were grouped in two divisions, the older ones with the master, the younger ones with the usher, so that William did not come directly under the master's instruction for some years, though as both upper and lower school were taught in the same room they would be well acquainted. Roche, however, can have had little influence on Shakespeare, for at the end of 1571 he resigned to become a lawyer in the town, and was replaced by a young Oxford graduate, Simon Hunt.

The hours were long, for according to one authority of the period, John Brinsley, master of Ashby-de-la-Zouch, 'there is none (no not almost of the least) but being used to it a while, they will sit very well in their places for two hours together, or two hours and a half, without any weariness'. Either the Eliza-bethan schoolboy differed from the neo-Elizabethan, or the good master was deceiving himself. In the summer William would have to be up by soon after five (an hour later in the winter) to wash, dress, comb his hair, say his prayers and have his breakfast before he heard the chapel bell begin to ring – the school was only a quarter of a mile away – then with his satchel and shining morning face report to the usher before the bell stopped at six o'clock. The day began with a reading from the Bible, the singing of a psalm and prayers, after which lessons lasted until nine, when there was a break of half an hour. Lessons then went on until eleven, 'or somewhat after, to countervail the time of the intermission at nine'. William would be home for dinner by half past eleven, but had to be in his place again at one o'clock for afternoon school, which lasted until five – or half past, 'to countervail the intermission at three'. School ended as it had begun, with prayers. It was a nine-hour day. Thursdays and Saturdays, however, were half-holidays, when recreations and sports were to be 'meet for gentlemen': shooting with the long bow, running, wrestling, jumping, but nothing clownish and above all no playing for money. Too much play, however, was not to be recommended, for 'experience teacheth that this draweth their minds utterly away from their books'. After all, the Elizabethan schoolboy was not so very different from his modern counterpart. There were holidays of about a fortnight at Christmas, Easter, and Whitsuntide; some forty days in the year. The master and usher were allowed another month, taken of course at different times.

Discipline was strict and punishment severe, for, as God had sanctified the rod, to spare the lazy and rebellious boy was to hate him, to love him was to correct. The first stage was a sharp reproof, and perhaps a loss of place in the form. If that failed, the boy was kept in, made to sit still and write exercises, if necessary every half-holiday until he showed himself truly sorry, for 'there is no hope to do any good till their stomachs be first broken'. There was one method that rarely failed to break the stubborn and unrepentant pupil. Three or four strong boys were ordered to seize the miscreant and hold him over a form so that he could stir neither hand nor foot, while the master administered half a dozen 'stripes or jerks' with a birch. The final sanction was expulsion.

The course was a gruelling one, virtually nothing but the learning of Latin, and in his first year William would spend all his time memorizing 'the accydence & princypalles' of Lily's Latin Grammar, the standard textbook. He would

learne by hart the parts of speach with their properties: the forming of Nombers, Cases, and Genders: the forming of diminutives in Substantives, of comparisons in Adjectives: so the forming of Nombers, Persons, Tenses and Moodes, in every Conjugation of all sorts of Verbes: whereof he shall rehearse afterwards some part ordinarily every day, illustrating the same with examples.

Shakespeare himself describes the kind of instruction he endured in his early days at the grammar school when, in *The Merry Wives of Windsor*, Mistress Page asks the Welsh schoolmaster, Sir Hugh Evans, to question her little son William 'in his accidence':

EVANS: William, how many numbers is in nouns?
WILLIAM: Two. . . .
EVANS: What is 'lapis', William?
WILLIAM: A stone.
EVANS: And what is 'a stone', William?
WILLIAM: A pebble.
EVANS: No, it is 'lapis'. I pray you, remember in your prain.
WILLIAM: Lapis.
EVANS: That is a good William. What is he, William, that does lend articles?
WILLIAM: Articles are borrowed of the pronoun, and be thus declined, Singulariter, nominativo, hic, haec, hoc.
EVANS: Nominativo, hig, hag, hog; pray you, mark: genitivo, hujus. Well, what is your accusative case?
WILLIAM: Accusativo, hinc.
EVANS: I pray you, have your remembrance, child; accusativo, hung, hang, hog. . . . What is your genitive case plural, William?
WILLIAM: Genitive case!
EVANS: Ay.
WILLIAM: Genitive, – horum, harum, horum. . . .
EVANS: Show me now, William, some declensions of your pronouns.
WILLIAM: Forsooth, I have forgot.
EVANS: It is qui, quae, quod: if you forget your 'quies', your 'quaes' and your 'quods', you must be preeches.

William Page escaped a breeching this time, but William Shakespeare may not always have been so lucky. And there was worse to come, for after his first year all examination, speaking, and writing was in 'pure Latin'.

He had just entered on this next stage of his scholastic career when he had a second chance to see the Queen. In August 1572 Elizabeth was on holiday, dallying in north Warwickshire, enchanted by the fireworks at Warwick Castle and the princely sports with which Leicester entertained her at Kenilworth, until at length she managed to tear herself away and on Saturday, the 23rd, a half-holiday, arrived at Charlecote. It was the eve of St Bartholomew, when the Catholic mob in Paris was turned loose on the sleeping Protestants, thousands of whom perished in the slaughter. It was a critical moment, and England prepared for war, for Elizabeth and her Privy Council were convinced that the massacre was part of a great Catholic plan concerted by France, Spain, and the Pope, and the prelude to invasion. They were wrong, but the people of Stratford, with the Queen and her ministers just across the river, must have felt almost at the centre of events, and Hunt and his usher would find it difficult to make their boys concentrate on numbers, cases, and genders.

Yet William had to concentrate, though now on the construing of easy sentences, probably *Sententiae Pueriles* and certainly Cato, first, as his usher instructed him, picking out a vocative case, then a nominative with its adjective, then the verb, and so on: '*Laeli*, O Lelius, *artes*, arts, *exercitationesque*, and exercises, *virtutum*, of virtues, *sunt*, are. . . .' And again Shakespeare parodies the pedantry of the Stratford schoolroom in the lovemaking of Lucentio in *The Taming of the Shrew*. Lucentio shows Bianca two lines of Ovid. 'Construe them,' she says, and Lucentio translates: '*Hic ibat*, as I told you before, *Simois*, I am Lucentio, *hic est*, son unto Vincentio of Pisa, *Sigeia tellus*, disguised thus to get your love.'

After Cato came Aesop, and the turning of every sentence inside out to arrive at its meaning:

Q.: Quid offendebat Gallus, dum vertit stercorarium?
R.: Offendit gemmam. . . .

And every fable was made a text for further moral instruction:

Q.: What Fable have you against the foolish contempt of learning and vertue, and preferring pleasure and play before it?
A.: The Fable of the Cocke, scratching in the dung-hill.

Cato and Aesop were considered the best of all books for the inculcation of virtue, except of course the Bible, and a constant exercise in school was the translating from English into Latin of the most exemplary passages in the Old Testament, particularly Genesis, Job, and Isaiah, the Psalms, Proverbs, and Ecclesiasticus, the books with which Shakespeare was to show himself the most familiar, suggesting that in after life he was no great student of the Scriptures.

In addition to the writing there was the speaking of Latin according to standard phrase books, in the manner of Holofernes and Sir Nathaniel, the schoolmaster and curate in *Love's Labour's Lost:*

HOLOFERNES: Anne intelligis, domine?
NATHANIEL: Laus Deo, bone intelligo.
HOLOFERNES: *Bone? bone* for *bene!*
NATHANIEL: Videsne quis venit?
HOLOFERNES: Video, et gaudeo.

All this memorizing and drill must have been irksome to the quick and exploring mind of an eager young boy, who undoubtedly preferred pleasure and play to learning, with which he certainly did not equate virtue, though perhaps Shakespeare found some fascination in the words with which he had to juggle, some inspiration even in the humdrum instruction of his usher, and might have written like his contemporary and friend, Michael Drayton:

> And when that once *Pueriles* I had read,
> And newly had my *Cato* construed,
> In my small selfe I greatly marveil'd then,
> Amongst all other, what strange kinde of men
> These Poets were; And pleased with the name,
> To my milde Tutor merrily I came,
> (For I was then a proper goodly page,
> Much like a Pigmy, scarse ten yeares of age)
> Clasping my slender armes about his thigh.
> O my dear master! cannot you (quoth I)
> Make me a Poet? When shortly he began,
> And first read to me honest *Mantuan.*

We could scarcely have a better picture than this, of <u>Shakespeare at the age of ten, when he first came across the poetry of the</u>

fifteenth-century Italian Latinist, Baptista Mantuanus. 'Ah, good old Mantuan!' exclaims Holofernes, quoting the first line of his eclogues, 'who understandeth thee not, loves thee not.'

Then we can imagine the gathering excitement of the little boy as he began the study of his first play, a comedy of Terence. What though the usher's method was a lingering anatomization of every line, each sentence merely a pretext for the illustration of Latin syntax, there were real characters, dialogue, wit, humorous situations, and a beautifully contrived form and structure, the five-act framework of classical drama. This was just the time when Stratford was becoming a regular centre for the summer visits of travelling companies of players, and between 1573 and 1576 the boy must have seen numerous performances by the players of the three great Earls, of Leicester, Warwick, and Worcester: old moral interludes and farces, very different from the shapely comedies of Terence and Plautus.

In the summer of 1575 Elizabeth was again in Warwickshire, lingering for almost the whole of July at Kenilworth, where Leicester diverted her with all the princely pleasures that England could afford. There were fireworks, pageants, plays, dancing, music, hunting, bear-baiting, rustic sports, the climax being a water-pageant of the Lady of the Lake, in which Triton rode upon a mermaid and Arion on a dolphin's back, singing 'a delectable ditty, and this in the evening of the day, resounding from the calm waters'. Kenilworth is only fifteen miles from Stratford, and John Shakespeare must have taken his son to see some of the pageantry, above all to the fireworks and water-pageant on that memorable Monday evening, apparently recalled in *A Midsummer Night's Dream*, when Oberon tells Puck how once he heard a mermaid singing on a dolphin's back.

> And certain stars shot madly from their spheres
> To hear the sea-maid's music.

Leicester's Men, the most privileged of all the companies of actors, the Queen's favourites who enlivened her Christmas Revels at Court, naturally played a large part in her summer revels at Kenilworth. Their leading member was James Burbage, and it may have been while performing on the improvised stages in the castle and its grounds that he conceived the idea of building a permanent home for his company in London. He was in the prime of life, in his early forties, an experienced actor and a one-time carpenter, just the man to build a wooden playhouse if he could raise the capital. This he did by the sweet and continual persuasion of his brother-in-law, and early in 1576 he took the lease of a plot of land in Shoreditch, beyond the City walls, on the great highroad leading to the north. By the summer of 1577 his playhouse was finished and Leicester's Men were in occupation. It was called 'the Theatre', for that is precisely what it was, *the* Theatre, the only public theatre in the country.

By this time, probably in 1575, Shakespeare had graduated from lower to upper school, from usher to master. If his promotion came on his eleventh birthday he would never or rarely have been taught by Simon Hunt, who resigned the mastership a few weeks before. It was a pity, for Hunt was a good scholar; but he had Catholic leanings and, after going to the English College for the training of Catholic missionaries at Douai, he went to Rome, where in 1580 he succeeded Father Parsons as English Penitentiary at St Peter's.

There is, however, no reason to doubt the ability of Hunt's successor, Thomas Jenkins, a Welshman of about thirty and a fellow of St John's, Oxford, incidentally a college that emphasized the importance of Greek. As Jenkins stayed at Stratford until 1579, it was he who was mainly responsible for Shakespeare's upper-school education, and we cannot help seeing an affectionate caricature of the man in the good Sir Hugh Evans, William Page's schoolmaster, doubtless a sound Latinist, though one who made the most delightful fritters of English.

It would, therefore, be one of Jenkins's first tasks to introduce his promising young pupil to the arts of Logic and Rhetoric, to 'the axiom, wherein every argument is disposed, the syllogism, whereby it is concluded', and to 'the fineness of speech in the rhetorical ornaments, such as comely tropes and

48

pleasant figures, and fit pronunciation and gesture', for every word, sentence, and emotion had its corresponding rhetorical action and pronunciation. And so the master taught the boy how to imitate Cicero phrase for phrase, trope for trope, and argument for argument. It was not a bad training for a poet and dramatist, though no doubt the originality of the boy's imagery, the similes and metaphors that were not to be found in the textbooks, puzzled and worried his tutor.

The object of rhetoric was to please, and by argument and reason to persuade; thus Longaville asks in *Love's Labour's Lost*:

> Did not the heavenly rhetoric of thine eye,
> 'Gainst whom the world cannot hold argument,
> Persuade my heart to this false perjury?

And what orator could be more pleasing and persuasive than Berowne? Shakespeare's early plays are full of the logic and rhetorical devices that he learned at school, and he characteristically burlesques the arts when it suits his purpose, as when Touchstone, 'honest Ovid among the Goths', argues:

> To have is to have; for it is a figure in rhetoric that drink, being poured out of a cup into a glass, by filling the one doth empty the other; for all your writers do consent that ipse is he: now, you are not ipse, for I am he.

Then there were the Latin poets, whom we may suspect that Shakespeare enjoyed more for their poetry than for the grammar, syntax, apothegms, logic, and rhetoric that Jenkins distilled from them: the *Eclogues*, *Georgics*, and *Aeneid* of Virgil, the *Odes* of Horace, and above all the *Metamorphoses* of Ovid, the poet whom he mentions and quotes most often, and the poet to whom his contemporaries compared him: 'the sweete wittie soule of Ovid lives in mellifluous and hony-tongued Shakespeare'.

It must have been a happy time for the boy. All was going well at home, and in 1575 his father considerably enlarged his property in Henley Street by the purchase of the two adjoining houses on the western side, with their gardens and orchards, so

49

forming a long half-timbered house, his shop at the east and a wing projecting into the garden at the back, a handsome and roomy home for his growing family. For by this time John and Mary Shakespeare had a family of five: William aged eleven, Gilbert nine, Joan six, Anne four, and a year-old baby, Richard. Gilbert would be in the lower school and old enough to be a companion, but there was no lack of other friends to play with, among them the cousins John and Hamnet Sadler, thirteen-year-old Richard Field, son of a tanner who lived in Bridge Street, and Richard Quiney, somewhat older.

With these and other school-companions he could practise archery on the Bankcroft, swim in the quiet waters of the river, or angle for perch and pike in the fishing-ground below the church, by the mill occupied by John Sadler's father. And here Edward Ingram kept his trammel and boats, which might be borrowed for expeditions up the river to Hampton Lucy and Charlecote, or downstream past Luddington and Weston-on-Avon towards Bidford. Or on foot there was the Forest of Arden to be explored, woodlands that still covered much of the country north and west of Stratford and reached almost to the outskirts of the town; and a mile or two beyond Clopton Bridge rose the low limestone escarpment of the Cotswolds, unenclosed uplands where the hare was coursed, with clumps of beeches on their heights and grey stone villages in the valleys. Forest, glade, river, and wold, trees, flowers, animals, and birds, oak, primrose, deer, and lark, they were all to be woven into the fabric of Shakespeare's poetry.

Then there were relations to be visited. Perhaps William did not make a point of going to see his uncle Henry Shakespeare, who was now farming at Ingon, two miles north of Stratford, the Snitterfield farm having been taken over by another of his uncles, Alexander Webbe. Henry was a quarrelsome character, and when Webbe died in 1573 and his widow Margaret married Edward Cornwall, the two men came to blows, for which affair Henry, who refused to appear in court, was fined. His fines were many, and a few years later he was excommunicated in Snitterfield church and pronounced *contumax*. It is true that few Elizabethans escaped trouble with the law, but it is significant that his brother John called none of his sons Henry. There were half a dozen other Arden aunts in addition to Margaret Cornwall. Alice Arden still lived at Wilmcote with her stepmother, and Katharine Arden's husband, Thomas Etkyns, farmed land between Wilmcote and Aston Cantlow. At Newnham, a mile to the east, lived Elizabeth and John Scarlet, and a mile to the west, at Little Alne, were John and Mary Fulwood, widow Arden's daughter, whose brother, John Hill, lived at Bearley, also the home of Agnes Arden and her first husband, John Hewins. The Ardens were thick in the Wilmcote area and within easy visiting distance for William, but his aunt Joan and her husband Edmund Lambert lived fifteen miles away in the Cotswolds, at Barton-on-the-Heath, where Christopher Sly was to come from.

Like many other Stratford worthies, Adrian Quiney for example, John Shakespeare aspired to change his rank of yeoman for that of gentleman and, like the Ardens, have a coat of arms. As an alderman, justice of the peace, and former bailiff of Stratford he had a strong claim; moreover he was a man of the necessary substance, the owner of a fine property in Henley Street and, thanks to his wife's inheritance, of land in Wilmcote, with an interest in an estate in Snitterfield; and then his wife was 'a daughter and heir of Robert Arden, a gentleman of worship'. In 1576, therefore, he applied to the Heralds' College, and Clarenceux sent him a 'trick' or sketch of arms as a suggestion for a possible grant. And that is all, for it was another twenty years before the grant was made.

What exactly happened we do not know, but it seems clear that in the winter of 1576 John Shakespeare suffered a sudden reverse of fortune. In September he attended a Council meeting as usual, but at the next one, in January 1577, he failed to appear. Only once before in the last thirteen years had he missed a meeting, but only once again was he to attend. Then in 1578–9 he disposed of his wife's estate. Her interest in the land at Snitterfield was sold to her nephew Robert Webbe for £4, the eighty-six acres of Asbies were let, and the other Wilmcote estate, consisting of fifty-six acres and a house, was mortgaged to her brother-in-law, Edmund Lambert, for £40, to be repaid in 1580. It was not repaid. Again in 1578, when John was called upon to contribute to the levy for the supply of additional soldiers he was presented for non-payment. His assessment of 3s. 4d., however, was only half the amount normally demanded of aldermen, and eventually he was excused payment altogether. Moreover, he was let off his poor-rate of 4d. weekly and the fine for nonattendance at Election Day in September 1578 when two other absentee members were severely mulcted, and apparently he was never called upon to pay a single fine for neglect of his duties. On the other hand, in 1580, he and a Nottingham hat-maker, John Audley, were bound over in the Court of Queen's Bench to give security against a breach of the peace. With a hundred and forty other men, mainly from the Midlands, they failed to appear, and John Shakespeare was fined £20 for his own default and another £20 for not bringing Audley into court. It was a singular affair and a crippling penalty.

Various reasons have been advanced to account for this apparent collapse of John Shakespeare's fortunes. Some see him as the victim of religious persecution, either as a fanatical Puritan or an uncompromising Catholic. It is true that in 1577 John Whitgift, a violently anti-Puritan prelate, became Bishop of Worcester, within which diocese Stratford lay, and that three years later, after the discovery of the secret Jesuit mission under Parsons and Campion, Parliament passed a ferocious Act making it high treason to proselytize or join the Roman Church, but there is no evidence that John Shakespeare was either Puritan or Catholic, his career suggesting rather that he was a middle-of-the-way man, conforming easily to the established church, and in any event all shades of religious opinion were represented on the Stratford Council. It is possible that for some reason he simply lost his grip, but the leniency and apparent sympathy with which he was treated by his colleagues suggest that he suffered some misfortune, an accident perhaps, that impaired his powers, the scope and profitability of his business, and his scale of living. This would account for his failure to pursue his application for coat armour and pride might well prevent his attending Council meetings. Fortunately he was able to retain his workshop and house in Henley Street.

The affairs of John Shakespeare, however, are important to us only in so far as they affected his eldest son. According to Rowe, 'the narrowness of his circumstances, and the want of his assistance at home, forced his father to withdraw him from school.' But this reads merely like the attempt of the Age of Reason to account for 'the small Latin and less Greek' with which Ben Jonson had credited Shakespeare, and, judging from his real and quite considerable knowledge of Latin and its literature, school textbooks, and rhetoric, it is much more likely that he stayed at school until he was sixteen, which would certainly be the wish of an ambitious father for a gifted son. If so, he would spend his last year under a new master, John Cottam, a Brasenose man who succeeded Jenkins in 1579. It is curious that the boy should have come under the influence of a series of masters with Catholic connexions. Simon Hunt left the school to go to Douai; Jenkins was at St John's with William Hartley, a seminary priest executed in 1588, and was almost certainly taught his college rhetoric, which he in turn taught Shakespeare, by the saintly martyr Edmund Campion; and John Cottam was the brother of Thomas Cottam, another Catholic martyr, executed in 1582, the year in which John was replaced at Stratford school by Alexander Aspinall, a good Protestant who was to remain there until his death forty years later. Incidentally, Roche, Cottam, and Aspinall were all Lancashire men.

It seems probable, therefore, that between 1577 and 1580, taught first by Jenkins then by Cottam, Shakespeare pursued his studies, perfecting his rhetoric, revising his Latin grammar, adding the *Satires* of Juvenal and *Ars Poetica* of Horace to his store of Latin literature, and writing Latin verses in imitation of the Latin poets, even perhaps English verses in imitation of Roger Ascham in his *Scholemaster*, a teacher who somewhat affected the letter, 'a figure much used by our common rimers':

Therefore, my heart, cease sighs and sobs, cease sorrow's seed to sow,
Whereof no gain but greater grief and hurtful care may grow.

Apparently the verse of the tragical mirth of Pyramus and Thisbe was not so much parody as plagiarism. Then, like the ideal scholar of another contemporary educationist, he might

ascend to the fourth degree, of Arithmetike and Geometrie. And according to the same manner, easely passe through these Artes in halfe a yeere, and so before the full age of sixteene yeeres be made fit to wade without a schoolemaister, through deeper mysteries of learning, to set forth the glorie of God, and to benefite his Countrie.

But then Shakespeare was not an ideal scholar; it is unlikely that he learned arithmetic and geometry, or that he was greatly interested in Latin grammar, or the endless moralizing and imitating of the ancients, or in wading through any deeper mysteries of learning. And it is certain that he was taught no science or geography, no modern history or modern language, no English literature or even English language, save incidentally by way of Latin. Yet, although he probably had no Greek at all, rather than less Greek, he had more than small Latin and as sound a literary training as most of his contemporaries, for university education was a professional one in medicine, law, or divinity, rather than a continuation of the liberal arts taught in schools.

In April 1579, William's younger sister died, the eight-year-old Anne, and a year later the last of the Shakespeare children was born, Edmund, possibly an unwanted child. In the following September Francis Drake put in to Plymouth on his return from his three-year voyage round the world.

CHAPTER 2

1580–7

MARRIAGE

*

WE can reconstruct the life of the Elizabethan schoolboy with some degree of certainty, but we cannot expect to discover much about the early career of an obscure young man, however great a genius, four centuries ago, and what happened to Shakespeare in the dozen years or so after leaving school must be mainly a matter of inference and conjecture. If he left school in 1580 he was ready for the university, for sixteen was then the normal age of entry. But there is no external evidence, no record of his name in any of the college books of Oxford or Cambridge, to show that he went there, and the internal evidence of his plays is all against it. Although he tells us more about the Elizabethan grammar school, its curriculum, text-books, and techniques, than any other contemporary dramatist, there is nothing to suggest that he was intimately acquainted with life at a university. Then, of course, if his father was in straitened circumstances, the chances are that he could not afford to send him to Oxford, the obvious university, being only forty miles from Stratford. Nor need we assume that a university education was necessary for the youth who was to write the poems and plays that he did. Once again, the universities trained boys for the three main professions of medicine, law, and the church, and Shakespeare already had a training that would fit him for most others.

We may take the evidence of R. Willis, his exact contemporary, the little boy who stood at his father's knee to watch the moral play of *The Cradle of Security*. All the learning he had, he tells us, was in the free grammar school at Gloucester, yet he came to be secretary successively to the Chancellor of the Exchequer, the Lord High Treasurer, and the Lord Keeper of the Great Seal: 'and this I note, that though I were no graduate of the university, yet I had so much learning as fitted me for the places whereunto the Lord advanced me'. Then there was Shakespeare's contemporary at Stratford, Richard Field, who in 1579 went to London as apprentice to Thomas Vautrollier, the best printer in England, and, when he took over his master's press, printed books in Latin, French, Italian, and Welsh, as well as passages in Greek and Hebrew. Again, there was Richard Quiney, another of Shakespeare's Stratford friends, a bookish man who certainly read Latin easily, and we have a Latin letter of 1598 written to him by his eleven-year-old son, presumably a pupil of Aspinall's at the grammar school, asking for two notebooks for himself and younger brother Thomas: '*ut provideres fratri meo et mihi duos chartaceos libellos quibus maxime caremus hoc presenti tempore*'. If Field turned out to be one of the best printers of the classics in London and young Quiney could write letters in Latin, we may be sure that there was little wrong with Stratford education and that William Shakespeare was well-equipped for most professions when he left school.

It must be remembered that the criticism and biographical sketches of Restoration times and the eighteenth century were based on the assumption that Shakespeare was a scarcely educated peasant, a genius it is true, but a sport of nature; Jonson had pronounced that he 'wanted art', and it followed, therefore, that he knew little or nothing about classical authors and authorities, and of the 'correct' way in which to write a play. Thus, according to Aubrey, John Shakespeare was a butcher, and it was only natural that William should be a butcher too, though of course when he killed a calf he would do it in a high style and make a speech. We can safely dismiss this romantic embroidery, though admittedly we might expect that under normal circumstances the eldest son would join his father in his trade. But circumstances were not normal; John and Mary Shakespeare must have realized that William was more gifted than most boys, that he had it in him to be something better than a master glover, and after all Gilbert was only two years younger and could come into the business in his stead. Then it is, to say the least, improbable that the height of William's ambition was to be a glover. If he could not go to Oxford to be trained for one of the learned professions, he could begin more humbly in Stratford, perhaps as a clerk in a lawyer's office. There were plenty of possible openings: William Court was a lawyer, so was his former schoolmaster, Walter Roche, or his father might well get him into the service of the town clerk, Henry Rogers.

If Shakespeare did begin his career in this way, as an articled clerk to an attorney, it would account for his remarkable knowledge of the law, legal terms and procedure. Of course, when he went to London he would pick up a good deal of legal jargon from the young men of the inns of court, but his knowledge seems to be something more professional than this, something so engrained that it appears not only in such deliberate mention as Hamlet's, 'Where be his quiddities now, his quillets, his cases, his tenures and his tricks? . . . his statutes, his recognizances, his fines, his double vouchers, his recoveries'; or in such self-conscious conceits as Venus's appeal to Adonis: 'Set thy seal-manual on my wax-red lips'; or in the punning of Pandarus: 'A kiss in fee-farm! . . . Words have no debts, give her deeds . . . What, billing again? Here's "In witness whereof the parties interchangeably – "'; but also in Lady Macbeth's grim, spontaneous imagery: 'But in them nature's copy's not eterne', and Macbeth's, 'Cancel and tear to pieces that great bond which keeps me pale!' The point need not be laboured, for there are few scenes in Shakespeare without some legal reference or image.

But whatever was Shakespeare's first occupation, we may be sure that he was reading, reading voraciously; not the Latin textbooks that he had studied at school, but any English books on which he could lay his hands. He would not be vastly entertained by the kind of literature to be found in the library of the former vicar, John Bretchgirdle, *Musculus upon Matthew* or *Homiliae Nauseae*, though he might find the Sternhold and Hopkins version of the *Psalms* slightly more appetizing, or even

The Actes of the Apostles, translated into English Metre by the 'peevish and humoursome' <u>Christopher Tye.</u> No doubt there was not a great choice in Stratford of reading for an imaginative boy, but at home there would be the Bible, probably the Genevan version, possibly Foxe's *Book of Martyrs* describing the persecutions of Mary's reign, a work scarcely calculated to reconcile the rival religious factions, and popular romances such as *Robin Hood*, jest-books like *The Hundred Merry Tales*, and collections of songs and ballads. If not at home, then on the shelves of neighbours he might find Chaucer's *Canterbury Tales* and Malory's *Morte d'Arthur*, dramatic poetry and romantic prose that the boy would devour with delight, while the adventure story in which Sir Thomas More wrapped the politics of his *Utopia* might be almost as absorbing. Perhaps he was able to borrow a copy of Froissart's *Chronicles*, a romantic history of the fourteenth century, and he might well come across the first, illustrated edition of Holinshed's *Chronicles of England, Scotland and Ireland*, published in 1577. Like John Foxe, who had been a tutor in the Lucy household at Charlecote, Raphael Holinshed had Warwickshire connexions, for he was the steward of Thomas Burdett of Bramcote, one of whose manors was at Packwood, near Stratford. Plays were probably a rarity in the town, though he might find a few interludes and moralities such as *Hickscorner* and *Wealth and Health*, or even *Cambyses*, 'a lamentable tragedy full of pleasant mirth', the knockabout nonsense of the comic villains Huff, Ruff, and Snuff.

A book that Shakespeare may have read while still at school was Arthur Golding's translation of the *Metamorphoses* of Ovid. Lumbering though Golding's rendering was, and of course forcing a Christian moral from the pagan's anything but moral fables, the stories fascinated Shakespeare; the subject of his first poem, *Venus and Adonis*, came from Ovid, and even when writing the last of his plays he remembered Golding's lines beginning, 'Ye airs and winds, ye elves of hills, ye brooks and woods alone.' And again as a schoolboy he might have read William Painter's *Palace of Pleasure*, another translation, a century of classical and Italian stories, many of them by Boccaccio and Bandello, whom, like the other Elizabethan dramatists, he was to plunder for plots when he wrote his plays. ugh

All these, however, belonged to the old age, to medieval and early Tudor times, and there was nothing in them to suggest the great flowering that was to come in the second half of Elizabeth's reign; for we must remember that just as there were no theatres until Shakespeare left school, so there was no drama, no prose, and no poetry of the new age. England was at the end of a barren century, and since Caxton had set up his press in Westminster just a hundred years before, apart from Skelton's pithy 'Skeltonics', there had been practically no poetry written that was to survive. If, however, Shakespeare was fortunate enough to pick up a little book published in 1557 he would find a taste of what was to come. This was the *Songes and Sonnettes* of the Earl of Surrey and Sir Thomas Wyatt, commonly known as *Tottel's Miscellany*, from the name of the publisher. It was a book that was to have the profoundest influence on Shakespeare, either direct or indirect, for Surrey's main contribution was a translation of part of the *Aeneid* into blank verse, the first as far as we know to be written in English, and Wyatt introduced the sonnet from Italy. Then both of them wrote lyrics, and we can imagine the excitement with which Shakespeare would read Wyatt's 'My lute awake!' and the unforgettable 'They flee from me, that sometime did me seek'.

Then, at the critical moment, Shakespeare's last year at school, came the first wonderful year of Elizabeth's reign. Drake was on his way back from the other side of the globe when, in 1579, Sir Thomas North published his translation of Plutarch, *The Lives of the Noble Grecians and Romanes*, John Lyly his *Euphues*, and Edmund Spenser his *Shepheards Calender*. It is improbable that Shakespeare found all these books in the early eighties, but it cannot have been long before he met them. North's *Lives* was to become the source of his Roman plays, his noble prose the fount of some of his finest poetry; Lyly's frothy euphuism was to be aped in *Love's Labour's Lost*, and Spenser's poetry, though it was another decade before the *Faerie Queene* appeared, was to inspire the writing of his early poems.

The boy was neither a scholar nor a bookworm, reading merely for information or because he had nothing better to do, but reading anything that excited his imagination and tearing the heart out of books in his search for what to him was new and valuable. And we may be sure that he was writing as well as reading, scribbling adolescent verses, fourteeners perhaps in imitation of Golding, or blank verse after the pattern of Surrey, or lyrics and sonnets in the manner of Wyatt, or a story from Ovid in the six-line stanza favoured by Spenser. And meanwhile, if we may trust Aubrey and the colouring of the monument in Stratford church, the boy of sixteen was growing up into a 'handsome, well-shaped' young man with auburn hair and hazel eyes, and many of his verses were addressed to a young woman who lived just across the meadows in the village of Shottery.

She was the daughter of Richard Hathaway of Hewland Farm, the thatched, half-timbered house now known as Anne Hathaway's cottage. Richard had married twice, and when he made his will in September 1581 Anne was twenty-five, the eldest of two families of children, with a brother and sister, Bartholomew and Catherine, aged twenty-three and eighteen, three young step-brothers, and a step-sister. A few days later Richard died, leaving the house to his widow, land to Bartholomew, who married before the year was out, and to Anne and Catherine 6*l*. 13s. 4d. each, 'to be paid unto her at the day of her marriage'. Twelve months later the twenty-six-year-old Anne was with child by the eighteen-year-old poet from Stratford.

It is no uncommon thing for a clever young man to be infatuated by a woman much older than himself – one thinks of Arthur Pendennis and the Fotheringay – but Anne Hathaway, aged twenty-six, a ripe age for a woman in Elizabethan times, fatherless in an overcrowded household of young children, the drudgery of which would fall largely on her shoulders, had every reason to encourage an ardent suitor, however young. It may be, therefore, that Stephen Dedalus (or James Joyce) was right:

He chose badly? He was chosen, it seems to me. If others have their will Ann hath a way. By cock, she was to blame. She put the comether on him, sweet and twentysix. The greyeyed goddess who bends over the boy Adonis, stooping to conquer, as prologue to the swelling act, is a boldfaced Stratford wench who tumbles in a cornfield a lover younger than herself.

And yet it is as unfair to blame Anne, who for all we know may have been just as infatuated by her golden lover as he was by her, as it is unwarranted and sentimental to absolve the hot-blooded boy from all blame by assuming that there was a pre-contract that amounted to a civil marriage and justified cohabitation before the marriage ceremony. There may have been some such pre-contract, but we do not know, and the haste with which the marriage was solemnized suggests that there was not. A young man had got a young woman with child, and the only decent thing he could do was to marry her as soon as possible.

By the middle of November Anne could no longer be in doubt as to her condition, and Shakespeare, as a minor, would have to explain the situation to his father and obtain his consent to marry her. Advent, however, was upon them, and the period when, from 2 December to 13 January, no marriage could be celebrated without a special and expensive licence, and then on 27 January began a similar Lenten season of inhibition, which would delay a normal wedding with thrice calling of the banns until after 7 April. There was no laxity about the enforcement of these regulations under Whitgift's régime. On Tuesday, 27 November, therefore, Shakespeare rode the twenty-five miles to Worcester, where at the bishop's registry he swore his reasons for desiring a dispensation and for a fee of a few shillings obtained a licence for the marriage after a single publication of the banns. A bond of surety was now required to safeguard the clergy against any lawful impediment such as consanguinity or marriage without the consent of the bride's 'friends', and on the following day two Shottery farmers, Fulk Sandells and John Richardson, signed the bond as sureties for £40. They were both friends of Anne's father, Richardson being a witness of his will and Sandells an overseer, responsible therefore for the payment of her £6 13s. 4d. on her wedding day. This must have followed almost at once. The only remaining day on which banns could be published was St Andrew's Day, 30 November, and on that Friday, therefore, or on Saturday, 1 December, they were married.

Where they were married we do not know, but it was probably at Temple Grafton, some three miles from Shottery, far enough away to escape inquisitive eyes. The clerk who made the entry in the Worcester register about the issue of the licence wrote that it was for the marriage of 'Willelmum Shaxpere et Annam Whateley de Temple Grafton', a pardonable error, for the man must have had the name Whateley very much on his mind, a long-standing tithe dispute involving a William Whateley having been before the Consistory Court on the same day. The names in the bond, an original document and not merely a clerk's entry, are clear enough: 'William Shagspere', another of the innumerable variations of the name, and 'Anne Hathwey of Stratford'. The Temple Grafton of the register was probably the name of the parish which Shakespeare swore was to be the scene of the marriage.

We may, if we wish, make a much more dramatic story out of it all: that Shakespeare really was in love with an Anne Whateley of Temple Grafton whom he was secretly going to marry with his licence, but was prevented by the two friends of the Hathaway family who followed him to Worcester and forced him to marry the woman he had wronged. But it would have been risky, indeed almost impossible, for a minor to have married a girl in this way; moreover, there is no record of Whateleys at Temple Grafton, and it is difficult to believe that Shakespeare, even allowing for the thoughtlessness and selfishness of youth, would have acted so like the young cads that he was to depict, Proteus for example, in his early plays.

There is no need to make a mystery of the affair. Shakespeare had got himself into a scrape, and his conduct, like the proceedings as a whole, was perfectly normal and regular, and in accordance with the custom of the age he would take his bride back to his parents' home in Henley Street. Already there were four children there: two little boys, Richard and Edmund, aged eight and two, but Gilbert, now sixteen, was probably learning his father's trade, and Joan at thirteen would be a welcome help to her mother. And the house was admirably suited to accommodate the young couple, for they could live almost independently in the wing that opened on to the garden at the back.

Shakespeare's courtship and hasty marriage coincided with an episode that must have added to the disturbance of that already sufficiently disturbed year, for at this time his father was threatened with some sort of violence at the hands of four of his fellow townsmen. Anyone thus threatened could go to a justice of the peace and make oath that he stood in fear of his life or some bodily hurt, whereupon a judge would order the sheriff of the county to attach the alleged offender and make him enter a bond to keep the peace. In the summer of 1582, therefore, John Shakespeare craved 'sureties of the peace against Ralph Cawdrey, William Russell, Thomas Logginge and Robert Young, for fear of death and mutilation of his limbs'. Little is known about Russell and nothing about Logginge, but Robert Young was a well-known dyer, and Ralph Cawdrey a substantial butcher, tenant of the Angel Inn, and at this time bailiff of Stratford. What happened further we do not know, but it may be significant that in September Alderman Shakespeare attended his first Council meeting since 1576 in order to register his vote for his old friend John Sadler as bailiff. It cannot have made life any easier for the Shakespeares to have been at enmity with Ralph Cawdrey.

Six months after his marriage and one month after his nineteenth birthday, Shakespeare's first child, a daughter, was born, and was christened in the parish church on its Feast Day, Trinity Sunday, 26 May 1583. She was called Susanna, an uncommon name suggestive of Puritanism, for it was a Puritan practice to give children biblical names. Apparently the Hathaways were a Puritan family, for when Anne's father made his will he asked to be 'honestly buried', and her brother Bartholomew also asked for a Puritan burial, 'hoping to arise at the Latter Day and to receive the reward of His elect'. It seems probable, therefore, that Anne herself was a Puritan, and that

63

it was she who persuaded her husband to agree to the name of Susanna. But whatever Anne's religious persuasion, if the young poet had felt cribbed and confined in Stratford before his escapade of the previous summer, he was now doubly trapped with a wife and child to support. Yet he was to fetter himself still more firmly, for at the beginning of 1585 Anne gave birth to twins, Hamnet and Judith, who were baptized on 2 February. Their godparents were almost certainly Shakespeare's friend, Hamnet Sadler, and his wife Judith.

In the following October another Shakespeare was born. This was the poet's cousin James, the short-lived son of his uncle Henry. Henry Shakespeare was again in trouble; he owed £5 to Christopher Smith of Stratford and another £22 to Nicholas Lane, a farmer and money-lender of Bridgetown on the other side of the river. Although his brother John had just lost £10 by standing surety for a local coppersmith who had failed to appear in court, he guaranteed £10 of Henry's debt, or so it was alleged by Lane, who sued him for that sum. John, however, denied the responsibility, contested the suit through all its stages, and when judgement was given against him appealed to a higher court. At the same time he embarked on another lawsuit. His brother-in-law, Edmund Lambert, died in April 1587, still in possession of the Wilmcote property that he had mortgaged to him ten years before as security for a loan of £40. It passed to his son John Lambert, to whom, in September 1587, according to a Bill of Complaint of the following year, 'John Shackespere and Mary his wife, together with William Shackespere his son' offered to sell the estate outright for a further payment of £20. Apparently William had some right of inheritance. The Shakespeares maintained that Lambert agreed but failed to keep his promise, and brought a Queen's Bench action against him for £30 damages. Lambert, however, denied the alleged arrangement and kept the property in spite of all attempts to recover it.

By this time John Shakespeare was no longer a member of the Stratford Council, for in 1586 a new alderman was appointed in his place, 'for that Mr Shaxspere dothe not come to the halles when they be warned nor hathe not done of longe tyme'. Perhaps it was Ralph Cawdrey who proposed the motion. It was mildly phrased, however, and the Council had been very patient, for Alderman Shakespeare had put in only one appearance during the last ten years.

The fortunes of the Shakespeares in the eighties were in sad contrast to those of the Quineys. John Shakespeare's old friend Adrian Quiney, the mercer, had thrice been bailiff of Stratford, and two years before John made his application had obtained a coat of arms and exchanged his rank of yeoman for that of gentleman. Then Richard Quiney, Adrian's son and the poet's slightly older contemporary, began his successful career. In 1580, when he was about twenty-two, he married Elizabeth Phillips, the daughter of a respected townsman, and in 1582 was elected a taster and constable, though he declined the office when his father was appointed bailiff for the third time. This was a month before William married Anne Hathaway. In 1586, however, at the meeting which deprived John Shakespeare of his rank of alderman, Richard accepted the post of chamberlain, and two years later he was himself an alderman, and in 1592 bailiff of Stratford.

This decline in his father's fortunes and rise in those of their friendly rivals must have been galling to Shakespeare and have added to his feeling of frustration, shackled as he was to a wife and three young children in a small provincial town. He had married in haste and there is reason to think that he repented at leisure. In 1585, when Hamnet and Judith were born, his wife was twenty-nine while he was still a minor, and though it is dangerous to read autobiography into his plays, one cannot help feeling that he was himself speaking in the character of Orsino when he wrote:

> Let still the woman take
> An elder than herself; so wears she to him,
> So sways she level in her husband's heart.

Then, towards the end of his career, he made the shepherd in *The Winter's Tale* protest:

I would there were no age between ten and three-and-twenty, or that youth would sleep out the rest; for there is nothing in the between but getting wenches with child, wronging the ancientry, stealing, fighting.

And then there is the warning of Prospero to Ferdinand:

> If thou dost break her virgin-knot before
> All sanctimonious ceremonies may
> With full and holy rite be minister'd,
> No sweet aspersion shall the heavens let fall
> To make this contract grow; but barren hate,
> Sour-eyed disdain and discord shall bestrew
> The union of your bed with weeds so loathly
> That you shall hate it both.

We need not assume that Shakespeare's marriage ever led to hate, or even disdain, but we can well imagine outbreaks of discord between the fretting and frustrated poet and his ageing, and perhaps puritanical, wife.

His thoughts would be all of London, the New Troy of Gloriana, the city of towers and palaces, temples and theatres, where there was scope for ambitious young men, and fortunes and reputations were to be won. Since his childhood he had heard stories of London and its wonders, for his father had often ridden there on Council business, and now Richard Quiney was returning with new accounts of its magnificence and wealth. And there was his other schoolfellow, Richard Field, the tanner's son of Bridge Street, whose career read like a fairy tale, for by the time he was twenty-six he had taken over Vautrollier's printing business and married his widow. There were even more tantalizing contacts with the capital. Every year one or two companies of actors called at Stratford on their summer tours before returning to London for their winter season.

The Earl of Worcester's Men were regular visitors, and were in Stratford in 1584 shortly after a misadventure at Leicester. On Friday, 6 March, they very properly asked the mayor for permission to play, but he told them that the time was not convenient and sent them away with a few shillings to pay for their dinner. Two hours later, having spent the mayor's money, presumably more on drink than on food, they again asked licence to play, and this time meeting with a curt refusal, they took their drum and trumpets and marched through the town shouting 'evyll and contemptyous words' and swearing they would play in Leicester whether the mayor gave them permission or not. Fortunately the affair ended happily and spent itself in nothing worse than noise, for when the effect of their drink had worn off they apologized, and the mayor generously promised not to report them to their patron, and even allowed them to play that night at their inn, provided they showed the audience his licence and publicly apologized for their insolent behaviour. There were eight men in the company, one of whom was eighteen-year-old Edward Alleyn. It was Shakespeare's first sight of the great tragic actor who was shortly to become the leading player of the Admiral's company, the main rivals of the fellowship that he was to join.

If a reputable company like Worcester's could behave with such insolence in the provinces, we can understand why there was such strict regulation of players. One of the chief aims of the Elizabethan Poor Law was to prevent vagrancy, particularly the wandering about the country of troops of men thrown out of work in this transitional period between feudalism and capitalism, when the gild system was breaking down, arable open fields were being enclosed for sheep pasture, and a single shepherd could take the place of half a dozen ploughmen. Hence it was that 'Comon Players in Enterludes whiche shall wander abroade' were classed as rogues and vagabonds along with rufflers, hookers, priggers, prancers, doxies, bawdybaskets, and others of the picturesque fraternity of the Elizabethan underworld, unless they had a licence to travel signed by at least two justices of the peace or were in the service of some peer of the realm. The penalties for vagabondage were discouraging: flogging and a hole bored through the ear with a hot iron for a first offence, more flogging and imprisonment for a second, the gallows for a third. All reputable companies of players, therefore, secured the patronage of a peer, and though

67

they were not paid by him, wore his livery and carried his licence to certify that they were his household servants.

The leading company in the seventies was that of the Queen's favourite, the Earl of Leicester, but in 1583 Elizabeth ordered her Master of the Revels to select a company for herself. These players are not to be confused with the old interluders whom Shakespeare had seen in Stratford as a small boy, and who had since died off. They were twelve of the best men conscripted from the other companies, three of them from Leicester's, who were grievously weakened as a result, two others being John Singer, a notable clown, and Richard Tarlton, a playwright as well as the most famous and popular comedian of his day, perhaps the original of Yorick, 'a fellow of infinite jest', whom Hamlet remembered so well. As members of the Queen's household, they wore the royal livery of a red coat and were sworn in by the Lord Chamberlain as Grooms of the Chamber, though without fee, for their duties were merely nominal and they were paid by Elizabeth only when they performed at Court. Their début was unpromising, for on their first summer tour, while playing at the Red Lion at Norwich, there was some misunderstanding with their audience, one of whom Singer felled and mortally wounded with a stage sword.

In 1587 Leicester's and the Queen's were both in Stratford, as well as three other companies, and the rewards they received from the bailiff for their performances in the Gild Hall are interesting. 'My Lord of Stafford's men' received 3s. 4d., 'another company' 3s. 4d., Essex's players 5s., Leicester's 10s., and the Queen's players 20s. That seems to be a fairly accurate assessment of the relative importance of the five companies. The plays they performed would be mostly nonsense, like *The Rare Triumphs of Love and Fortune*, in which Venus and Fortune squabble over a couple of lovers, or perhaps the Queen's put on Tarlton's *Seven Deadly Sins*, quaintly described as 'a most deadly but most lively play', in which King Gorboduc and his tedious family were resurrected. Tarlton belonged to the older generation of playwrights, authors of moral interludes, and the theatre still awaited the arrival of the new men who were to revolutionize the drama. There was not much longer to wait, and one of them, a young poet of twenty-three, was probably among the audience that watched the wretched fare offered by Stafford's Men, Essex's Players, and the rest in Stratford in that summer of 1587.

There has been much ado about Shakespeare's 'lost years', either the seventeen years between the collapse of his father's fortunes and the first definite mention of his name in London, or, more narrowly, the seven years between the christening of Hamnet and Judith and Robert Greene's attack on 'Shake-scene' in 1592. Some think he went to Italy, where he gained his (far from accurate) knowledge of Italian life and topography. One critic marvels 'at his intimate description of Italian life, explicable apparently only on the supposition that he was an eye-witness of the scenes he describes'; another finds *The Taming of the Shrew* enveloped in 'a pure Paduan atmosphere', another that *Othello* is equally pure Venetian. Even Shakespeare's geographical blunders are adduced as evidence of his minute knowledge of the Italian scene, as when Valentine goes by water from Verona to Milan, from which inland town Prospero was to be hurried aboard a bark to cry to the roaring sea. Some think that he went to the wars and trailed a pike in the Spanish Netherlands.

By 1585 the situation there was serious. The revolt of Philip of Spain's Protestant subjects had been almost crushed by his troops, who were now besieging Antwerp and commanded sixty miles of coast opposite England from which to launch an invasion. At last Elizabeth was forced to act and, after some characteristically hard haggling with the Netherlanders, sent an inadequate expeditionary force too late to save Antwerp. It was commanded by the pleasure-loving Earl of Leicester, who was supported by his thirty-year-old nephew, Sir Philip Sidney, and his twenty-year-old stepson, the Earl of Essex, his General of the Horse. It was a futile campaign, largely given up by the dilatory Leicester to revelry, and by Essex to pageantry and tournaments, while Sidney chafed at the delay and constantly urged action. The climax came in September 1586 at Zutphen, where Essex behaved with great gallantry, and Sidney, 'the miracle of the age', was mortally wounded. By November, Leicester was back in England. Apparently he had taken some of his players with him, for on St George's Day, Shakespeare's twenty-second birthday, he entertained the citizens of Utrecht with an after-dinner show of 'dauncing, vauting and tumbling, with *The Forces of Hercules*, which gave great delight to the strangers'. A few weeks before, Sidney had written from Utrecht to Sir Francis Walsingham: 'I wrote a letter to yow by Will, my lord of Lester's jesting plaier, enclosed in a letter to my wife . . . I since find that the knave delivered the letters to my ladi of Lester.' This has been taken as a reference to Shakespeare, but as we know that the jesting player who was to succeed Tarlton in popular favour, 'Mr Kemp, called Don Gulihelmo', was at Dunkirk in the previous November, we can be quite sure that it was he, Will Kempe and not Will Shakespeare, who bungled the delivery of Sidney's letters.

We can weave any romance we fancy about these early years of Shakespeare. A seventeenth-century historian wrote that Fulke Greville, Lord Brooke, was 'Shakespear's and Ben Johnson's master', and, if we have not faith enough in genius with a grammar-school education, we can imagine him, like Michael Drayton, as a page or singing-boy in some great nobleman's household, where he received his breeding and acquired his knowledge of music. Or we may imagine if we wish, that after the failure of his father's fortunes he sailed round the world with Drake, voyaged to the Levant, was ship-wrecked on the sea-coast of Bohemia, and made his way to Venice, where the Earl of Southampton helped him and became his patron. There is, of course, nothing to support such flights of fancy, though it is just possible to make a case for Aubrey's claim that Shakespeare 'had been in his younger yeares a Schoolmaster in the Countrey'.

When Alexander Houghton of Lea, in Lancashire, made his will in 1581, he left his brother Thomas all his 'Instrumentes belonging to mewsyckes and all maner of playe clothes yf he be mynded to keppe and doe keppe playeres'. If, however, his brother would not

> keppe and manteyne playeres then yt ys my wyll that Sir Thomas Heskethe knyghte shall hauc the same Instrumentes and playe clothes. And I most hertelye requyre the said Sir Thomas to be ffrendlye unto ffoke Gyllome and William Shakeshafte nowe dwellynge with me and eyther to take theym vnto his Servyce or els to helpe theym to some good master.

Fulke Gyllome was a gildsman who played in the Chester miracles, and it is just conceivable that William Shakeshafte is William Shakespeare, using a variant of his name, for in the Snitterfield records his grandfather is sometimes called Shakeschafte, and that he was a player and tutor in the service first of Houghton and then of Sir Thomas Hesketh of Rufford, near Liverpool. Certainly Hesketh had a company of players in 1587, for that Christmas they were at Knowsley, the Lancashire seat of the Earl of Derby, among whose guests were his illegitimate daughter Ursula and her husband, Sir John Salisbury, later to be celebrated in *Love's Martyr*, the volume to which Shakespeare may have contributed the poem known as 'The Phoenix and Turtle'. Moreover, he probably became one of Derby's players for a time, and it is interesting to note that when he and his fellow actors came to arrange their shares in the Globe theatre in 1599, they did so with the help of Thomas Savage, a Rufford man who was the cousin of Thomas Hesketh's widow.

It is an odd series of coincidences, but almost certainly it is no more. There is no clear connexion between William Shakespeare of Warwickshire and William Shakeshafte of Lancashire; there were Shakespeares and Shakeshafts in the north of England as well as in the Midlands; there seems to be no reason why the poet should have adopted the Snitterfield form of his grandfather's name, which, as far as we know, he never did on any other occasion, and there is nothing in the plays to suggest a knowledge of the Lancashire scene, customs, or dialect. Then, when Houghton made his will, Shakeshafte was 'now dwellynge' with him; that was on 3 August 1581, and yet Susanna

71

must have been conceived soon after the end of that month. It is not impossible, but it is most improbable; the story simply does not ring true; it is the wrong shape. The brilliant and ambitious Stratford boy would scarcely bury himself more remotely in the country with a company of inferior provincial players; we do not even know that he wanted to be an actor, but we do know that he wanted to write, and his objective would be London, not Lancashire.

If there is any truth in the story that he became a schoolmaster or usher 'in the country', there were plenty of places near Stratford where he might have found employment for a time, and there is a late tradition that before going to London he lived at Dursley, an old market town at the foot of Stinchcombe Hill in the Cotswolds, and certainly there are references to this area in *Henry IV*: to Woodmancote, or Woncot, a village adjoining Dursley, to the Vizar family of the town and the Perkes family of Stinchcombe. But all this is little more than surmise, and until we have real evidence of Shakespeare's whereabouts in the eighties we must assume that he was in Stratford until at least 1587. He was certainly there in 1582 when he married Anne Hathaway, in 1584 when he begot Hamnet and Judith, almost certainly there when they were christened, and probably, though not necessarily, in 1587, when according to his father's account he was a party to the verbal offer to sell the Wilmcote property to John Lambert. We should, then, imagine him in 1587 as working in Stratford, possibly in a lawyer's office, living with his parents in Henley Street, reading omnivorously, writing eagerly, and, in spite of his inner conflict, enjoying himself hugely within the limits of his modest, but beautiful, environment. If he was no longer in love with his wife, there were the three children, and much as he wanted to get away to a sphere that offered scope to his exploring spirit, he would be reluctant to leave them. It must be remembered that the bonds, both of love and duty, that tied him to Stratford were strong – there is plenty of evidence of this in his later life – and that in 1587 he was still a very young man.

Then came the crisis: possibly a violent quarrel with Anne,

precipitated perhaps by her puritanical, churchwarden brother Bartholomew, who cannot have approved of his writing; possibly some escapade that involved him with Sir Thomas Lucy of Charlecote and gave rise to the poaching legend chronicled by a Cotswold parson a century later; or more probably and simply, the urge to get away and seek his fortune at this time of crisis in the political and literary history of England suddenly became irresistible. If so, opportunity coincided with desire. In 1587 his schoolfellow Richard Field became master of the Vautrollier press, and Shakespeare might ask for, or Field offer him, an opening. Then, in the same year there were the five companies of players in Stratford. Essex's, Stafford's, and presumably the 'other company' were all provincial troupes, but Leicester's and the Queen's had their headquarters in London, and it is likely enough that either of them would accept the services of a handsome, well-shaped young man if he offered them, particularly of a writer who might polish up an old play to make it presentable. It is as good a conjecture as any that he joined the Queen's Men and arranged to meet them in London at the beginning of their winter season.

But whether Shakespeare joined the players in Stratford, or went to see if Richard Field could give him an opening in his business, whether he had some other introduction, or simply set off to seek his fortune, it is clear that he must have gone to London at about this time, leaving his wife and children in the care of his parents. There was no question of desertion; London was only ninety miles away, a two days' journey, and he could easily return to Stratford in case of emergency. He was going, full of confidence, to restore the fortunes of his family, but above all he was going because the great literary revival was in the air, because, although he was not conscious of it, London had need of him; in short, because he must.

CHAPTER 3

1587–8

LONDON

*

WHEN Shakespeare crossed Clopton Bridge on his way to London, he could take the road to Banbury and Aylesbury, though he probably took the more westerly route through Oxford, a town that must always have drawn him, and so up the chalk escarpment of the Chilterns and down their gentle beech-covered slopes to High Wycombe and the valley of the Thames. As he approached the river he would see the great bulk of Westminster Abbey with its recent addition, the delicately traceried Chapel of Henry VII, and here, bordering the water, was the great Hall of Rufus and Richard II and the other remains of old Westminster Palace, where Parliament met, the Lords in their chamber and the Commons in St Stephen's Chapel. For Westminster was the seat of government, where the Queen had her principal palace and the great nobles their town houses. Just beyond the old palace was the new one of Whitehall, Cardinal Wolsey's old house enlarged by Henry VIII, which Shakespeare would pass on his right as he walked up the road to Charing Cross. Most prominent was the great dining-hall where plays were performed, and where within a few years he would himself act in his own plays. There were two gateways across the road, connecting the main buildings with lodgings in St James's Park, where also were the cockpit, tenniscourt, and tiltyard. At Charing Cross the road turned east and here became the Strand, running parallel to the river, and Shakespeare, his mind working ever in correspondences and images, must have been struck by the general resemblance to Stratford: a town on the bank of a swan-crowded river, and a single bridge at one end. If Westminster Abbey were Holy Trinity Church, he might have been walking up High Street, past his old school, the Gild Chapel and New Place, towards Henley Street and Clopton Bridge. But it was a resemblance only in plan; the scale, in every sense of the word, was so much grander. On his right, instead of the Stratford almshouses, were the great houses of the nobility, Durham House, recently given by Elizabeth to her new favourite, Sir Walter Raleigh, Russell House, the Savoy, Somerset House, built in a new classical style that he had never seen before, Arundel House, Leicester House, and on his left were rows of smaller houses backed by Convent Garden and the open country.

At Temple Bar he entered Fleet Street and the precinct of the lawyers, the region of the inns of court, of the Middle and Inner Temple, Lincoln's Inn and Gray's Inn, colleges that made London into a third university town, where lawyers learned their business and the young nobility and gentry to manage their estates. There was gaiety too, music, dancing, and acting in their halls, for they were the nurseries of courtiers as well as of conveyancers, whence they got their name of inns of court. Like the Oxford and Cambridge colleges, they had family and territorial connexions, and many Westcountrymen entered the Middle Temple: Raleigh was there and his Cornish cousins the Carews, and it was the favourite inn of those coming up from Stratford: Fulke Greville, the Combes, the Rainsfords of Clifford Chambers, the Hales family of Snitterfield; and Shakespeare's 'cousin', Thomas Greene, was to enter the inn a few years later.

The houses here became thicker, the streets narrower and more crowded, and after crossing the Fleet River, beside which was the Bel Savage Inn, he would climb the hill to the old fortified town, and at Ludgate pass through the walls and enter the City. Here within the walls, which ran from Blackfriars, a suppressed Dominican priory by the river, in a great northern arc back to the river at the royal stronghold of the Tower a mile farther down, in a maze of narrow streets and tall, huddled houses, lived some 200,000 of the Queen's subjects, proud of their independence. For distinction must be made between aristocratic Westminster and London proper, the City of merchants and master craftsmen, apprentices and journeymen, 'the storehouse and mart of all Europe', ten times more populous than any other town in England. It was governed by a Lord Mayor and Corporation jealous of any interference by the Court and Privy Council at Westminster, though they were themselves continually trying to extend their authority into the rapidly expanding suburbs beyond the walls and south of the river in Southwark, for the town was bursting with the influx from the provinces.

Facing Ludgate was the west end of the Gothic cathedral of St Paul's, its door plastered with notices put up by those looking for employment, its nave cluttered with gossips, while in St Paul's Churchyard were bookshops and many of the printing houses, among them, at the Sign of the White Greyhound, Richard Field's. East of St Paul's, Cheapside, the street of goldsmiths and butchers, cut through the City to its centre, where Sir Thomas Gresham had built his Royal Exchange in a novel and wholly Flemish style, not far from his house in Bishopsgate Street. This was part of the great road that ran through the City from north to south, from Bishopsgate in the northern wall into Gracious Street and so to London Bridge, Southwark, and the Channel ports, the busiest thoroughfare in London, therefore, well provided with inns for travellers and carriers, the Bull, Cross Keys, the Bell, and Boar's Head. Northwards the road ran through the rapidly growing suburb of Shoreditch, and about half a mile from Bishopsgate was James Burbage's Theatre, now ten years old, and close to it the Curtain, another playhouse, built by Henry Laneman, strategically sited rather nearer the City to skim off his rival's audience. However, the two proprietors had recently made an agreement to work their theatres together and pool the profits.

For all Englishmen, London Bridge was one of the wonders of the world, a street built over the river, supported on twenty-one stone piles, with twenty arches through which small boats could pass and the waters roared at the ebb of tide. The houses were built as high as those on the land, but so close together that they joined at the top, and here the mercers and haberdashers had their shops, and over the southern gateway, impaled on poles as a warning to travellers and foreigners, grinned the shrinking heads of executed traitors. London Bridge, however, was not the only means of crossing the river, for some 2,000 licensed watermen fiercely competed for passengers, whom they ferried from bank to bank for a fee of a penny – and a tip.

Southwark was dominated by the tower of St Mary Overy, or St Saviour's as it was renamed at the Reformation, the church in which Chaucer's friend, old John Gower, lay in effigy on his canopied tomb, and where Shakespeare's youngest brother was one day to be buried. But Bankside was less remarkable for its piety than as a place of entertainment and compulsory penance for those who took their pleasures too lightly. A low-lying region of swamp, open drains, and scattered houses running westward along the river bank towards Lambeth Marsh, it consisted of two 'liberties', areas outside the direct control of the City Corporation, the Liberty of the Clink, in which was Winchester House, the London residence of the Bishop of Winchester, and beyond that the Liberty of Paris Garden, with its stairs where watermen landed their passengers from the Liberty of Blackfriars on the other side of the river. The Clink was one of the five prisons of Southwark, and gave its name to the liberty, in which, surrounding Winchester House, was a concentration of brothels or stews, many of them with armed guards at their doors and seductive arbours in their gardens. One of the landlords of the stews was Philip Henslowe, an astute man of business who had married his master's widow, with whose money he was buying up property in this promising district, and in 1587 was just completing the building of the first Bankside theatre, the Rose. The playhouse was close to the Beargarden, a triple-galleried circus in which bears and other animals were baited, a royal sport of which Henslowe was soon to become joint-master. It was a lucrative monopoly, for the Master of her Majesty's Game received £5 whenever the Queen was present, in addition to the profits made out of public baiting and the granting of licences.

There are various contemporary descriptions of the sport, including a poster advertising a typical Thursday entertainment, Thursday being the day when theatres were closed, or supposed to be closed, for the benefit of baiting. Five dogs were to bait a bear for a stake of £5, 'and also to wearie a bull dead at the stake, and for your better content shall have plasant sport with the horse and ape and whipping of the blind bear'. The whipping of the blind bear, Harry Hunks, 'till the blood ran down his shoulders' was a humorous interlude, as was the baiting by dogs of a horse with an ape tied to its back.

Into the same place [wrote a Spanish diplomat] they brought a pony with an ape fastened on its back, and to see the animal kicking amongst the dogs, with the screams of the ape, beholding the curs hanging from the ears and neck of the pony, is very laughable.

More innocent diversion was provided at the end of the entertainment by fireworks, as when a rocket was fired at a large suspended rosette, from which fell apples and pears and small crackers that exploded when the spectators rushed into the arena to gather the fruit.

The Beargarden and the Rose might almost be taken as symbols of Elizabethan society, a society of violent contrasts in which vice neighboured virtue and corruption elbowed innocence. As the churches were encompassed by brothels, palaces by slums, so brutality was a violent foil to kindliness, passion to patience, greed to generosity, falsehood to truth, melancholy to mirth, awareness of mortality to the joy of living, and these people who yelled with delight as the bulls tossed the dogs, and laughed to see the beating of a blind and weeping bear, whose silks and satins were stained with the spittle of their frenzied lips, were those who had come from an edifying sermon full of high morality, and thrilled to the celestial music of Tallis and Byrd, who hurried from a public execution, where they spat upon the wretch who was to die, to listen to the poetry of *Hamlet* and *Lear*. It was a proud, mercurial, quarrelsome, litigious, vivid society, a medieval people magically vitalized by contact with the Renaissance, quivering with energy, straining at the leash of the past, prepared to shock and overrun the three corners of the world.

It was a noisy society too:

> There squeaks a cartwheel; here a tumbril rumbles;
> Here scolds an old bawd; there a porter grumbles.
> Here two tough car-men combat for the way;
> There two for looks begin a coward fray.
> Two swaggering knaves here brabble for a whore;
> There brawls an ale-knight for his fat-grown score.

In the old days people had been content to walk, but now carts, drays, and new-fangled coaches jostled and lumbered over the cobbles of the narrow streets, to the great endangering of life, and given any pretext for rejoicing, or at the first rumour of alarm, the Londoners would run to the towers of their 120 churches and set all their bells rocking and clashing in their steeples.

There were many pretexts for rejoicing, many rumours of alarm in 1587. Without any formal declaration, the twenty years' war with Spain had begun when Leicester took his expeditionary force to the Netherlands, and when in February 1587, after another Catholic plot against her life, Elizabeth at last consented to the execution of her cousin, Mary Queen of Scots, Philip of Spain began his preparations for invasion. For was he not the rightful king of England, a descendant of John of Gaunt, to whom Mary had assigned her claim to the English throne, to the exclusion of her twenty-year-old son, James VI of Scotland? At Cadiz, therefore, he assembled his invincible Armada, which was nearing completion when, in April, Drake sailed into the harbour and burned the bulk of the shipping, returning to Plymouth with a great East Indian carrack, all her silken treasure intact. Although the Armada was not destroyed, there was little chance of its sailing that year; and this was the situation that greeted Shakespeare when he arrived in London, the scene described apparently in *Hamlet*, for like Marcellus the raw provincial boy might well have asked:

> Why this same strict and most observant watch
> So nightly toils the subject of the land,

79

> And why such daily cast of brazen cannon,
> And foreign mart for implements of war;
> Why such impress of shipwrights, whose sore task
> Does not divide the Sunday from the week;
> What might be toward, that this sweaty haste
> Doth make the night joint-labourer with the day?

Shakespeare had arrived in London at the most thrilling moment in its history; thrilling, however, not only because danger, anxiety, expectancy, and hope were in the air, but also because the long-awaited dramatic revolution was imminent.

For in that memorable decade of the eighties, while Drake was raiding the Spanish Main, Sidney writing his sonnets to *Stella* and the *Arcadia* to his 'most dear lady and sister', Mary, Countess of Pembroke, at Wilton House, while Spenser in Ireland was writing *The Faerie Queene*, the young men who were to prepare the way for Shakespeare, still entangled in Stratford, were gathering in London. First was John Lyly, an Oxford man, author of the sophisticated romance *Euphues*, the affected style of which made him the most fashionable writer of the age; then, turning his talents to the drama and purging his prose of its wanton excesses, he wrote two exquisite gossamer comedies, *Campaspe* and *Sapho and Phao*, for the singing-boys of the Chapel Royal and Paul's, who presented them before the Queen in 1584. These were soon followed by *The Arraignment of Paris*, another Court play for the Chapel Children, but mainly in rhyming verse interspersed with lyrics for the high treble voices of the boys. The author was George Peele, like Lyly an Oxford man, though far less reputable, who specialized in writing pageants for the City companies on the occasion of the Lord Mayor's installation. Yet another Oxford man, who had still to make his name as a dramatist was a former Lord Mayor's son, Thomas Lodge, who also had a reputation for loose living and was soon in trouble with the Privy Council. From Cambridge came a more brilliant and more dissipated Bohemian, Robert Greene, who, having added a foreign to a native depravity, abandoned his wife and child and settled in a London slum with his mistress, the sister of a notorious thief, to make a living by writing 'love pamphlets' in the popular euphuism of the period. From Cambridge, too, came Greene's young friend, Thomas Nashe. Finally, there was Thomas Kyd, who, though not a university man like the others, had been at Merchant Taylors' School with Spenser and Lodge, before taking up his father's profession of scrivener.

All these men, collectively known as the University Wits, were in revolt against the false classicism and pedantry that men like Gabriel Harvey, a Cambridge don, were trying to impose on English verse and the native drama, though with the exception of Lyly they were as yet scarcely more articulate than the obscure grammar-school boy from Stratford who had recently arrived in the capital. The explosive material was there, but the divine spark that was to fire it had yet to be struck.

Then, in the summer of 1587, perhaps while Shakespeare was making his way from Warwickshire, another young man, his exact contemporary, arrived in London from Cambridge, where he had just taken his degree. This was Christopher Marlowe, the Canterbury grammar-school boy. Earlier in the year the Admiral's Men had been in Cambridge, where, like Shakespeare in Stratford a few years before, he may have met the leading tragedian Edward Alleyn, who had left Worcester's for a more distinguished company, and if so it would not be long before he was introduced to Philip Henslowe at the Rose on Bankside, where the Admiral's were playing. For apparently Marlowe had come from Cambridge with the manuscript of a play in his pocket, written with Alleyn in mind as the tragic hero, and naturally he wanted to see it produced. Henslowe and Alleyn read the play and bought it, and one afternoon at the beginning of the winter season the Admiral's presented the first part of *Tamburlaine the Great*. It was perhaps the most momentous performance in the history of the English theatre, for, rejecting both the buffoonery of the native drama and the pedantry of pseudo-classical plays, Marlowe made a synthesis of the best elements in both, the vigour and action of the one, the form and structure of the other, and in his Prologue trumpeted the manifesto of the new Elizabethan dramatists:

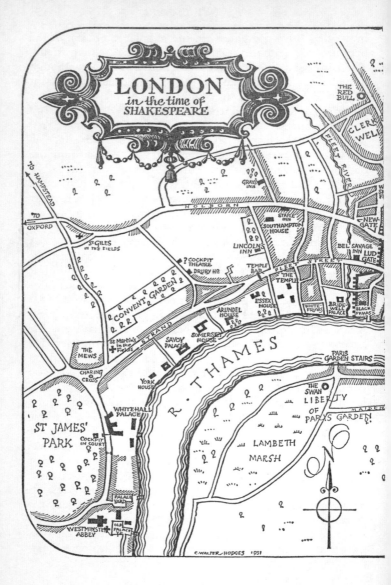

LONDON
in the time of
SHAKESPEARE

THE RED BULL

CLERKEN WELL

FLEET RIVER

TO HAMPSTEAD

TO OXFORD

HOLBORN

GRAYS INN

STAPLE INN

NEW GATE

SOUTHAMPTON HOUSE

St GILES IN THE FIELDS

LINCOLNS INN

BEL SAVAGE INN LUDGATE

? COCKPIT THEATRE
DRURY He

TEMPLE BAR

FLEET STREET

THE TEMPLE

WHITE FRIARS

BRIDE WELL PALACE

CONVENT GARDEN

ESSEX HOUSE

ARUNDEL HOUSE

BLACK FRIARS

St Martin's in the Fields

SAVOY PALACE

SOMERSET HOUSE

THE STRAND

THE MEWS

R. THAMES

PARIS GARDEN STAIRS

CHARING CROSS

YORK HOUSE

THE SWAN

LIBERTY OF PARIS GARDEN

ST JAMES' PARK

WHITEHALL PALACE

COCKPIT IN COURT

LAMBETH MARSH

PALACE YARD

WESTMINSTER ABBEY

OLD PALACE YD

C. WALTER HODGES 1951

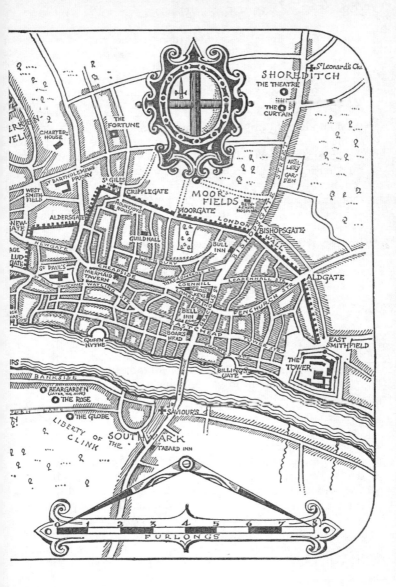

SHOREDITCH

St Leonard's Chu.

THE THEATRE

THE CURTAIN

THE FORTUNE

CHARTER-HOUSE

ARTILLERY GARDEN

ST BARTHOLOMEWS PRIORY

ST GILES

WEST SMITH FIELD

CRIPPLEGATE

MOOR FIELDS

BETH LEM HOSPL

ALDERSGATE

MOORGATE

NEWGATE

MOUNTJOYS HOUSE

LONDON WALL

BISHOPSGATE

LUDGATE

GUILDHALL

BULL INN

ST PAUL'S

CHEAPSIDE

MERMAID TAVERN

WATLING ST

CORNHILL

LOMBARD ST

LEADENHALL ST

ALDGATE

CHURCHYARD

THREADNEEDLE ST

FENCHURCH ST

BELL INN

QUEEN HYTHE

EAST CHEAP

BOARS HEAD

EAST SMITHFIELD

THE TOWER

BILLINGS GATE

BANKSIDE

BEARGARDEN (LATER, THE HOPE)

THE ROSE

THE GLOBE

ST SAVIOUR'S

LIBERTY OF THE CLINK

SOUTHWARK

TABARD INN

0 1 2 3 4 5 6 7 8

FURLONGS

> From jigging veins of rhyming mother-wits,
> And such conceits as clownage keeps in pay,
> We'll lead you to the stately tent of war,
> Where you shall hear the Scythian Tamburlaine
> Threatening the world with high astounding terms.

There followed the equally high astounding action, in which the conquering Tamburlaine made menageries of kings, footstools of defeated emperors, and starving princes dashed out their brains against their cages. There was plenty of excitement for the groundlings, cruelty enough to make them forget the delights of the Beargarden, and though there was no comedy, though much of the verse was mere fustian and noise, the rest of the extravagant melodrama was poetry, a thundering blank verse the like of which had never before been heard on the English stage, charged with heavenly imagery and reverberating with remote mysterious names like those on the lips of seamen returning from the Indies and Cathay. The play closed on a quieter note:

> Then sit thou down, divine Zenocrate;
> And here we crown thee Queen of Persia,
> And all the kingdoms and dominions
> That late the power of Tamburlaine subdued.
> As Juno, when the giants were suppressed,
> That darted mountains at her brother Jove,
> So looks my love, shadowing in her brows
> Triumphs and trophies for my victories.

After this speech the rapt astonished Londoners must have left the theatre still with the whirling verses in their heads and eagerly anticipating the promised sequel. Marlowe had made the fortunes of Alleyn, Henslowe, and the Admiral's, though that was nothing; he had that afternoon demolished both the knockabout theatricals of clowns and the desiccated dramaturgy of dons, setting up in their stead the drama of poets. He had done for the adult companies what Lyly had done for the boys', but his was a much more momentous achievement, for the great playhouses of the people were far more important than the small semi-private theatres of the children, and it was the full-blooded poetic drama, beyond the compass of boys, that was to be the glory, as it was also the reflection, of the Elizabethan age.

The long-awaited spark had fallen, and the effect was immediate. All the poets of London must have heard one of the early performances of *Tamburlaine*, and most of them returned to their lodgings to emulate the play and its titanic hero. Greene, a rapid writer, was the first in the field with his *Alphonsus*, containing frank allusions to 'mighty Tamburlaine'. It was probably written for the Queen's before the end of the year, and was closely followed by Lodge's *Wounds of Civil War* for the Admiral's, a tedious tragedy in which the author tried to repeat the success of Marlowe's famous scene, when Tamburlaine is drawn in his chariot by 'the pampered jades of Asia', the Kings of Trebizon and Soria, but his 'Sylla in his chair triumphant of gold, drawn by four Moors' was only a shadow of the mighty original. Peele's contribution was a spectacular *Battle of Alcazar*, again for the Admiral's, but this, like *Alphonsus* and *The Wounds of Civil War*, paled before the sun of Kyd's *Spanish Tragedy*, a play that was to rival *Tamburlaine* in popularity and influence, and to be revived again and again in the course of the next fifteen years. Kyd had the brilliant idea of modernizing Seneca, of seizing on the sensational elements that were merely reported by messengers in pseudo-classical plays, murder and madness, blood and ghosts, and sweeping them from the wings on to the stage. To these ingredients he added the theme of vengeance, and the tragedy of revenge, or tragedy of blood, was born, the model for innumerable popular plays, of which *Hamlet* is only the most famous.

Shakespeare, too, must have seen *Tamburlaine* at the Rose and been swept away on the torrent of Marlowe's verse, something very different from anything he had ever experienced in Stratford when watching the puerile plays that formed the pre-Marlovian repertory of the travelling companies. They can have done little to inspire him with the ambition to become a professional playwright, and it may well be that he had no such intention when he went up to London. But *Tamburlaine* was a revelation, an exaltation, and after that experience he could have no doubt as to his true vocation. Yet, if he was an actor and factotum with the Queen's he would have very little time for original work, and for the first year or so his dramatic activity would perforce be confined mainly to revising and patching up old plays, and even new ones, to make them topical and popular, and perhaps his reaction to *Tamburlaine* was the rewriting of part of a new history of *Henry VI*. His opening lines were certainly inspired by that play, and a finer tribute to Marlowe than anything written by the University Wits:

> Hung be the heavens with black, yield day to night!
> Comets, importing change of times and states,
> Brandish your crystal tresses in the sky,
> And with them scourge the bad revolting stars
> That have consented unto Henry's death!

It is pure Marlowe, the raging grief of Tamburlaine for divine Zenocrate:

> Raise cavalieros higher than the clouds,
> And with the cannon break the frame of heaven;
> Batter the shining palace of the sun,
> And shiver all the starry firmament!

I suspect that by the end of 1588 the Queen's Men had added the play to their repertory, and that Shakespeare's revised version quite eclipsed Greene's *Alphonsus*.

The Queen's, like any other actors' company, was an association of men who invested their money in a common stock of properties, costumes, and plays. Properties were the least valuable part of the stock: weapons, musical instruments, and so on, while some plays demanded a special feature such as the Admiral's Hell Mouth, cage for Tamburlaine's victims, and cauldron for boiling the Jew of Malta. Costumes, on the other hand, were exceedingly valuable, for materials were very expensive, velvet, for example, costing £1 a yard, at least £30 of our money. Plays they bought outright from the dramatist, generally for £6 or £7, and it was the book-keeper's responsibility to copy out the 'parts' and guard the precious manuscript so that it did not fall into the hands of another company, which, in the absence of copyright laws, would then be able to perform it. The total value of the stock might be as much as £700 of Elizabethan money, and the players divided the profit according to the number of shares they held, which might be one or more, or only a fraction of one. There were normally about ten of these 'sharers' or 'full adventurers', as they were called, one of whom acted as business manager. They employed minor actors, or 'hirelings', for about 6s. a week, and some of the sharers made a few more shillings by training boys to play women's parts and hiring them out to the company. Then in addition to the book-keeper or prompter, there was a tireman who looked after the properties and wardrobe, a stagekeeper who swept up the litter, and one or two musicians.

If Shakespeare was with the Queen's, or any other company, it would be as a hireling, for he cannot have brought much money with him from Stratford, and it would be some years before he had saved £50 or so to buy a share when a vacancy occurred. And it would be some time before he mastered his profession, before he was a sufficiently trained actor to take a leading part, for Elizabethan acting was not natural and realistic but declamatory and formalized, full of conventions and traditional gestures to emphasize the meaning of the words. We cannot expect, therefore, to find his name in any of the lists of actors at this early stage of his career, and he is not mentioned as one of the fellowship of the Queen's led by Tarlton, though it is probable that John Heminge, who was to become one of his greatest friends, was a member. He would, in short, be learning his profession, beginning at the bottom of the ladder, and getting acquainted with the rhythm of an actor's life.

At this time the City inns were still used as playhouses in the winter months, when the road out to the Theatre and Curtain in Shoreditch and the lanes of Bankside became too miry to attract a profitable audience. The Queen's favoured the Bull and Bell in Bishopsgate Street and the Bel Savage in Ludgate Hill, and in the square yard of one of these, surrounded by galleries for the spectators, they performed their repertory of plays, giving special attention to those that they were to present at

Court before the Queen during the Christmas Revels. These lasted from the beginning of November until the beginning of Lent, though under Elizabeth the great period of revelry and plays was the Twelve Days of Christmas, from the Feast of St Stephen to Twelfth Night, 26 December to 6 January, and in 1587–8 the Queen's performed on both these days. They also put on a tumbling turn, relic of the time when players were acrobats as well as actors, and on 18 February they presented another play. This was a last fling before the austerities of Lent, when plays were expressly forbidden, though as it was difficult to enforce the order in the liberties and suburbs this was the time when the companies left the inns for the public playhouses beyond the jurisdiction of the London Corporation. The Queen's normally rented the Theatre from Burbage until July or August, when they went on tour in the provinces, for this was the period of plague, and there were few summers when the theatres were not closed for a season by order of the Privy Council to prevent it spreading. In the autumn they returned to the Theatre before retreating to one of the City inns and again beginning their rehearsals for the Revels.

As no Elizabethan thought it worth while to describe the theatres of the period and there is only one illustration of an interior, a sketch of the Swan, we know little about them, and very little about the first three, the Theatre, Curtain, and Rose. We gather that the Theatre was built mainly of timber, that it had 'about three galleries', that there was a tiring-house or dressing-room for the actors, that it was round, an amphitheatre, and that is about all. However, from the Swan sketch, illustrations of theatre exteriors, the contracts for the building of the Fortune and Hope, and from various allusions in the literature of the period, it is possible to make some sort of reconstruction of an Elizabethan playhouse. Another aid is our knowledge, scanty though it is, of the medieval theatre, of which the Elizabethan was a development.

The medieval theatre was a 'round' in which religious, and no doubt secular, plays were still acted in some parts of the country in Shakespeare's day. These rounds were simply open arenas, fifty or sixty feet in diameter, encircled by wooden stands or earthen banks into which steps were cut to accommodate the audience. Two of these earthen rounds may still be seen in west Cornwall, and from the stage directions and plans given in their manuscripts we can tell pretty well how the Cornish miracle plays were produced. Ranged round the arena or 'plain' were a number of small tents or 'houses', rather like bathing-tents, each representing a locality in the play, and here the characters remained when they were not performing. Good characters were at the south, powerful worldly characters such as kings at the west, and evil ones at the north, next to Hell's Mouth, the working jaws of a fearful monster, belching smoke and fireworks and devils. Heaven was at the east, with a throne for God and another tent beside it where angels played and sang. Most of the action took place towards the middle of the plain so that all had a fair chance of seeing and hearing, and here was the principal locality of the play, represented by some piece of scenery, a ship perhaps, or a chapel. A large open space was necessary for many of the more spectacular episodes, as when the Duke of Cornwall's host of twenty men defeats the heathen army of fifteen, whose leader escapes on horseback ('horse aredy' the prompter notes in his script), as well as for the acrobatics of the stock comic characters, the torturers, and devils.

Morality plays were presented in much the same way by travelling companies of actors who set up their movable theatre on the outskirts of a town, as we can tell from the plan illustrating the fifteenth-century *Castle of Perseverance*. In the middle of the plain is the Castle, and around it are the 'houses': the World at the west, Flesh at the south, the Devil north, Covetousness north-east, and Heaven at the east.

This medieval method of production is beautifully illustrated in a French miniature of about 1450 by Jean Fouquet, who depicts the central scene in the play of the martyrdom of St Apollonia. The grisly martyrdom is being enacted in the middle of the plain, round which is a wooden gallery with canvas houses for Heaven, musicians, and a king, Hell being a monster's mouth from which devils are emerging. There are spectators in the gallery between the actors' houses, and beneath it other spectators are standing, while some squat in front round the edge of the plain.

The medieval theatre, then, was a theatre in the round, and as this method of production of miracles and moralities lasted well into the sixteenth century, in Cornwall at least as late as 1602, we should expect Tudor interludes and early Elizabethan plays to have been presented in a similar fashion in the halls of schools, colleges, great houses, and palaces: a central stage, generally raised so that use could be made of traps, with one or two houses set against the wall. The most important spectators would sit on the dais close to the 'front' of the stage, while facing them at the lower end of the hall would be the less privileged members of the audience. That this was the method of production at Court in Shakespeare's day seems clear: for example, the Revels Office accounts have such entries as 'sparres to make frames for the players howses' and 'canvas to cover diuers townes and howses'; then, when *Gorboduc* was produced at Whitehall in the winter of 1561, the hall was 'to be furnished with skaffolds to sit upon, for ladies to behold the sports, on each side', and for the Revels of 1601, exactly forty years later, the Office of Works was responsible for 'framing and setting up a broade stage in the midle of the haule'.

Presumably this was also the manner of production in the private theatres, 'private' being used to distinguish the small roofed theatres of the boys from the open 'public' playhouses of the adult companies. The boys of the choir school attached to St Paul's were trained by their master and acted in a circular theatre, probably the chapter house, and in 1576, the year of the building of the Theatre, the Master of the Children of the Chapel Royal leased a large room in one of the buildings of the suppressed priory at Blackfriars and converted it into a theatre for his boys. By 1582 the Paul's boys were acting at Blackfriars with the Chapel children, and it was this joint company that presented the plays of Lyly at Court. According to their lease they were supposed to use their room only for Court rehearsals, but in fact they gave public performances there as well, so that their landlord complained that they had turned it into a regular theatre, thereby spoiling the amenities of the neighbourhood as well as disfiguring the house itself. His complaint was not unreasonable if the singing boys behaved like those in the dancing-school next door, who 'cutt upp the lead with knifes or boored yt through with bodkyns wherby the rayne cometh throwghe', and by 1584 he had recovered possession. For sixteen years after this, the end of the first Blackfriars theatre, the adult companies had no public competition from the boys, and even at Court they were less in demand owing to the rise of the Queen's Men, the dramatic revolution of the late eighties and the new plays written by Marlowe and his contemporaries for the adult actors.

One would expect the inn-yard presentation of the boisterous Tudor and early Elizabethan interludes and farces, before audiences very different from those in private halls and theatres, to resemble even more closely that of the medieval round: a few tents ranged round the walls, and the audience confined to the galleries and standing room below them, where they were roped off as in the Cornish rounds, so that the performers had most of the yard for their medley of histrionics and acrobatics, for it must be remembered that many of these early plays were as heavily laced with horseplay as the late miracles and moralities. In the Coventry miracles Herod leaped off the stage to rage 'in the strete also', and in the highly moral *Castle of Perseverance* Belial has 'gunne-powder brennynge In Pypys [burning in pipes] in his handis & in his eris & in his ars whanne he gothe to battel'. Fireworks and devils, battles and tumbling were what the early audiences were accustomed to and expected, and the yard was certainly the place for such things; almost it might be said, no yard no audience, for it would be almost like a circus without an arena.

When, therefore, James Burbage built the first public, open-air theatre in 1576 he had a number of models to work from, chief of which were the inn-yard theatres, the medieval rounds, and the Bankside Beargarden. The sketch of the Swan, built twenty years later, gives us a general idea of the interior of a

tectum

porticus

orchestra

mimorum aedes

ingressus

proscaenium

planities siue arena

quintum sed spectari et spectari, historiam romanam oni destinatum, in quo multi vrsi, tauri, et stupendae magnitudinis canes, distructis canci et septis alitibus, qui ad

THE SWAN THEATRE

From the drawing of J. de Witt, *c.* 1596

typical Elizabethan playhouse. Like the Beargarden, it was a wooden amphitheatre of three galleries enclosing an arena or yard some fifty to sixty feet in diameter. The stage was not in the middle, but a platform, perhaps five feet high, set against a flat wall at one side of the building and projecting into the yard. Two stout columns at the yard end supported a canopy over the stage at the level of the gallery roof, and above this was a loft from which, through traps, aerial flights could be made, cannon balls rolled to simulate thunder, and other quaint devices practised. There were also traps in the stage communicating with the space below, which was (unlike the Swan sketch) either concealed by hangings or more probably boarded in. In the wall at the far side were two doors leading on to the stage, and above them two galleries on a level with the upper and middle gallery encircling the yard.

It is this wall, blank at the bottom save for its two doors, that is the main problem in reconstructing the method of Elizabethan staging, for somehow there must have been a way of representing scenes 'above' and 'within'. For example, there must have been a balcony for the production of *Romeo and Juliet*, and there must have been some sort of curtained 'inner stage' within which, according to the original stage direction, 'Prospero discouers Ferdinand and Miranda playing at Chesse'.

The orthodox solution is that the wall was that of the tiring-house or actors' dressing-rooms, as it is in fact labelled in the Swan sketch: 'mimorum aedes', the actors' building. Then, the lower gallery is said to be an upper stage, which would normally have a balcony in front of it; the upper gallery (hidden by the canopy in the sketch) was for the musicians, and between the two doors was a curtained recess forming a small inner stage. In this way we get the 'above' and 'within' that Elizabethan plays sometimes demand. And yet there is no authority for these suppositions. In the Swan sketch the lower gallery is divided into a number of boxes or 'rooms' apparently occupied by spectators; there is no balcony, and there is no sign of an inner stage between the doors.

Another solution has recently been advanced by Dr Leslie

Hotson.* According to this, the Elizabethan production of plays in the public as well as in the private theatres and halls was, like the medieval, in the round, so that the galleries over the stage contained seats, the best seats, occupied by gallants and their ladies. The tiring-house, he maintains, was under the stage, as it was in the medieval pageants, the great two-tiered wagons on which scenes from miracle plays were enacted in some big towns such as York and Coventry. The long edge of the rectangular stage was against the wall and the scenic action was transverse, that is across, not from wall to yard. At each end of this tennis-court-like stage was a row of two or three small 'houses', some of them with two storeys, running from near the back wall to the columns supporting the canopy at the yard end. Most entries were from traps within the 'houses'. His stage, in fact resembles that in the Fouquet miniature, for if we imagine ourselves beside the king's throne, where the best seats are, on our right will be Heaven and good characters, on our left Hell and evil characters, an arrangement symbolized by the opposing rows of houses on the Elizabethan stage, those on the right, as seen from the best seats, the galleries under the canopy known as the 'lords' room', representing good, those on the left or sinister side representing evil. These curtained and, if necessary, two-storeyed houses supplied the necessary 'within' and 'above' for a play's production.

I think Dr Hotson is right in essentials, though mistaken in some of his emphasis and detail. The Elizabethan theatre *was* a development of the medieval round and retained many of its conventions of staging; but it is very improbable that the space below the stage was anything more than an extension of the tiring-house, which in the Swan sketch is shown as being beneath the lords' room, while the stage is open underneath. This, it is true, could be an error, as the sketch was made from memory, but what are we to make of Henslowe's memorandum about ceiling 'the rome ouer the tyerhowsse' at the Rose? It is certain, I think, that houses were erected on the stage, though they were by no means always necessary, and their curtains

* *Shakespeare's Wooden O*, 1959.

would be used as little as possible, for their continual drawing would be a distraction and, when drawn around, an obstruction for a great part of the audience. Then, entries from below stage through traps would be very rare except for comic business and ghostly visitations. The two doors in the tiring-house wall would give the effect of opposition and conflict, Montagues entering by one, Capulets by the other, and similarly with Lancastrians and Yorkists, English and French, Greeks and Trojans, fairies and mortals.

Moreover, when Burbage built his experimental Theatre, at a time when horseplay and acrobatics were so popular, I suspect that he used the yard much as his medieval predecessors had used the plain for their moralities. As late as 1590, in *Soliman and Perseda* there are the directions, 'Enter Basilisco riding of a mule', and 'Piston getteth up on his ass, and rideth with him to the door', and how effective it would have been if in Shakespeare's bustling 1 *Henry VI*, when the French 'leap over the walls in their shirts', they had jumped into the yard from one end of the stage while the English scaled the other. And was Tamburlaine on his way to Babylon simply drawn on to the stage by the pampered jades of Asia, or did he flog his royal steeds triumphantly around the yard? No doubt there was a period of experiment, but it could end only in one way; it was more profitable to fill the yard with groundlings, and after the dramatic revolution, when plays became much more a matter of words than of clowning and acrobatics, it could generally be dispensed with. Yet it seems probable that the two alleys between the ends of the stage and the side-galleries were sometimes closed to the groundlings, and that, for example, Romeo 'leaped the orchard wall' into the Capulet garden by vaulting on to the stage from one of them.

Experiment and experience would lead to other changes, as when in 1595 the throne, or state, another medieval relic, apparently on a dais between the doors in the tiring-house wall, was stored in the loft at the Rose, a device perhaps copied from the Swan, leaving room for the gallants to sit on their hired stools 'under the state of Cambises himself'.

The theatre for which Shakespeare wrote, therefore, was very different from ours: not an Italianate theatre of illusion with proscenium arch, front curtain, scenic wall, and elaborate scenery, but a theatre of medieval conventions in which the audience's imagination supplied the background to the actors and their words: a bare framework was a battlement or balcony, the empty stage anything from Cleopatra's palace to the Forest of Arden; above it were the Heavens and below was Hell, and the yard itself could be pressed into service as required. It was a theatre in which the actors were surrounded by their audience, all of whom could see and hear, whether they sat on stools on the stage, or in the lords' room above, or in the side-galleries, or stood in the cheaper galleries or the yard. Above all, it was an infinitely flexible theatre in which any sort of action at any level could be represented, the production of a play having the speed and fluidity of the cinema, the technique of which Elizabethan staging so closely resembled.

The public playhouses were 'open' to make use of the daylight, for effective artificial lighting would have been almost impossible. A flag flew from the top of the theatre to show that there was a performance, which usually began at two o'clock in the afternoon. Three trumpet soundings announced the beginning, and at the third sounding the Prologue appeared, dressed in the traditional black, for it was the clergy who used to introduce the miracle plays, and then, again like the cinema, the action flowed without a break for change of scene to its conclusion two or two and a half hours later.

Entrance to the first public theatres cost a penny, which gave access to the yard, and perhaps part of the bottom gallery, where the groundlings stood, another penny paid at an inner door securing a seat in one of the upper galleries, and a third penny a seat with a cushion. A full house would be worth £7 or £8. The admission pennies paid at the main entrance were the players' profits, the gallery takings the owners' rent, both being collected by 'gatherers' with boxes (hence the modern 'box-office'), Burbage himself operating at one of the inner doors of his Theatre, where he was said to 'thrust some of the money devident betwene him and his ffellowes in his bosome or other where about his bodye'. Perhaps the trick was already an old one, another survival from the medieval rounds, but it persisted until the closing of the theatres in 1642, by which time prices had risen enormously, and gatherers 'seem to scratch their heads where they itch not, and drop shillings and half-crown pieces in at their collars'. Hirelings were often employed as gatherers, and perhaps Shakespeare began his career as a box-holder at the door of the Theatre.

The theatres did not escape the attention of the Puritans, those zealous Protestants with a passion for preaching and a singularly joyless creed that laid special emphasis on the observance of the Sabbath; indeed they opened their attack as soon as the Theatre, Curtain, and Blackfriars theatre were completed. It began with a sermon preached at Paul's Cross by Thomas White in November 1577: 'The cause of plague is sin,' he thundered, 'and the cause of sin is plays; therefore' – but there was no need to finish the syllogism. Sodom is exceeded, and 'the sumptuous Theatre houses' are the sinks of 'theft and whoredom, pride and prodigality, villany and blasphemy, schools of vice and dens of thieves'. This broadside was followed a month later by another parson, John Northbrooke:

> Satan hath not a more speedy way, and fitter school to work and teach his desire, to bring men and women into his snare of concupiscence and filthy lusts of wicked whoredom, than those places and plays and theatres are; and therefore necessary that those places and players should be forbidden and dissolved and put down by authority, as the brothel houses and stews are. . . . Many can tarry at a vain play two or three hours [the preacher added disarmingly] when as they will not abide scarce one hour at a sermon.

The earthquake of 1580 that 'shaked the scenical Theatre' was of course seized upon as a sign of God's wrath, though in fact the only casualties were two children who were listening to a sermon in church, a detail omitted by the Puritans. Then the Beargarden disaster one January Sunday in 1583 furnished further shot for the offensive against these Heathenishe Enterludes and Playes. For surely it is to be feared, beesides the distruction bothe of bodye and soule, that many are brought unto, by frequenting the Theater, the Curtin and such like, that one day those places will likewise be cast downe by God himselfe.

Phillip Stubbes was even more outspoken in his *Anatomy of Abuses*: the players are 'idle lubbers, buzzing dronets, painted sepulchres and doble dealing ambodexters'; playhouses 'Venus pallace and sathans synagogue'; and as for plays, are they not a

prophanation of the Lord his sabaoth? Doo they not draw the people from hering the word of God, from Godly lectures and sermons? Do they not maintaine bawdrie, infinit folery, & renue the remembrance of hethen ydolatrie? Do they not induce whordom & unclennes? nay, are they not rather plaine devourers of maydenly virginitie and chastitie? For proofe whereof, but marke the flocking and running to Theaters & curtens, daylie and hourely, night and daye, tyme and tyde, to see Playes and Enterludes; where such wanton gestures, such bawdie speaches, such laughing and fleering, such kissing and bussing, such clipping and culling, Suche winckinge and glancinge of wanton eyes, and the like is used, as is wonderfull to behold.

The Puritans had a power of invective and a knowledge of bawdry exceeded only by Shakespeare.

One sympathizes with the Puritan attack on bearbaiting, 'that cruell and lothsome exercise, that unholy spectacle', but not with their attempt to equate the 'pleasure to see one poore beast to rent, teare and kill another' with that of seeing the plays, however paltry, put on at the public theatres. 'The Lord of his mercie open the eyes of the maiestrats to pluck down these places of abuse,' concluded Stubbes: Beargarden, theatres, and all.

But the eyes of the magistrates were already open: the City fathers were overwhelmingly Puritan, and nothing would have pleased them better than to pluck down the theatres. Fortunately, however, they were outside their control: the Theatre and Curtain in the suburb of Shoreditch, the boys' theatre in the Liberty of Blackfriars, while Henslowe was very prudently building his Rose among the stews in the Liberty of the Clink. Moreover, the theatres had powerful supporters, among them Sir Philip Sidney, who, in his *Apology for Poetry*, defended comedy as an exposure of the common errors of life, and tragedy as a teacher of whatever is most worthy to be learned. But, far more important, the Queen and her Privy Council in Westminster were determined that the theatres of the City should remain open, for were they not nurseries of the Court, places of rehearsal for her entertainment during the winter Revels? Elizabeth, every inch a humanist, detested the philistinism of the Puritans as heartily as their narrow theology, and resisted their attack on her players as stubbornly as that against her bishops. It was for this reason that she formed her own company of players, and ordered the Lord Mayor to license them to play on weekdays within the City if they wished. The Corporation replied by licensing the Queen's Men, and no other company, to play at the Bull and Bell inns on holidays. But it was no use. The Queen made her meaning icily clear, and her players were allowed to perform on workdays as well as holidays. The result was, of course, as the Corporation complained, that 'all the places of playeing were filled with men calling themselves the Quenes players'.

The Queen and Privy Council looked on with an indulgent eye, yet they were not prepared to tolerate other forms of abuse by the players. There must, for example, be no criticism of the government or of the established religion in their plays, no political meetings in their theatres, no brawls within, and no riots without, or they would be closed. Moreover they would be closed in time of plague. The Corporation enthusiastically agreed, and suggested that they should be allowed to open when weekly deaths in London had been less than fifty for a period of twenty weeks. It was their final stratagem in this phase of their struggle; weekly deaths were very rarely under fifty, and the theatres would hardly ever have been able to open their doors. The Council ruled that they should be closed only when *plague* deaths exceeded thirty a week, and for the moment the Corporation had to be satisfied with that.

99

This then was the position in London when Shakespeare celebrated his twenty-fourth birthday in April 1588. The great city, driven by a sense of urgency, was throbbing with excitement, and all was in a state of confused though purposeful activity, for every citizen knew that Spain was preparing another Armada and that one day that summer it would be seen bearing down on the Channel ports to pour its sea-borne army into England. It was the fulfilment of the century-old prophecy that the year was to be one of eclipses, unparalleled marvels, and disasters, the world's grand climacteric, perhaps even the end of all things:

> When from the Virgin Birth a thousand yeares
> With full five hundred be compleat and told,
> The Eightie Eighth a famous yeare appeares,
> Which brings distress more fatall then of old.
> If not in this yeare all the wicked world
> Do fall, and land with sea to nothing come;
> Yet Empires must be topsie turvie hurl'd,
> And extream grief shall be the common summe.

But Shakespeare and the other young poets in the capital were thrilling to another excitement in which dread had no part, the new creative spirit released by Marlowe, flaming amazement from the stage and heavens of the Rose, shaking the air with the defiant music of Tamburlaine and Faustus. They can have had little love for the puritanical City fathers who were trying to quench that flame and silence that music, and if Anne Shakespeare had a similar horror of plays and playhouses we can understand why her husband set off for London alone, and never, so far as we know, brought her and her family to share his life there. No doubt she did not think of her young husband as one of 'those Schoole-masters in bawderie, roisters, brallers, bosters, loiterers, ruffins', but theatres could well be for her synagogues of Satan, and she might tremble for his safety and be quite unable to sympathize with his work.

Although there was no plague that summer the Queen's Men went on tour, and on 19 July were at Bath, the day on which the long-expected Armada was sighted off Scilly, a huge crescent of 150 ships hung with black, presaging tragedy and the over-throw of England. But that night Admiral Howard and Drake beat out of Plymouth Sound, and a week later the 'Spanish floating Babel' was in flight round the gale-beaten coasts of Britain, half of it never to return

It was the one decisive action of the twenty years war, but it was enough; Spain had lost control of the seas, all the Americas and Indies lay open to Drake and his fellow seamen, and the Spanish empire, though not topsy-turvy hurled, began rapidly to crumble. But 'that admirable year Eighty-Eight' was decisive in other ways as well. A few days after the destruction of the Armada the Earl of Leicester died and was replaced at Court by his stepson, the fascinating auburn-haired Earl of Essex, who had just come of age, and the infatuated fifty-five-year-old Elizabeth at once took him into favour, heaped honours upon him, and installed him close to Whitehall by the river, in Leicester House, renamed Essex House.

The literary scene also underwent a change as more young poets poured into London from the provinces. Shakespeare's Warwickshire contemporary, Michael Drayton, arrived at about this time, as did George Chapman, who joined Marlowe as a member of the circle that surrounded Raleigh at Durham House. The young Earl of Southampton, patron of poets, aged only sixteen, came down from Cambridge in 1589 to enter Gray's Inn, from the same college as the brilliant 'young Juvenal', Thomas Nashe, and his friend Robert Greene. Meanwhile the great sequence of Marlowe's plays was enacted at the Rose, *Doctor Faustus, The Jew of Malta, Edward the Second*, and in 1590–1 the first three books of *The Faerie Queene* were published as well as the dazzling prose and poetry of Sidney, now four years dead, the *Arcadia*, and his sonnets to *Stella*. Never before had London known such a state of literary ferment, never had there been such a stimulus to write, such a creative spirit abroad as after the defeat of the Armada, at the dawn of England's greatness when all things seemed possible, and when, like Shakespeare, to be young was very heaven.

CHAPTER 4

1588–94

THE LORD CHAMBERLAIN'S SERVANT

*

ALTHOUGH Shakespeare may have been little more than a raw provincial boy when he arrived in London, it would not be long before any awkward angularities were rubbed away, for it would be difficult to imagine a more liberal education than that offered an actor in one of the favoured companies after the dramatic revolution and congregation of poets in the capital, a far more liberal education than that of a man who went to the university and then became a parson or a schoolmaster in the country. A Warwickshire dialect would be no disadvantage, for men were then proud of their native speech, all sorts of accents were heard at Court, and the great Sir Walter Raleigh himself gloried in his Devonshire burr.

First, there was the fellowship of the players, not all of them educated men it is true, but some of them had graduated from the boys' companies where they had been trained by men like Lyly and Sebastian Westcott, perhaps even Tallis and Byrd. The very training in their profession was an education, their instruction in the arts of rhetoric and music, of graceful movement, and the delivery of a blank-verse line. Then, in their theatres they met the poets who wrote their plays, and Shakespeare would have additional opportunities of meeting writers of all kinds, the men whose work was published by Richard Field. And not the least important element in an actor's education was travel. 'Home-keeping youth have ever homely wit,' says Valentine sententiously in *The Two Gentlemen of Verona*, and if Shakespeare was with the Queen's between 1588 and 1591 he saw far more of England than the majority of his countrymen saw in a lifetime, visiting Faversham and Dover in Kent, Bath, Gloucester, Ludlow, and Bridgnorth in the West

Country, Leicester, Coventry, and Nottingham in the Midlands, Norwich, Ipswich, and Aldeburgh in East Anglia, 'the furthest parte of Langkeshire' and perhaps even Scotland to play at the Court of James VI. They certainly played at three of the houses of the Earl of Derby, and this intimacy with the aristocracy and acquaintance with their homes was a great polisher of manners. But the nobility were to be met in greater numbers in London, not so much the middle-aged and staider members in their town houses, as their sons at the inns of court, lively young men like the Earl of Southampton, who two or three afternoons a week rode out to the Theatre or crossed the Thames from Blackfriars to Paris Garden to visit the Rose, and boasted of their friendship with the players. And sometimes during their Christmas revels they would invite the players to give a performance in the hall of one of their inns.

Travel, the conversation of poets, and companionship of courtiers were part of an actor's everyday life, yet in a sense all were but prologue to performance at Court, for the fiction still held that companies of actors, the London companies at least, were licensed simply to supply entertainment to the Queen, all other performances being merely rehearsals for the Revels. These were under the direction of the Master of the Revels, Edmund Tilney, who had an office and clerks, a wardrobe, workrooms for tailors, carpenters, and property makers, 'togeather with a Convenient place for the Rehearsalls and settinge forthe of Playes and other Shewes for those Services'. As Tilney had been responsible for the formation of the Queen's Men, he took a particular interest in their activities and the plays they had to offer, and in the three winter seasons between Christmas 1588 and Lent 1591 they gave nine performances at three of the royal palaces, Whitehall, Richmond, and Greenwich, far more than any other company. These Court performances were financially important, for the players received £10 for every appearance before the Queen, considerably more rewarding than a full house at the Theatre. If Shakespeare was with them he was well acquainted with the great riverside palaces, their guards, grooms, ushers, and ceremonial, and he must have caught a glimpse of the dancing in the great hall, of the Queen herself dancing with the youthful Essex, before she took her seat and the play began. We can understand, therefore, how it was that the young man who had left Stratford a few years before, quite ignorant of life in the Court, was able to write his first plays on the theme of kings and princes, the three parts of *Henry VI*, and one cannot help wondering if these were the three plays presented by the Queen's at Richmond between 1 January and Twelfth Night 1591. They were certainly written by the following year.

At the beginning of 1592, shortly before Edward Alleyn married his stepdaughter, Philip Henslowe began to keep a diary or account book in which he entered, in his inimitable spelling, the names of the companies who rented the Rose, their plays, and his receipts as owner of the theatre, sometimes adding the word 'ne' to indicate a play that was in some way a new one, either a first performance, or newly corrected, or recently bought by him, for Henslowe collected his own stock of plays. Thus, on Saturday 'the 19 of Febreary' he began to record the four months' season of 'my lord Stranges mene', who opened with a performance of Greene's *Friar Bacon and Friar Bungay*:

Feb 19	Fryer Bacune	17s. 3d.
21	Mulomurco	29s.
22	Orlando	16s. 6d.
23	Spanes comodye, Donne Oracoe	13s. 6d.
24	Syr John Mandevell	12s. 6d.
25	Harey of Cornwell	32s.
26	the Jewe of Malltuse	50s.

There was no performance on Sunday, the 20th, though they gave one on Thursday, the 24th, ignoring the Privy Council's strict renewal of the order not to play on Thursdays and so seduce spectators from the neighbouring Beargarden, 'to the greate hurte and destruction of the game'. (The case was altered when Henslowe and Alleyn, his partner as well as son-in-law, acquired an interest in the Royal Game a few years later.) They also ignored the regulation about not playing in Lent, and throughout the season, which lasted until 23 June, they played every day except Sundays, Good Friday, and two other days, 105 performances altogether, the lowest receipts being 7s. for a revival of Lodge's and Greene's *Looking Glass for London*, the highest £3 16s. 8d. for a 'ne' play on Friday, 3 March, *Harey the VI*. This is the first mention anywhere of a Shakespeare play, which may have been any of the three parts of *Henry VI*, though most probably the first of the trilogy. Henslowe's average takings for the season were £1 14s. It should be observed that there was no continuous run in the Elizabethan theatre; the same play was rarely given twice in one week, and as the season progressed new plays replaced the least popular ones in their repertory, so that Strange's presented twenty-three plays in their eighteen weeks at the Rose. Of these the most popular were 'Jeronymo' (*The Spanish Tragedy*), played every week but two, that is sixteen times; *The Jew of Malta* with ten performances; *Henry VI*, such a draw that it was given three times in eight days and fifteen times in all; and 'Tittus & Vespacia', possibly *Titus Andronicus*, 'ne' on 11 April (receipts £3 4s.), after which it was repeated six times. Shakespeare, Marlowe, Kyd – and the rest nowhere. Their four plays account for forty-eight performances to packed houses, half the total number, whereas Greene's two plays were given only three times altogether, *Friar Bacon* being dropped after a second performance that brought in only 15s. 6d., while *Orlando Furioso* was never repeated after its first unprofitable production.

While Strange's were acting at the Rose, Tom Nashe was writing his *Pierce Penilesse*, a biting and explosive satire in which among other things he gave a half-mocking, half-serious, defence of the theatre, worth quoting for its glimpse of an Elizabethan audience:

For whereas the after-noone beeing the idlest time of the day; wherein men that are their owne masters (as Gentlemen of the Court, the Innes of the Courte, and the number of Captaines and Souldiers about London) do wholy bestow themselves upon pleasure, and that pleasure they devide either into gameing, following of harlots, drinking, or seeing a Playe: is it not better that they should betake them to the least extreame, which is Playes?... As for the hindrance of Trades and Traders of the Citie by them, that is an Article foysted in by the Vintners, Alewives and Victuallers, who surmise, if there were no Playes, they would have all the companie that resort to them lye bowzing and beere-bathing in their house every after-noone.

And then more seriously, 'What if I proove Playes to be no extreame; but a rare exercise of vertue?' The plot, he argues, is often taken from English history, and in the play the valiant acts of our forefathers are revived, an inspiration to their degenerate descendants.

How would it have ioyed brave Talbot (the terror of the French) to thinke that after he had lyne two hundred yeares in his Tombe, hee should triumphe againe on the Stage, and have his bones newe embalmed with the teares of ten thousand spectators at least (at severall times) who, in the Tragedian that represents his person, imagine they behold him fresh bleeding?

Evidently Nashe took a particular interest in *Harey the VI*, of which Lord Talbot was the hero.

By the time *Pierce Penilesse* was published in August, Nashe's friend Robert Greene was on his deathbed. Sunk in destitution and despondency, he was living in physical and spiritual squalor among the dregs of the London underworld, profiting from his seamy experience by writing pamphlets exposing the tricks of his companions, an occupation that led to the exposure of his own trickery in selling *Orlando Furioso* to the Queen's and then, when they were on tour, to the Admiral's, an exploit that may account for its single performance at the Rose. He was unrepentant, protesting that it was only tit for tat, the players themselves swindling the playwrights whose work they bought. Then, after a supper of pickled herring and Rhenish with Nashe, the wretched and embittered young poet died.

A few weeks later his last pamphlet was published 'at his dying request' by his friend Henry Chettle. This was his *Groatsworth of Wit*, an autobiographical sketch in which he describes his declension from an 'Arch-plaimaking-poet' to a destitute pamphleteer, sucked dry by the players who, recently vagabonds, now strutted about like gentlemen of great living. Then, addressing 'those Gentlemen', that is those university men, Marlowe, Nashe, and Peele, he launches his savage attack on the players.

Base minded men all three of you, if by my miserie ye be not warnd: for unto none of you (like mee) sought those burres to cleaue: those Puppets (I meane) that spake from our mouths, those Anticks garnisht in our colours. Is is not strange, that I, to whom they all haue beene beholding: is it not like that you, to whome they all haue beene beholding, shall (were yee in that case as I am now) bee both at once of them forsaken: Yes, trust them not:

And then he singles out one player for his final invective:

for there is an upstart Crow, beautified with our feathers, that with his *Tygers hart wrapt in a Players hyde,* supposes he is as well able to bombast out a blanke verse as the best of you: and beeing an absolute *Iohannes fac totum,* is in his owne conceit the onely Shake-scene in a countrey.

The reference to Shakespeare is apparent, for Greene's quotation is a parody of a line in the third part of *Henry VI*, 'O tiger's heart wrapped in a woman's hide', but this personal assault is something different from the general abuse of players and must have been occasioned by some specific injury, either real or imagined. We know of none, but the outburst becomes comprehensible if Shakespeare was an actor with the Queen's, the company to which Greene sold most of his plays; a good actor too, though merely a hireling, a *Johannes fac totum,* an upstart crow strutting in the feathers of Greene's poetry as if they were his own. As all too often they were, for one of the functions of this Jack-of-all-trades was to patch and rewrite plays for his company, and the history of Henry VI, Joan of Arc, and Talbot that had drawn 10,000 spectators to the theatre was scarcely recognizable as the one that he had written with Peele and Nashe, so much of his work had this Shakescene rewritten. Moreover, this young upstart actor had had the audacity to purloin his subject, to continue his history, and write two more (highly successful) plays of *Henry VI*, as though a mere grammar-school boy could pen blank verse like a university man! But Greene was wrong; the first phase of the dramatic revolution was almost over, and the future lay with men who, whether university graduates or not, happened to be poets with a genius for play-writing.

Chettle was himself an author and minor playwright, and three months after Greene's death published his *Kind-Harts Dreame*, a tract containing 'five apparitions, with their invectives against abuses reigning'. One of the apparitions was Robert Greene, 'of face amible, of body well proportioned, his attire after the habite of a schollerlike Gentleman, onely his haire was somewhat long'; but more important than the invective of apparitions was Chettle's apology addressed to the living. Marlowe had resented Greene's remarks about his atheism in the *Groatsworth of Wit*, and accused Chettle of mischiefmaking by not deleting the offending passages, which, as editor, he was entitled to do. In his preface Chettle stoutly defended himself, but added that he regretted having published the passage about the upstart crow, a man whom he did not then know but had since made a point of meeting.

I am as sory [he wrote] as if the originall fault had beene my fault, because my selfe have seene his demeanor no lesse civill, than he exelent in the qualitie he professes: Besides divers of worship have reported his uprightness of dealing, which argues his honesty, and his facetious grace in writing, that aprooves his Art.

It is the first portrait we have of Shakespeare: courteous as he is excellent an actor, upright and honest as his writing is witty and graceful, and well acquainted with many people of rank and importance.

At this time, the end of 1592, Shakespeare was twenty-eight and had been some five years with the 'quality', that is the players, though it is improbable that he was still with the Queen's. In the autumn of 1588 their great comedian, Tarlton, died, an irreparable loss, and from that time their fortunes began slowly to decline. For competition was growing, their greatest rivals being the company of Lord Admiral Howard, for whom Alleyn was playing the great tragic heroes of Marlowe. Then there was another rising company under the patronage of Lord Strange, the Earl of Derby's heir, one of whose members was Richard Burbage, younger son of James Burbage, a determined young man who makes his first appearance in a brawl at the Theatre in 1590, when widow Brayne, as relict of James's late partner, claimed one half of the gallery takings and advanced with her supporters to seize them. James and his wife, 'looking out at a wyndoe upon them', called them whores and murdering knaves; their elder son Cuthbert joined in the abuse, but Richard seized a broom, paid one of their opponents his share with a beating, and 'scornfully and disdainfullye played with the nose' of another. This was the man who was to rival Alleyn as the greatest tragedian of the age, and when Shakespeare saw him act he must have thought that he could do for his projected plays what Alleyn was doing for Marlowe's.

By the end of 1590 Shakespeare had three or four plays to his credit, and it was probably these, with his revision of other men's work, that kept the Queen's together, enabling them to hold their own against the competition of the Admiral's, and account for the five plays they gave at Court during the Revels of 1590–1. He would now be in a position to buy a share in the Queen's if he wished, but they had nobody approaching the stature of Alleyn, whereas Strange's had Burbage, and in 1591 he transferred his allegiance and bought a share in that company. This, at least, appears to be the most likely reconstruction of events. If John Heminge accompanied him and Augustine Phillips was already a member of Strange's, the famous fellowship that was to perform his plays was already beginning to assemble. That Christmas Strange's gave six performances at Whitehall, the Queen's only one, and only once again did they appear at Court. Soon they were reduced to selling their plays, either to Henslowe or the publishers, including *The True Tragedy of Richard III*, *The Troublesome Reign of King John*, *The Famous Victories of Henry V*, and *King Leir*, anonymous plays in some of which Shakespeare must have acted and may have had a hand as reviser, and all of which he was either to rewrite or use as sources for his later work. In May 1594 Henslowe lent his nephew £15 to buy a share in 'the Quenes players when they broke and went into the contrey to playe'. They seem never to have returned to London and to have become merely a provincial company. The Admiral's and Strange's had proved too strong for them.

Shakespeare, then, was probably acting at the Rose with Strange's in that memorable spring of 1592, and already Burbage was doing for him what Alleyn was doing for Marlowe, playing the titanic heroes, or villains, of his tragedies, for the negro Aaron in *Titus Andronicus* is the counterpart of Barabas in *The Jew of Malta*. It is a young man's play, in the writing of which Shakespeare drew on his schoolboy knowledge of Seneca and Ovid's *Metamorphoses*, pedantically larding his text with scraps of Latin like any University Wit: 'O, 'tis a verse in Horace; I know it well,' says Chiron, 'I read it in the grammar long ago.' It was also a deliberate attempt to win popular favour at the first assault, to out-Tamburlaine Tamburlaine and surpass *The Spanish Tragedy* in horror. There is a human sacrifice, murder, execution, rape, a cutting out of tongues, chopping off of hands, slitting of throats, eating of human flesh, and in the last scene all but two of the remaining characters are killed, leaving Titus's eldest son to the not unurgent business of ordering well the state, which he begins by condemning Aaron to be stood breast-deep in earth and famished. Yet it was not only the cruelty, violence, and horror that fascinated the Elizabethan audience, the play had a structure and held together, suggesting that its author was a born dramatist, as it had verse revealing beyond doubt that he was also a born poet:

> The green leaves quiver with the cooling wind,
> And make a chequer'd shadow on the ground:
> Under their sweet shade, Aaron, let us sit,
> And, whilst the babbling echo mocks the hounds,
> Replying shrilly to the well-tuned horns,
> As if a double hunt were heard at once,
> Let us sit down and mark the yellowing noise;

And, after conflict such as was supposed
The wandering prince and Dido once enjoy'd,
When with a happy storm they were surprised,
And curtain'd with a counsel-keeping cave,
We may, each wreathed in the other's arms,
Our pastimes done, possess a golden slumber;
Whiles hounds and horns and sweet melodious birds
Be unto us as is a nurse's song
Of lullaby to bring her babe asleep.

Shadow, echo, yellow, Dido, melo: it is characteristically Shake-spearian music, anticipating Lorenzo's 'Dido with a willow', Viola's 'willow . . . halloo . . . babbling gossip', and Gertrude's 'willow grows . . . crow-flowers . . . melodious lay'. How popular the play was is attested not only by its success at the Rose in 1592 and its revival in 1594, but also by Jonson's squib in *Bartholomew Fair*:

He that will swear *Jeronimo* or *Andronicus* are the best plays yet shall pass unexcepted at here, as a man whose judgement shows it is constant and hath stood still these five-and-twenty or thirty years.

That was written in 1614, and if Jonson's figures are anything more than round numbers it means that *Titus Andronicus* was written by 1589.

The first part of *Henry VI*, of which Shakespeare was probably only the reviser, altering here, adding a touch there, and completely re-writing some of the scenes, was popular for another reason, or rather another emotion. It was not a tragedy of blood and revenge like *Titus Andronicus* and its prototype *Jeronimo*, pandering to man's baser nature, but a history appealing to the triumphant nationalism of the Elizabethans who had just scattered the Spanish Armada and carried the war into the Spanish peninsula itself. For most of the audience the Frenchmen were Spaniards, and although the play ended with the defeat of the English in the Hundred Years War it seemed somehow more in the nature of a victory: the cowardly French were always running away, all their successes were equally cowardly stratagems, Talbot died a hero's death, that is like an Englishman, and Joan of Arc was a sorceress and common trollop – a quite unShakespearian touch. But as Shakespeare rewrote and reread his Holinshed and Halle the theme of the Wars of the Roses took shape in his mind, and he prepared his audience for a continuation of the disastrous history of Henry VI's reign. Thus, in the middle of the French wars and jarring factions of the English nobility, comes the still, dramatic relief of Talbot's loyal address to the King:

> I have awhile given truce unto my wars,
> To do my duty to my sovereign:
> In sign whereof, this arm . . .
> Lets fall his sword before your highness' feet,
> And with submissive loyalty of heart
> Ascribes the glory of his conquest got
> First to my God and next unto your grace.

It is an adumbration of the philosophy that Shakespeare was to develop throughout his work, a philosophy derived from the Middle Ages and a commonplace to the Elizabethans: that of an ordered universe at the heart of which was God, while on the terrestrial plane was the King, another fixed centre about which all subjects should revolve in orbits orderly as those of the sun, planets, and stars about the earth. But if order gave place to disorder, chaos was come again. It was this theme of chaos and its consequences that Shakespeare developed in the next two parts of *Henry VI*.

It is a scene of pitiless ferocity in which all the main characters are cheats, liars, braggarts, bullies, murderers, and the trilogy ends with the murder of Lancastrian Henry and his son by the Yorkist brothers, the new King Edward IV, and the Dukes of Gloucester and Clarence. The verse with its imagery from stones, snakes, wolves, tigers, and other beasts of prey reinforces the inhumanity of the action, the Duke of York's famous speech before being butchered by Queen Margaret being as good an example as any:

> O tiger's heart wrapp'd in a woman's hide!
> How couldst thou drain the life-blood of the child,
> To bid the father wipe his eyes withal,

> And yet be seen to bear a woman's face?
> Women are soft, mild, pitiful and flexible;
> Thou stern, obdurate, flinty, rough, remorseless.
> Bidst thou me rage? why, now thou hast thy wish:
> Wouldst have me weep? why, now thou hast thy will:
> For raging wind blows up incessant showers,
> And when the rage allays, the rain begins.

Shakespeare had not forgotten his training in rhetoric at Stratford, the 'comely tropes and pleasant figures' that Thomas Jenkins had taught him. It is splendid oratory and, spoken with 'fit pronunciation and gesture', splendid theatre, but it is not the stuff from which characters are created. All rant the same hyperbolic high-astounding verse, and the people we remember are the humble prose-speakers, the followers of Cade: George Bevis, John Holland, Dick the butcher, and Smith the weaver.

But Shakespeare had joined Strange's so that Burbage could play the great character that he had in mind for the fourth part of what was now to become a tetralogy, the play that was to make all whole, stop civil wounds, and restore divine order by the marriage of Lancaster and York. So, while Strange's were acting at the Rose in the early summer of 1592, Shakespeare began to write his *Tragedy of King Richard the Third*:

> Now is the winter of our discontent
> Made glorious summer by this sun of York. . . .

He was gaining confidence, discarding the influence of Marlowe, and Richard's verse is rarely the high-pitched rhetoric of *Henry VI*, but more natural, almost at times colloquial, and out of this new easy language Shakespeare created his first great character – for it must always be remembered that his characters are only words – a melodramatic villain it is true, but a credible and most memorable villain.

The glorious summer of 1592, however, was to turn into a long winter of discontent. Alarmed by the thousands flocking to the Rose, the London Corporation appealed to Archbishop Whitgift for his help in 'the refourming and banishing of so great evill out of this Cittie'. Whitgift, implacable opponent of the Puritans, was an unpromising ally, and all he could suggest was a bribe to the Master of the Revels; but when on 11 June, a Sunday, there was a riotous assembly of apprentices on Bankside under pretence of meeting at a play, the Privy Council, fearing further disturbances, ordered the closing of the theatres until Michaelmas, and on 23 June Strange's season at the Rose came abruptly to an end. They petitioned the Council, pointing out that they could not afford to take their whole company on tour and that to split it would break up the fellowship, 'whearebie wee shall not onlie be undone, but alsoe unreadie to serve her maiestie'. But their appeal was in vain. A few weeks later plague descended on London, the worst visitation since the year before Shakespeare's birth, and the theatres remained closed, 'the doors locked up, the flags taken down, like houses lately infected, from whence the affrighted dwellers are fled, in hope to live better in the country'.

The players, too, had to go into the country, following their drums and trumpets in their lumbering wagons, competing with the provincial companies and earning only a fraction of what they received daily in their London theatres. The depleted Strange's made for Cambridge, where the 'Mayor's Play' brought in 20s., then turned west to Oxford for a beggarly 6s. 8d., and so to Coventry and Gloucester. They were home, however, by Christmas, when they gave three performances at Hampton Court, the palace to which Elizabeth had withdrawn to escape infection, and on 29 December began another season at the Rose. Their repertory was the same as before, with the addition of two plays that Henslowe marked as 'ne', 'the Gelyous comodey' and 'the tragedy of the Guyes', presumably Marlowe's *Massacre at Paris*.

The season, however, was tragically brief. Infection returned, plague deaths mounted, and on 31 January the Rose was closed again after a Council order forbidding all assemblies of people within seven miles of the City, except for preachings (the Puritans would not forgo those) and divine service at church. Rather than risk a repetition of their recent experiences in the country, the players hung about in London for a time, hoping that the outbreak would subside, but as the weather grew warmer the sickness increased at an alarming rate and the Council issued orders to the Corporation. No children were to go to school from infected houses; constables were to provide women carrying red rods to attend the sick; sextons were to set up notices on the doors of infected houses; scavengers were to cleanse the streets every day except Sunday, and all were to join in a common hunt for dogs – a fatal injunction, for it was the dogs that killed the plague-carrying rats. Then, all infected houses were to be closed for a month, the sound being shut in with the sick and dying, an order that led to scenes like those described by Dekker, of 'some fearfully sweating with coffins, to steal forth dead bodies lest the fatal hand-writing of death should seal up their doors'. There were to be 11,000 plague deaths in London that year.

It was no place for the players in 1593, and Pembroke's were already on their way to the west country, Sussex's to the north, when on 6 May the Privy Council issued a special licence to Strange's authorizing them to exercise their quality of playing in any uninfected town beyond the seven-mile limit surrounding London. The actors named were 'Edward Allen, servaunt to the right honourable the Lord Highe Admiral, William Kemp, Thomas Pope, John Heminges, Augustine Phillipes and George Brian, being al one companie, servauntes to our verie good Lord the Lord Strainge'. Adversity had made an odd confusion, for here was Alleyn leading five of Strange's Men, his rivals, presumably with one or two hirelings and boys, into the wilderness. Richard Cowley, another member of Strange's, joined them at Bristol with a letter for Alleyn from his wife, and in September Henslowe sent him news of Pembroke's: 'they ar all at home and have ben this v or six weackes, for they cane not save ther charges with travell as I heare & were fayne to pawne ther parell'. 'I praye ye, son,' he added, 'commend me heartely to all the reast of youre fealowes for I growe poore for lacke of them.' It was true enough, for Henslowe grew fat on the players, and the Rose had been closed for eight months.

There was, however, an easing of the plague at Christmas, and though there was only one performance at the Revels at Hampton Court, the last melancholy appearance of the Queens', Sussex's managed to get in two short seasons at the Rose before they gave up the struggle and, like the Queen's, possibly with them, 'went into the country'. Pembroke's were in the pawn-broker's hands, the Queen's and Sussex's in the provinces; the Admiral–Strange combination under Alleyn was all that was left of the London players.

When, therefore, the plague had almost spent itself, having killed a tenth of London's citizens in its two years' desolation, and Henslowe was allowed to open an isolated little theatre at Newington Butts, he made another entry in his Diary:

In the name of god Amen begininge at Newington my Lord Ad-meralle men & my Lorde Chamberlen men As ffolowethe 1594

June	5	Heaster & Asheweros	8s.
	6	the Jewe of Malta	10s.
	7	Andronicous	12s.
	8	Cutlacke	11s.
	10	Bellendon ne	17s.
	11	Hamlet	8s.
	12	Heaster	5s.
	13	the Tamynge of A Shrowe	9s.
	14	Andronicous	7s.
	15	the Jewe	4s.

The Lord Chamberlain's is not another company, but Strange's under another name. Lord Strange had become Earl of Derby on his father's death in September 1593, but had himself died in the following April, and his company had therefore to look for another patron. They were fortunate in finding one in Henry Carey, Lord Hunsdon, for not only was he a first cousin of the Queen, but also her Lord Chamberlain, master of the Master of the Revels, and ultimately responsible for her enter-tainment and control of the theatres. Strange's, then, or Derby's as they had been for a few months, were the Chamberlain's when they began to play at the small, inaccessible Newington theatre, where even *The Jew of Malta* brought in only 4s. on a Saturday afternoon.

By this time the two companies had been reorganized and were sharing the Newington theatre, acting perhaps on alternate days, simply because it was the only one available. Then, in the middle of June, all restrictions were withdrawn, and Henslowe triumphantly carried off his son-in-law and the Admiral's to the Rose, while James Burbage gave an equally cordial welcome to his son Richard and the Chamberlain's at the Theatre. The Theatre, however, was still too remote in the winter, and in October Lord Hunsdon wrote to the Lord Mayor:

> Where my nowe companie of Players have byn accustomed for the better exercise of their qualitie, & for the service of her Maiestie if need soe requier, to plaie this winter time within the Citye at the Crosse kayes in Gracious street; These are to requier & praye your Lo. (the time beinge such as, thankes be to god, there is nowe no danger of the sicknes) to permitt & suffer them soe to doe; The which I praie you the rather to doe for that they have undertaken to me that, where heretofore they began not their Plaies till towardes fower a clock, they will now begin at two, & have don betwene fower and five, and will nott use anie Drumes or trumpettes att all for the callinge of peopell together, and shalbe contributories to the poore of the parishe.

By the autumn of 1594, therefore, the two companies had settled in, the Chamberlain's playing at the Theatre in spring and summer, and at the Cross Keys in winter, while the Admiral's, in less need of alternative winter quarters, played throughout the year at the Rose on the other side of the river. The great rivalry had begun. The Admiral's had the better theatre and they had Alleyn; but the Chamberlain's had Burbage and one incomparable advantage, William Shakespeare, who as a sharer wrote exclusively for them; the Admiral's, on the other hand, had lost their great dramatist, for in the spring of 1593 Marlowe had been killed in a brawl in a Deptford tavern.

That Shakespeare was a full adventurer with the Chamberlain's we know from the accounts kept at Court by the Treasurer of the Chamber, for early in 1595 he was one of the three sharers who were paid £20 for the presentation of two plays by the company at Greenwich Palace during the Christmas Revels: 'To Willm̄ Kempe Willm̄ Shakespeare & Richarde Burbage seruauntes to the Lord Chambleyne . . . for twoe seuerall comedies or Enterludes shewd by them before her Matie in xrmas tyme laste paste.' We do not know, however, what he was doing during the two plague years that threw the theatrical world into such confusion, between the summer of 1592 when Strange's were playing at the Rose and the summer of 1594 when they reappear as the Chamberlain's playing at Newington.

Yet, although there are no records of Shakespeare's whereabouts, it is not difficult to reconstruct events with some degree of probability. When Strange's were driven into the country in 1592 they complained that their company was so great that they could not afford to take all their members, and one obvious and potentially most profitable economy would be to leave their actor-dramatist behind to write a play for them against their return. Nothing could have suited Shakespeare better, and when they set out for Cambridge he would take the more westerly road that led to Oxford and Stratford. Aubrey tells us that he 'was wont to go to his native country once a year', but he cannot have had many opportunities of seeing his family for the last five years, when as a hireling he would have to do as he was told, and in any event was too busy acting, writing, and making a name for himself to have time for more than one or two brief visits to his home, and we cannot doubt that now his first thoughts would be, if not for his wife and parents, at least for his children.

He would be welcome indeed, for he arrived at a critical time. The Spaniards had occupied Britanny to support the Catholics in the French civil war, and as they now had another base from which to launch an invasion, commissioners were sent into the English counties to collect the names of those who did not attend church and ask them the reason why. In the spring of

1592 the Warwickshire commissioners found in Stratford three Catholics suspected of relieving priests, including William Clopton, eleven more Catholics who paid their monthly fine instead of attending church, six who were too decrepit to attend, and nine others who 'it is sayd coom not to churche for fear of process for debtte'. One of these was John Shakespeare, not a Catholic recusant deliberately absenting himself from church, but fearful of appearing in the streets lest he should be arrested for debt. His son, by now a successful actor-dramatist, had returned with money in his purse, and this is the last we hear of John Shakespeare's financial troubles.

Shakespeare's father was now in his sixties, 'a merry cheek'd old man', his mother some ten years younger, and, as far as we know, all their children were still living with them in Henley Street. Gilbert was twenty-six, Joan, not yet married, twenty-three, Richard eighteen, and Edmund only twelve, eager to follow his eldest brother to London and become an actor. Shakespeare himself was only twenty-eight, but Anne was thirty-six, approaching forty, a great age for the young poet who had recently written,

> When forty winters shall besiege thy brow
> And dig deep trenches in thy beauty's field,
> Thy youth's proud livery, so gazed on now,
> Will be a tatter'd weed, of small worth held.

And the young father's children were growing up: Susanna was nine, and the twins, Hamnet and Judith, seven, Hamnet just old enough to go to his old school, of which Alexander Aspinall had been master for the last ten years.

After the strenuous though intoxicating years in London it must have been a great happiness once again to be united with his family, to revisit the scenes of his youth, the river, the Forest of Arden and the Cotswolds, and to renew his friendship with his former companions, with Hamnet Sadler, Juline Shaw, Henry Walker, Richard Quiney, elected bailiff in October, and the rest. There were pleasures and diversions in plenty, and he would be unlikely to miss Queen Elizabeth's visit to Oxford in

September, when two Latin plays were presented in Christ Church hall, one of them a comedy, the *Rivales*, which may have set him wondering about writing an English comedy on a theme of Plautus. He had friends in the university, young Henry Willoughby, for example, an undergraduate at St John's, but his main object in riding the forty miles to Oxford may have been to see a dearer friend, one whom he had first met three years before when he was a student at Gray's Inn, the eighteen-year-old Earl of Southampton, now a courtier in the Queen's retinue and, according to the academic Latin poem celebrating the occasion, 'No other youth who was present was more beautiful than this Hampshire prince, or more distinguished in the arts of learning, although as yet the tender down scarce bloomed on his cheek'. It may have been as he rode home to Stratford that Shakespeare composed the sonnet beginning, 'To me, fair friend, you never can be old':

> three winters cold
> Have from the forests shook three summers' pride,
> Three beauteous springs to yellow autumn turn'd
> In process of the seasons have I seen,
> Three April perfumes in three hot Junes burn'd,
> Since first I saw you fresh, which yet are green.

His four months' stay in Stratford, however, was by no means altogether a holiday, and he had work to do for his company before he settled down to write something entirely for his own satisfaction. First of all, therefore, he finished *Richard III*, his children serving as models for the children in the play, and then turned to the narrative poem that he had in mind, *Venus and Adonis*, almost certainly written in the autumn of 1592 when he was in Stratford with sufficient leisure for such an enterprise. It was the tenth anniversary of his courtship and marriage. The poem could scarcely have been written if he had been touring England from east to west with a cry of players, and amid all its artifice there are simple touches of nature that suggest a renewed acquaintance with his native countryside: the comparison of the shy Adonis to a 'dive-dapper peering through a wave', of Venus's quick withdrawal of her eyes to the sudden shrinking of a snail within its shell, its 'tender horns being hit', and above all the description of the dew-bedabbled hare, coursed by hounds over the Cotswold uplands.

Thus, when the plague abated in December and Shakespeare rode back to London to rejoin Strange's for the Revels at Hampton Court, he carried two manuscripts in his saddle-bag. It is improbable, however, that *Richard III* was acted that winter, for there would be insufficient time for rehearsal for a Court performance, and the season at the Rose was too brief for its addition to their repertory before plague closed the theatres again at the end of January. But Shakespeare had time to see *Venus and Adonis* into the press before he returned to Stratford at the beginning of May, when Alleyn led the rump of Strange's into the country. Beautifully printed by Richard Field, it was published apparently in the autumn, when the plague was beginning to abate. This we learn from the letter of a crazy soldier, William Renoldes, who was convinced that the Privy Council caused certain books to be published to persuade him that the Queen was in love with him. In his letter, dated 21 September 1593, he wrote:

Also within thees few dayes ther is a nother booke made of *Venus* and *Adonis* wherin a queene represents the person of *Venus,* which queene is in great love (forsothe) with *adonis*, and greatly desiares to kise him, and she woes him most intierly, telling him although she be oulde, yet she is lustie freshe & moyst, full of love & life (I beleve a goodell more than a busshell full) and she can trip it as lightly as a phery nimpfe vppon the sandes and her foote stepes not seene, and much ado with red & whyte.

There was indeed. The poem was dedicated 'to the Right Honourable Henrie Wriothesley, Earle of Southampton, and Baron of Titchfield':

Right Honourable, I know not how I shall offend in dedicating my vnpolisht lines to your Lordship, nor how the worlde will censure mee for choosing so strong a proppe to support so weake a burthen, onelye if your Honour seeme but pleased, I account my selfe highly praised, and vowe to take aduantage of all idle houres, till I haue honoured you with some grauer labour. But if the first heire of my inuention proue deformed, I shall be sorie it had so noble a godfather: and neuer after eare so barren a land, for feare it yeeld me still so bad a haruest, I leaue it to your Honourable suruey, and your Honor to your hearts content which I wish may alwaies answere your owne wish, and the worlds hopefull expectation.

Your Honors in all dutie,
William Shakespeare

It is a formal enough epistle, dignified and restrained, not at all in the adulatory vein of so many of the dedications addressed by other poets to this promising young patron of literature; yet we should scarcely expect Shakespeare, a member of a despised profession, to unlock his heart in a dedication and publicly parade his intimacy with one of the greatest peers of the realm. On the other hand, we should expect some offering from a poet to the object of his devotion, and it seems probable that the 'lovely boy' to whom Shakespeare was at this time addressing his sonnets was the one to whom he dedicated the 'first heir of his invention', his first published work. We should also remember the story ascribed to Davenant, that Southampton gave Shakespeare 'a thousand pounds, to enable him to go through with a purchase which he heard he had a mind to'. The sum is fantastically large, but if there is any truth in the story it suggests a gift far in excess of anything that a patron was expected to do for his protégé.

Henry Wriothesley belonged to the new nobility which had profited from the dissolution of the monasteries, his grandfather having acquired great wealth and the abbeys of Titchfield and Beaulieu in Hampshire. His father married Mary Browne, daughter of the first Viscount Montague, and there were two sons and a daughter of the marriage, Henry being the second son. He was born at Cowdray House in Sussex on 6 October 1573, almost ten years after Shakespeare, and in 1581, after the death of his elder brother and his father, became third Earl of Southampton at the age of eight. With no brothers and no uncles, he was now the only hope of his house if the princely line was to be perpetuated, and everything was done to make him worthy of his heritage. He became a royal ward, the great Lord Burghley himself acting as his guardian, and when only twelve he was sent to St John's College, Cambridge, where he graduated M.A. in 1589. By this time he had entered his name at Gray's Inn and appointed the famous scholar John Florio, translator of the *Essays* of Montaigne, as his tutor in Italian. His marriage was an all-important question, and when he was only sixteen Burghley offered him the hand of his granddaughter, Lady Elizabeth Vere; but it was no love-match and after some hesitation Southampton refused to change his single state. When *Venus and Adonis* was published, therefore, he was still a bachelor and one of the most handsome and accomplished noblemen at Court, a favourite of the Queen and a friend of Essex, a patron of poets and young-looking for his years, which were only nineteen.

He was, in fact, just such a youth as Shakespeare had been describing in his sonnets since reading Sidney's sequence to *Stella* which inspired the vogue of sonneteering, a 'sweet boy' with 'a woman's face', an Adonis far above the poet in rank, whose duty it was to marry and beget an heir. This is the theme of the early sonnets:

> Who lets so fair a house fall to decay,
> Which husbandry in honour might uphold
> Against the stormy gusts of winter's day
> And barren rage of death's eternal cold?
>   O none but unthrifts, dear my love, you know:
>   You had a father, let your son say so.

It is also the theme of Venus:

> Torches are made to light, jewels to wear,
> Dainties to taste, fresh beauty for the use,
> Herbs for their smell, and sappy plants to bear;
> Things growing to themselves are growth's abuse:
>   Seeds spring from seeds and beauty breedeth beauty;
>   Thou wast begot; to get it is thy duty.

Even the verse forms are the same, for the six-line stanza of

Venus and Adonis is merely the sestet of a sonnet; and as a footnote it is worth remarking that Shakespeare implies that his young friend's father is dead though his mother is living: 'You *had* a father' and,

> Thou art thy mother's glass, and she in thee
> Calls back the lovely April of her prime,

a graceful compliment to the widowed Countess of Southampton.

The 'lovely boy' of the sonnets is the Adonis of the poem, 'more lovely than a man', shy, wayward, and 'frosty in desire', reluctant to take a wife and incapable of loving even the Queen of Love. *Venus and Adonis*, in fact, is an allegory on a theme of the sonnets, an allegory with a moral, for Adonis dies without an heir: 'To grow unto himself was his desire.' The secondary significance would not be lost upon Southampton though it could mean nothing to the world, which seized upon the rich eroticism of the poem, coupling it with Marlowe's *Hero and Leander* as a 'luscious marrowbone pie for a young married wife', and even younger lovers slept with the verses underneath their pillows. Although too literary, enamelled, and rhetorical to please the austerer palate of today, it is a highly accomplished poem, and how popular it was in Elizabethan times is proved by the ten editions through which it passed before the end of the reign. It is not too much to say that *Venus and Adonis* made Shakespeare's reputation.

Of course we should not take everything that Shakespeare wrote to Southampton either too literally or too seriously. There is more than an element of convention and playfulness both in the matter and manner of the poems, and Southampton would take them for what they were, the expression of the poet's regard, the good looks, civil demeanour, and genius of whom attracted him, while Shakespeare, dazzled by his rank and flattered by his friendliness, was genuinely fond of the handsome, generous, and accomplished boy. Nor is there reason to suspect anything unnatural or perverted in their relationship (the twentieth sonnet should be sufficient refutation) which seems to have been merely the innocent affection, or passion, to use the Elizabethan word, that one young man so often feels for another, a passion that Shakespeare idealized in his sonnets, making them a vehicle for his meditations on love and friendship, life and death, and all-devouring Time. And after all, these are the things that matter, the poetry of the sonnets, not the shadows that may so doubtfully be traced upon their surfaces, for at least a score of them are among the greatest poems, some would say *are* the greatest short poems, in our language.

Perhaps it was while seeing *Venus and Adonis* into the press and hopefully waiting with his fellows for the theatres to re-open at the beginning of 1593 that Shakespeare wrote *The Comedy of Errors*. It was a new venture, his first essay in comedy, involving many modifications both of style and structure. As it was based on two Latin plays by Plautus, the action was con-fined, in the classical manner, to a single day, so that one of the characters, old Aegeon, had to explain the initial situation to the audience in a speech of a hundred lines. Shakespeare was to repeat this classical 'unity of time' in his last play, and it is inter-esting to compare Prospero's opening narrative in *The Tempest* with the similar – and yet how different – one of Aegeon, for both are descriptive of shipwreck. Then, his one tragedy and four histories, *Titus Andronicus* and the *Henry VI–Richard III* tetra-logy, had been written almost entirely in blank verse, and the bright, metallic Marlovian rhetoric was scarcely a medium for comedy and farce. Shakespeare, therefore, experimented with new forms, with prose and doggerel for broad comedy and with rhyme for his chief characters. This new, and so Shake-spearean, lyrical note in the plays is first unmistakably heard in the love-making of Antipholus of Syracuse (III.ii), where, as in the sonnets, the harmony is extended from the line to the passage as a whole by assonance or half-rhyme:

> Sweet mistress – what your name is else, I *know not*,
> Nor by what *wonder* you do hit of mine –
> Less in your *knowledge* and your grace you show not
> Than our earth's *wonder*; more than earth divine. . . .

> Against my soul's pure truth why labour you
> To make it *wander* in an *unknown* field?

It is unashamedly undramatic, for Shakespeare has forgotten the play in the excitement of the poetry, but it was a foretaste of what was to come; and though *The Comedy of Errors* is not a great play – incidentally it is much the shortest – it is very good fun, and proved that Shakespeare was a master of comedy as well as of tragedy.

Strange's may have taken the new comedy on tour, and again they would leave its author behind to write another play for them while they were so unprofitably employed in the provinces, and after six months in plague-stricken London Shakespeare would be ready to escape once more to Stratford. Before writing another play, however, he had to fulfil the promise made to Southampton of taking advantage of all idle hours to honour him with some graver labour, a labour that might prove to be a repetition of his former success as a narrative poet. The subject that he had been pondering for his next long poem was *The Rape of Lucrece*, like *Venus and Adonis* a story out of Ovid, and his treatment of the successful rape was much the same as that of the frustrated seduction, an extended exercise in rhetoric. The hundred-line dispute between the ravisher's frozen conscience and hot-burning will is prologue merely to a debate of twice the length with his virtuous victim, and the rape itself little more than a pretext for the heroine's three-hundred-line apostrophes to Night, Opportunity, and Time. Although the death of Lucrece is more dramatic than that of Adonis, the reader is quite unmoved by a tragedy that is as remote from life, as withdrawn and formal, as a Byzantine mosaic. And as beautiful: for again there are passages of poetry that might have come out of the sonnets, and no praise could be higher than that.

It is interesting to note that, as Caroline Spurgeon observed, under one of the arches of Clopton Bridge there is still an eddy that may have suggested the image in *The Rape of Lucrece*:

> As through an arch the violent roaring tide
> Outruns the eye that doth behold his haste,

Yet in the eddy boundeth in his pride
Back to the strait that forced him on so fast;

and the Induction of Shakespeare's next play, *The Taming of the Shrew*, is full of allusions to the Stratford neighbourhood, for the immortal tinker Christopher Sly, born at Barton-on-the-Heath, home of Shakespeare's cousin John Lambert, haunts the alehouse at Wincot at the foot of the Cotswolds, where he owes fourteen pence to the fat proprietress Marion Hacket. We are introduced to a troupe of travelling players, of whom Sly asks, 'Is not a comonty a Christmas gambold or a tumbling-trick?' A few years earlier, before the dramatic revolution, that would have been a fair definition of a comedy, but 'No,' says Shakespeare in the person of one of his characters, 'it is more pleasing stuff. It is a kind of history.' And with that the players begin the history of Katharina and Petruchio, the shrew and the shrew-tamer: the scene, Padua.

The Taming of the Shrew is the first of a group of plays with an Italian setting, which leads some to think that Shakespeare must have gone to Italy during the plague years 1592–4, though how he managed to write such a phenomenal amount on his travels is another matter. There was no need to go to Italy; he could get all the information he wanted from Florio, whom almost certainly he knew through their common patron Southampton, just as Ben Jonson got his Venetian information for *Volpone* from 'his worthy Freind Mr John Florio: the ayde of his Muses'. It is quite possible that Florio taught Shakespeare some Italian as well as French, not difficult languages to read for anybody with his knowledge of Latin. But he rarely read a foreign book, Latin, Italian, or French, if an English version were available – he certainly preferred Florio's translation of Montaigne's *Essays* to the original, and there is a copy inscribed with what may be a genuine signature, 'Willm. Shakspere' – for he was a rapid reader as he was a rapid writer, impatient to get to the heart of a matter unless the book was one to be digested, like the *Faerie Queene* or the sonnets of Sidney. In any event, Christopher Sly is pure Warwickshire Shakespeare, the taming an old and well-known story, and for the Bianca sub-plot there was '*Supposes*: A Comedie written in the Italian tongue by Ariosto, and Englished by George Gascoyne of Grayes Inne Esquire, and there presented'. It is characteristic of Shakespeare thus to interweave three strands of different material to make a whole.

Although the Queen's was the only company commanded to perform at the Revels, so ironically named in that tragic plague-winter of 1593, Shakespeare would return to London with the work he had written in Stratford, and Strange's (or Derby's since Lord Strange's succession to the earldom in September) would get in a January season at the Theatre or Curtain while Sussex's were playing at the Rose. What they performed we do not know, for, to our infinite loss, Henslowe was the only theatre owner to keep a record, but by now *The Comedy of Errors* must have been in their repertory, and probably *The Taming of the Shrew*, though there would be little time for rehearsal. And again, as a year before, Shakespeare took his poem to a publisher, though not this time Field, who was really a printer, but to John Harrison, to whom Field transferred *Venus and Adonis*. However, Field printed *The Rape of Lucrece*, again beautifully, for Harrison, who registered it on 9 May 1594 – for all books had to be registered with the Stationers' Company – a few days before it was issued and on sale in Paul's Churchyard. Shakespeare prefixed an argument, or synopsis of the story, and another dedication to Southampton, and these, with the *Venus and Adonis* dedication, are the only non-dramatic prose of his that we possess. The *Lucrece* dedication reads:

The loue I dedicate to your Lordship is without end: whereof this Pamphlet without beginning is but a superfluous Moity. The warrant I haue of your Honourable disposition, not the worth of my vntutored Lines makes it assured of acceptance. What I haue done is yours, what I haue to doe is yours, being part in all I haue, deuoted yours. Were my worth greater, my duety would shew greater, meane time, as it is, it is bound to your Lordship; To whom I wish long life still lengthned with all happinesse.

Your Lordships in all duety.
William Shakespeare

This epistle, with its emphasis on love and duty, should be compared with the twenty-sixth sonnet, beginning:

> Lord of my love, to whom in vassalage
> Thy merit hath my duty strongly knit,
> To thee I send this written ambassage,
> To witness duty, not to show my wit.

The 'written ambassage' may be merely the sonnet itself, but more probably it is the copy of *Lucrece* that Shakespeare sent to Southampton, enclosing the poem that freely expresses in verse the love that could only be hinted at in the dedication.

The theatres had been closed for most of the time since the beginning of February, and when *Lucrece* was published Shakespeare's company was in the provinces, at Ipswich on 8 May and at Winchester on the 16th, where they were called 'the players of the Countess of Derby', the Earl having died in April. Shakespeare himself, we must assume, was again left behind to write another play with an Italian setting. This was *The Two Gentlemen of Verona*, his first romantic comedy, a kind of play that he was to make peculiarly his own and that was to culminate in *Twelfth Night*. Julia, indeed, is a first sketch of Viola; like Viola she disguises herself as a page to serve the man she loves, only to discover his perfidy, for Proteus orders her to take the ring she had given him to Silvia, and Julia asks:

> It seems you loved not her, to leave her token.
> She is dead belike?

That trick of voice is Viola's precisely:

> My brother he is in Elysium.
> Perhaps he is not drown'd. What think you, sailors?

Of course *The Two Gentlemen of Verona* is not to be compared with *Twelfth Night* as a work of art, yet it has the excellent fooling of Launce and his dog, the first of Shakespeare's incomparable lyrics, 'Who is Silvia?', and there is the poetry of Proteus:

> For Orpheus' lute was strung with poets' sinews,
> Whose golden touch could soften steel and stones,
> Make tigers tame, and huge leviathans
> Forsake unsounded deeps to dance on sands.

This is something very different from the poetry of Shakespeare's master, Marlowe, and with characteristic impartiality he puts this princely splendour into the mouth of the first of his caddish young heroes.

By the beginning of June, Derby's, now the Chamberlain's, were back in London playing at Newington with the Admiral's, among their plays being 'Andronicous', 'Hamlet' and 'The Tamynge of A Shrowe'. The first is Shakespeare's *Titus Andronicus*, but this *Hamlet* is a lost play, written probably by Kyd and almost as popular as his *Spanish Tragedy*, for just as 'Hieronimo, go by, go by' was a catch-phrase of the time, so was 'Hamlet, revenge!', though our only, and tantalizing, glimpse of the play is Lodge's allusion to 'the Visard of ye ghost which cried so miserably at ye Theator like an oister wife, Hamlet, reuenge'. The ghost in Shakespeare's play, it will be remembered, does not cry 'Hamlet, revenge!' 'The Tamynge of A Shrowe' is more of a problem. Shortly before the Chamberlain's produced it at Newington the play was registered and published as 'A Pleasant Conceited Historie, called The taming of a Shrew. As it was sundry times acted by the Right honorable the Earle of Pembrook his seruants'. ('A pleasant conceited history' – 'More pleasing stuff, a kind of history'.) Single plays were normally published in quarto form, and this quarto of 1594 is very different from the play published in the first collected edition, the Folio of 1623, as *The Taming of the Shrew* (*The* Shrew, not *A* Shrew) and it looks as though somebody with a knowledge of the plot had turned a dishonest penny. A company could always raise capital by selling a play, though as this was equivalent to making a present of it to their rivals, few plays were sold in normal times. But the plague years of 1592–4 were not normal times; companies were driven to raise money by selling their stock, and in 1594 at least eighteen plays were published and another ten registered for future publication. We know that Pembroke's were in a bad way and had to pawn their costumes, so it may be that one or two of their number had seen an early performance of *The Shrew*, made a synopsis of the story, rewritten it in pedestrian blank verse heavily laced with borrowings from Marlowe, performed it, perhaps in the provinces, and sold it to a publisher for a few pounds.

In the absence of copyright laws, such practices were only too common, and at about the same time as the publication of *A Shrew* a 'bad' quarto of *2 Henry VI* was on sale in the shop of Thomas Millington, a stationer who did not ask too many questions about the ownership of plays, which in any event were not treated as serious literature, like sermons for example, and the most reputable stationers rarely dealt in them. Millington's quarto was called 'The First part of the Contention betwixt the two famous Houses of Yorke and Lancaster', and it seems to have been vamped up from memory by an actor who had doubled the parts of Suffolk and Cade, for their speeches are more accurate than the rest, which is so bad that it was long mistaken for an old play rewritten by Shakespeare as the *2 Henry VI* of the Folio. Millington wisely refrained from adding the name of the author and of the company who performed it.

On the other hand, early in 1594 Millington published a good quarto of *Titus Andronicus* as 'The Most Lamentable Romaine Tragedie of Titus Andronicus: As it was Plaide by the Right Honourable the Earle of Darbie, Earle of Pembrooke, and Earle of Sussex their Seruants'. During the plague years, when companies split and combined to weather the storm, plays became almost common property and were performed by a bewildering succession of companies; but as 'tittus' was first acted by Strange's, as Derby's is first named in the quarto list, and as it dropped out of the Admiral's repertory when their alliance with the Chamberlain's broke up, it looks as though it was their property and that they sold it to raise money when they reorganized in the winter of 1593–4.

Four of Shakespeare's works, then, were published in the

first half of 1594, by which time the plague was over, the Chamberlain's at the Theatre in friendly rivalry with the Admiral's at the Rose, and Shakespeare resuming his work as a player. But Burbage, Heminge, and his other colleagues would realize that he was far too valuable an asset to be much employed in acting, for their fortunes depended primarily on the plays that he wrote for them, and it is unlikely that he was often cast for very exacting parts, unlikely that he was allowed to waste his time travelling about the country on summer tours, and no doubt Rowe was not far wrong when he wrote that 'the top of his performance was the Ghost in his own *Hamlet*'.

It is now possible to review the members of the Chamberlain's company who, on that June day in the atrocious summer of 1594, were welcomed at the Theatre by James Burbage and his partner, his elder son Cuthbert. There were eight sharers altogether, six of whom at least had been with Strange's when Alleyn led them into the provinces in the previous year. The two exceptions were Shakespeare and Richard Burbage, now a man of twenty-six who had recently made his name in the part of Richard III, and was already rivalling Alleyn as the greatest tragedian of the day. Then there was Will Kempe, after Tarlton's death the most popular of all actors, whimsically described by Nashe as 'that most Comicall and conceited Cavaleire Monsieur du Kempe, Jester monger and Vice-gerent generall to the Ghost of Dick Tarlton'. After entertaining Leicester on his Netherlands campaign, he had visited Denmark before joining Strange's, with whom he acted in the anonymous comedy, *A Knack to Know a Knave*, with its scene of 'Kemps applauded Merrimentes of the men of Goteham', a feeble anticipation of Dogberry, whose part he was later to play as well as Peter in *Romeo and Juliet*. Kempe's comedy was broad clowning, though he excelled at a jig, the song and dance, often bawdy, with which comedies, and sometimes even tragedies, were brought to a riotous conclusion. Thomas Pope was an acrobat as well as a clown, excelling as a dialect-speaking rustic, but apparently George Bryan played more serious parts, though there is no record of his performances with the Chamberlain's, whom he soon left for a post at Court as Groom of the Chamber. Richard Cowley is also a shadowy character, apparently an actor of no great distinction, for though he stayed with the company for twenty-five years little is known about him save that he played Verges to Kempe's Dogberry. Augustine Phillips appears to have been a peculiarly attractive man, the most loyal of colleagues and a great friend of Shakespeare's, to whom no doubt he was endeared by being a musician, the composer of 'Phillips his gygg of the slyppers', though it is as a player of graver and more stately parts than Kempe's that we imagine him. The business manager of the company was John Heminge, a Droitwich man aged about thirty-five, and if the tradition is true that he created the part of Falstaff, we have some idea of the kind of part he played.

There were two or three boys trained to play women's parts, one of them being Samuel Gilburne, apprenticed to Phillips, whom he was eventually to succeed as a sharer. Among the hirelings was John Sincler, a wafer of a man for whom Shakespeare wrote a number of small parts: Pinch, 'a mere anatomy', in *The Comedy of Errors*, the diminutive beadle ('thou atomy') in 2 *Henry IV*, Shadow, thin as the blade of a penknife, and the apothecary in *Romeo and Juliet*. More important were William Sly and Henry Condell. Sly seems to have been an actor of more than common ability and succeeded Bryan as a sharer shortly before Condell succeeded Pope. Condell is imperishably associated with Heminge, for not only were they neighbours in St Mary Aldermanbury, family men and fellow officers in the parish church, but they were the longest lived of the original Chamberlain's fellowship, the only two who remained to help to edit the collected edition of Shakespeare's plays.

As it was agreed that Shakespeare's contribution to the fellowship was to be writing rather than acting, and as Southampton would come of age in October, it was only appropriate that he should write a play to celebrate the event, perhaps even to be acted at his house on his birthday. This, of course, is merely surmise, for we do not know that *Love's Labour's Lost* was written for Southampton, but it was almost certainly written at about this time and for some courtly occasion; it is too stylized to have been written primarily to please a popular audience and too full of literary allusions that would be, in more senses than one, above the heads of the groundlings in a public theatre. 'The tender juvenal' Moth, for example, may be the 'young Juvenal' Nashe of Greene's *Groatsworth of Wit*, and Holofernes the conceited Cambridge don Gabriel Harvey, then engaged in a wordy war of pamphlets with Nashe occasioned by the death of Greene, and there may be a touch of Lyly in the fantastic Armado. Nobody, however, could complain that Shakespeare had only one way of writing, for nobody could say what he was going to do next, and it was in part his variety that made him so popular. He had written English histories, a tragedy of revenge, Plautian comedy, farce, romantic comedy, and here was a comedy derived from the Italian *commedia dell' arte*, with its stock characters of bragging *capitano*, pedantic *dottore* and *zanni*, or buffoons. And throughout was his incomparable poetry in all its freshness, prodigality, and variety: blank verse, rhyme, sonnet, and lyric.

Love's Labour's Lost, having no change of the courtly scene and no violent action, would be just the play to present before the Queen at the Revels of 1594, and on St Stephen's night, 26 December, we can imagine Shakespeare and his fellows nervously and impatiently waiting in an ante-chamber for the dancers in the Great Chamber of Greenwich Palace* to take up their positions on the recently erected scaffolds surrounding the diminutive stage, at one end of which the Queen, still handsome despite her sixty-one years, false auburn hair, and black teeth, seated herself in her canopied chair of state, the Earl of Essex standing beside her. Then the flourish of trumpets summoning the players, and after their obeisances, the play. We may try to reconstruct the cast: Shakespeare as the King, Burbage as Berowne, Phillips and Bryan as Longaville and Dumain, Kempe perhaps as Armado, and Heminge, Cowley, and Pope as Holofernes, Dull, and Costard, with the young boy Samuel

---

* 'Makeinge readye the great chamber wth degrees ... for the Playes and Maskes at cristemas.' *Works Accounts.*

Gilburne as Rosaline. Or, in this comedy, did Shakespeare play the lead, reversing parts with Burbage? It would have been most fitting had he done so.

The Chamberlain's gave another command performance on the following night, this time perhaps *The Comedy of Errors*, the play they were to present the next evening at Gray's Inn. As these were the first Revels that the inns of court had held since the beginning of the plague, their Grand Night was a particularly wild one, the young men being so excited that by nine o'clock they were clambering on the stage and making such a tumult that their guests from the Inner Temple, offended by their entertainment, left the hall. Their withdrawal somewhat sobered their hosts, who fell to dancing with their lady guests, and then, as at Court, the dancing done, 'a Comedy of Errors (like to Plautus his *Menechmus*) was played by the Players'. 'So that Night was begun, and continued to the end,' the Gray's Inn chronicler recorded, 'in nothing but Confusion and Errors; whereupon it was ever afterwards called *The Night of Errors*.' The next day the men of law held a mock trial in which they found a sorcerer guilty of causing the confusion, and of foisting 'a Company of base and common Fellows to make up our Disorders with a Play of Errors and Confusions'. Shakespeare and his companions were little older than their hosts, and we may be sure that they enjoyed the revels to the full, and that many of the errors in their comedy that night were unintentional.

It was only fitting that the Chamberlain's should give the Court play celebrating the wedding of the Earl of Derby and Elizabeth Vere a month later, for the new Earl was the younger brother of their former patron, Lord Strange. This was the last of the six plays of the Revels that Christmas. The Chamberlain's had given three, and the Admiral's three. So far, the honours were even.

CHAPTER 5

1595–7

DEATH OF HAMNET

*

SHAKESPEARE was not quite thirty-one when, in March 1595, Kempe, Burbage, and he, as representatives of the Chamberlain's, were paid for the first two comedies they had presented at Court that Christmas: £6 13s. 4d. for each performance, and £3 6s. 8d. 'by way of Her Majesty's reward', the customary gratuity when the Queen herself was present. Court performances were an important item in a player's income, for £10 divided among eight sharers was, though not princely, a considerable sum. They would, it is true, have to pay their hirelings and boys, but there were few other expenses, as the Revels Office supplied properties, 'houses' and their silken hangings, and even costumes if necessary. A sharer, therefore, might expect £1 for each performance, the equivalent of at least £30 today, so that three Court performances meant something like £100. After the lean years of the plague, the year 1595 promised to be a good one, and Shakespeare could look forward to an income such as he had never before enjoyed. He might expect some £40 as his share of the takings at the Theatre, and if he wrote another two plays and sold them to his company – he seems to have averaged two plays a year throughout the nineties – that would mean at least another £12. What were his receipts from the sale of his poems we do not know, but *Lucrece* was proving almost as popular as *Venus and Adonis*, and his total income must have been in the nature of £60, or £1,800 of our money. It is not very much when compared with the fabulous sums received by popular entertainers today, and it would be considerably less if there were to be an outbreak of plague or if the theatres were closed for any other reason; on the other hand there was no income tax, and so there was money enough to restore the fortunes of his family in Stratford.

More important than money, however, was the happiness that came with success and the elation of creative activity. In the last seven years he had written nine plays and two long poems and poured out his heart in a century of sonnets that would, he dared to hope, outlast marble and the monuments of princes. His name was already one to conjure with, and one enterprising stationer was on the point of publishing an ancient piece of fustian called *The Lamentable Tragedie of Locrine*, relying on the addition of his initials to sell it. There was the thrill of the applause from a packed house at the Theatre when one of his plays was presented, the excitement of a few words of congratulation from the Queen herself after a Court performance, the satisfaction of knowing that his published poems were appreciated by the public, his unpublished sonnets by his friends, and above all the intoxicating knowledge that he had within himself an inexhaustible vein of poetry that had as yet scarcely been exploited. All things conspired to make him happy, as they also conspired to make him successful.

The plague years had brought about a dramatic revolution less triumphant than that carried through by the University Wits after the Armada, for not only had the London companies been reduced to two, but many of the dramatists themselves had gone. Greene had died in squalor in 1592; in the following year Marlowe had been stabbed to death and buried obscurely in a Deptford churchyard; Kyd had perished almost as miserably as Greene towards the end of 1594; Peele was on his deathbed, Lyly a disappointed man who had abandoned literature for politics. Lodge had turned physician and written his last play. Nashe was left, but he was a pamphleteer, novelist, and inspired journalist rather than a playwright, and at the beginning of 1595 Shakespeare was without a rival in the dramatic field.

As Shakespeare wrote entirely for the Chamberlain's, this was a serious matter for Henslowe at the rival Rose. He painted his theatre, added a porch to the tiring-house door, and paid his carpenters £7 for 'mackinge the throne in the heuenes', a device for raising that cumbersome property into the loft over the stage, whence it could be let down when required, much to the gratification of the groundlings; but paint, spectacle, and apparatus were no substitute for plays. It is true that plays of a sort were to be had, and at this time, the beginning of 1595, the Admiral's added half a dozen to their repertory: *The French Comedy* (presumably to vie with *Love's Labour's Lost*), *The Mack, Olympo, Hercules* . . . all lost, long forgotten, their authors unknown, and almost the only Admiral's plays that have survived from this period are the tragedies of Marlowe, then growing old-fashioned, but revived again and again in a desperate attempt to compete with the new work that flowed from Shakespeare's pen: *Romeo and Juliet, Richard II, A Midsummer Night's Dream, King John, The Merchant of Venice*. . . . But if the Admiral's could not compete with the Chamberlain's in quality they could at least outstrip them in quantity, and in the three years 1594–7 they added fifty-five new plays to their stock, or, it would be truer to say, Henslowe added them to his stock. Henslowe was a wealthy man with money lucratively invested in the neighbouring stews, and in partnership with Alleyn he began to take over the management of the Admiral's, not only buying plays, properties, and costumes for them, but also advancing loans both to the company and individual actors, some of whom he bound to himself by contract. He sought out new and impecunious dramatists from whom he commissioned work, needy writers who could touch up old plays, and these too he got into his power by advancing money and making them sign away their freedom. His fully developed system was one of mass production with carefully planned division of labour, whereby four or five dramatists put a play together, each concentrating on his particular speciality: tragedy, comedy, farce, pathos, and so on. Plays rolled off the assembly-line with factory-like precision, and because of this rapid turnover they were cheap, highly competitive commodities that could be refashioned or scrapped if they proved to be failures.

The Admiral's soon became a very different kind of organization from the free association of the Chamberlain's, a theatrical despotism, more or less benevolent, as opposed to a democracy; but it was efficient, and Henslowe gradually collected a very promising team of workers. The foreman was the veteran Anthony Munday, acknowledged to be the 'best plotter', and other recruits were Henry Chettle, the printer who had vouched for Shakespeare's civil demeanour and honesty, young Thomas Heywood and Thomas Dekker, and even George Chapman. Indeed, almost every dramatist except Shakespeare passed through, or served his apprenticeship in, the Henslowe workshop.

One of their products has been preserved in manuscript, *The Booke of Sir Thomas More*. 'Book' was a technical term for the manuscript of a play, which, having been modified by the company and annotated by the book-keeper, was submitted to the Master of the Revels for his approval as the acting version, or 'allowed book', which might then be used as the prompt-copy. *Sir Thomas More* appears to have been written by Munday, Chettle, Heywood, and Dekker, and then sent to Edmund Tilney for his endorsement as Master of the Revels; Tilney, however, questioned a number of passages, for the theme was a delicate one, dealing with Elizabeth's father, and he returned the book for alteration, whereupon the authors rewrote the offending lines and called in another man to revise a scene in which More pacifies the anti-alien rioters of 1517. This unknown reviser is thought by some to be Shakespeare, for the handwriting resembles that of his signatures, the only certain writing of his that we possess, and the verse itself, in style, thought, and imagery, might well be his. Here is Sir Thomas More telling the rioters what would happen if they succeeded in driving the foreign craftsmen out of the country:

> you had taught
> how insolenc and strong hand shoold prevayle
> how ordere shoold be quelld, and by this patterne
> not on of you shoold lyve an aged man
> for other ruffians as their fancies wrought
> with sealf same hand sealf reasons and sealf right

woold shark on you and men lyke ravenous fishes
woold feed on on another.

The image of mankind preying on itself like monsters of the deep is a common one in Shakespeare, and generally associated, as here, with the concept of chaos brought about by the forcible upsetting of the divinely established order; and the verse, too, is Shakespearian, though characteristic of a later date than 1595. Yet it seems improbable that Shakespeare would revise a scene for the rival Admiral's, unless it was to help Chettle and his young colleagues out of a difficulty, a characteristically generous gesture one would think; or perhaps Henslowe refused the play for the Admiral's, the joint-authors offered it to the Chamberlain's, and Shakespeare began to see what he could make of it. Whatever happened, the play was abandoned, yet it remains an interesting example of a typical Henslowe product in the making, and if the three pages of the scene by the unknown reviser really were written by Shakespeare they are a priceless aid to textual criticism, for if we know how Shakespeare wrote we know the kind of error that compositors would make in setting up his plays for the press.

Although at the beginning of his career Shakespeare was probably a dresser of other men's work, those times were long past, and when the theatres reopened in 1594 he found himself at the top of his profession, the creative vein growing rapidly deeper and richer, his imagination incandescent, and from his teeming brain the words poured into his plays and sonnets, for at this time he was as much in love with words as he was in love with life, playing, juggling, and jesting with them, twisting them into strange shapes and usages, and coining new ones of his own. He was in fact just such a wild, witty, attractive young man as Berowne in *Love's Labour's Lost*, and in Berowne we have, I think, a portrait of the thirty-year-old Shakespeare, not a deliberate and altogether accurate likeness, of course, but a half-mocking and unconscious projection of himself. Rosaline describes him:

Berowne they call him; but a merrier man,
Within the limit of becoming mirth,

> I never spent an hour's talk withal:
> His eye begets occasion for his wit;
> For every object that the one doth catch,
> The other turns to a mirth-moving jest,
> Which his fair tongue, conceit's expositor,
> Delivers in such apt and gracious words,
> That aged ears play truant at his tales,
> And younger hearings are quite ravished;
> So sweet and voluble is his discourse.

Mirth, wit, gracious words, sweet discourse; these, we feel, are the qualities in Shakespeare that so ravished young hearings like Southampton's and appealed to the ears of graver men of worship. It is, however, Berowne's eye that begets his wit, and it is abundantly clear that for Shakespeare the eyes were the most precious of all possessions, beautiful in themselves and themselves the fount of beauty in this delightful world. 'Precious' is the Shakespearian epithet for the eye from Rosaline's 'dear and precious eyesight' and Romeo's 'precious treasure of his eyesight' to Othello's 'darling like your precious eye' and Edgar's tragic punning image of the blind Gloucester 'with his bleeding rings, Their precious stones new lost'. Love, says Berowne, 'adds a precious seeing to the eye', and,

> From women's eyes this doctrine I derive:
> They sparkle still the right Promethean fire;
> They are the books, the arts, the academes,
> That show, contain and nourish all the world.

And he adds,

> Small have continual plodders ever won,
> Save base authority from others' books.

Like Berowne, Shakespeare was no student, no scholar, no burrowing bookworm, though he was an omnivorous reader, at this time lingering over the poetry of Spenser and his fellow-countryman Drayton, skimming through the pages of Daniel's *Civil Wars between Lancaster and York*, and rereading Arthur Brooke's old-fashioned *Tragicall Historye of Romeus and Juliet*, the poem that suggested the play that he was then writing:

another experiment, the application of his lyrical poetry to tragedy. Berowne had forsworn taffeta phrases, silken terms, and three-piled hyperbole, but fortunately Shakespeare himself was unable to curb his exuberant fancy and abandon them yet awhile, and the result was the sequence of comedies, histories, and tragedies of his lyrical period, from *Romeo and Juliet* to *The Merchant of Venice*.

Berowne's jesting is within the limit of becoming mirth; it is Boyet and Costard who talk greasily, but Mercutio, the young man with whom we identify Shakespeare in *Romeo and Juliet*, and the character which he himself probably played, far exceeds that limit in his jesting. His speech is full of what editors delicately call indelicate quibbling, and what the reader, if he understands, calls sheer bawdiness; but we do Shakespeare a great disservice if we ignore these things and mentally purge his plays of anything unfit to be read aloud by a gentleman to a company of ladies, substituting for the Elizabethan poet the image of a Victorian clergyman. Perhaps he sometimes stuffed his lines with spicy sallets to make them savoury, to tickle the taste of his audience, but the flavour was a rare and witty one, not gross; his bawdiness is never prurience or sniggering indecency, but the frank and spontaneous expression of a healthy young man who accepted life and saw it whole. And if we are to see Shakespeare whole, we must admit the fact that in his youth he was the bawdiest of Elizabethan dramatists.

It is equally mistaken to assume that because Shakespeare is England's national poet he is also its national saint, or at least an edifying model of the domestic virtues. The boy who tumbled a woman among the sheaves of a Stratford harvest-field may well have failed to remain faithful to a wife much older than himself, from whom he was separated for the greater part of the twenty-odd years he lived in London. Nearly all Shakespeare's nicest young men are impulsive, ardent, generous, and passionate: Hotspurs not Bolingbrokes – Hotspur himself, Berowne, Mercutio, Benedick, Hamlet. 'Give me that man that is not passion's slave,' says Hamlet to Horatio, and as Hamlet admired those whose blood and judgement, passion

and reason, were so well commingled that they were not slavish
dancers to the pipe of Fortune, so Shakespeare admired the
self-possessed and calculating Bolingbrokes (though he loved
the Hotspurs) and in his sonnets chid Fortune as the guilty
goddess of his harmful deeds. We cannot wonder, then, that
Shakespeare, impetuous as his more lovable young heroes,
with an eye like Berowne's for beauty's tutors, should have
been entangled by a woman's eye.

She appears in the hundred and twenty-seventh sonnet, a
married woman, light in behaviour but dark in complexion, an
unfashionable colour in the reign of the fair-haired Elizabeth:

> Thine eyes I love, and they, as pitying me,
> Knowing thy heart torments me with disdain,
> Have put on black, and loving mourners be,
> Looking with pretty ruth upon my pain. . . .
> Then will I swear beauty herself is black,
> And all they foul that thy complexion lack.

If the sonnets really are to be treated as an autobiographical
record of Shakespeare's early friendship and love, the Dark
Lady seduces his young friend, to whom he writes:

> Gentle thou art, and therefore to be won,
> Beauteous thou art, therefore to be assailed;
> And when a woman woos, what woman's son
> Will sourly leave her till she have prevailed?

and to his mistress:

> Beshrew that heart that makes my heart to groan
> For that deep wound it gives my friend and me!
> Is't not enough to torture me alone,
> But slave to slavery my sweet'st friend must be?

And then:

> Two loves I have of comfort and despair,
> Which like two spirits do suggest me still:
> The better angel is a man right fair,
> The worser spirit a woman colour'd ill.
> To win me soon to hell, my female evil

> Tempteth my better angel from my side,
> And would corrupt my saint to be a devil,
> Wooing his purity with her foul pride.

In sixteenth-century France and England sonnets were often fashionable exercises in imaginary love, and it may be that the Dark Lady is no more than a dramatic fancy; yet she seems to be more than a phantom of a poet's brain, a real woman whom Shakespeare passionately loved and at times as passionately detested, driving him to feel that lust is the expense of spirit in a waste of shame. Who she was we do not know, but perhaps we hear of her as the black-eyed Rosaline who was Romeo's first love, and meet her as the Rosaline of Berowne:

> A whitely wanton with a velvet brow,
> With two pitch-balls stuck in her face for eyes;
> Ay, and, by heaven, one that will do the deed,
> Though Argus were her eunuch and her guard.

Perhaps we hear of her again, or more probably of some more fleeting love, in a poem written by Henry Willoughby, a twenty-year-old undergraduate of St John's College, Oxford. *Willobie his Avisa*, published towards the end of 1594, is nothing as a work of art but may mean something in the biography of Shakespeare, for in the prose argument Willoughby describes how he fell in love with the virtuous and invincible Avisa and, unable to endure the burning heat of his desire, confided his passion to 'his familiar friend W. S., who not long before had tried the courtesy of the like passion, and was now newly recovered of the like infection'. W. S. assured him that the lady might be won, comforting him,

with an impossibility, either for that he now would secretly laugh at his friend's folly, that had given occasion not long before unto others to laugh at his own, or because he would see whether another could play his part better than himself; and in viewing afar off the course of this loving comedy he determined to see whether it would sort to a happier end for this new actor than it did for the old player. But at length this comedy was like to have grown to a tragedy by the weak and feeble estate that H. W. was brought unto. . . .

Then in the poem Willoughby describes how, while waiting hopelessly beside the inn where the married Avisa lives, his friend W. S. approaches:

> But yonder comes my faithful friend,
> That like assaults hath often tried.

He tells him his grief, and W. S. replies:

> Well, say no more; I know thy grief,
> And face from whence these flames arise;
> It is not hard to find relief
> If thou wilt follow good advice.
>   She is no saint, she is no nun:
>   I think in time she may be won.

The last two lines are a variation on a favourite theme of Shakespeare's, and W. S. goes on to explain the ways in which a woman may be won.

Of course, the theatrical imagery of the argument, and 'actor' and 'player', may be used merely figuratively, or if literally, the reference could be to any actor whose initials were W. S., Shakespeare's colleague William Sly, for example. Yet young Willoughby might well describe Shakespeare, ten years his senior, as an old, or experienced, player, and the case for his being the W. S. of *Avisa* is strengthened by the commendatory verses prefixed to the poem, for they contain the first literary mention of Shakespeare by name:

> Yet Tarquin pluckt his glistering grape,
> And Shake-speare paints poor Lucrece' rape.

And the case is further strengthened by the fact that Willoughby was a near kinsman of Thomas Russell, the friend whom Shakespeare was to appoint one of the overseers of his will.

Thomas Russell was born in 1570, the second son of Sir Thomas Russell, a wealthy and aristocratic landowner of Strensham, a village near Tewkesbury on the River Avon. His father died when he was a child, leaving him two of his extensive manors, one being Alderminster on the Cotswolds, four miles south of Stratford on the road to Oxford and London. After two years at Oxford, in 1590 he married Katherine Bampfield, a Somerset girl, and in the same month Henry Willoughby's elder brother married Katherine's sister. Although it was another few years before Russell finally settled at Alderminster, he was a frequent visitor to his manor, and it may have been then that he met Shakespeare – John Shakespeare was a dealer in wool, and Russell's Cotswold sheep supplied it – and when Henry Willoughby went up to Oxford he may well have asked the poet to call on his kinsman, who was interested in literature and an admirer of *Lucrece*, on his way through the town.

It looks, therefore, as though the W. S. of *Avisa* really may be the thirty-year-old Shakespeare, like Berowne a lover whose eager senses are all quickened by a woman's beauty:

> A lover's eyes will gaze an eagle blind;
> A lover's ear will hear the lowest sound. . . .
> Love's feeling is more soft and sensible
> Than are the tender horns of cockled snails;
> Love's tongue proves dainty Bacchus gross in taste.

From the unconscious reflection of himself in his imagery, it is clear that all his physical senses were most delicately developed and attuned, making him a lover of the world, its sights and sounds and scents, its tastes and contacts. Most of his images, his comparisons in simile and metaphor, spring from nature, but many of them spring with equal spontaneity from the arts, particularly from music, for after nature and words he loved music; his mistress is 'my music'; the stars and planets sing in their turning spheres; harmony and concord symbolize the divinely established order, and the man who has no music in himself is in a pitiful state of discord and confusion, fit for treasons, stratagems, and spoils. Altogether, the picture we have of Shakespeare at the beginning of his long association with the Chamberlain's, on the threshold of his greatest achievements, is one of a young man healthy in mind and body, ardent and impulsive, yet proudly and harmoniously balanced.

He had probably finished *Romeo and Juliet* by the time the

Chamberlain's went on their summer tour in East Anglia, and he returned to Stratford for a season with the newly begun manuscript of *Richard II*, a difficult play to write, as it dealt with the deposition of a king, a theme that would, unless very carefully treated, be little to the liking of Elizabeth. He would find Stratford still recovering from the ravages of the great fire of 1594, and while he was there see an even more disastrous conflagration, which brought the total loss to 200 houses and other buildings, while £12,000-worth of goods were destroyed and 400 people rendered homeless. Many of the houses of leading townsmen were burned, including those of Adrian Quiney, Abraham Sturley, Hamnet Sadler, and Thomas Rogers, the new bailiff, and the Shakespeare house in Henley Street narrowly escaped destruction. Richard Quiney, however, went to London where he obtained a patent from the Privy Council authorizing the Stratford Corporation to collect money from the neighbouring towns and shires to relieve the distress, and from the ashes rose a new and fairer Stratford, with half timbered gabled houses such as that of Thomas Rogers, now called Harvard House. It was in August 1595, shortly before the second fire, that 'Master Shakespeare', very probably the poet, bought a book that belonged to Margery Young, Richard Field's sister, whose husband, a Stratford dyer, had recently died.

Shakespeare was back in London by November to rehearse for the Revels, bringing with him his completed tragedy of *Richard II*, and on Sunday, 7 December, the courtier and diplomatist, Sir Edward Hoby, wrote to Sir Robert Cecil, Lord Burghley's son, asking him to supper on the following Tuesday at his house in Canon Row, Westminster, where 'K. Richard shal present him selfe to your vewe'. A fortnight later Elizabeth moved from Whitehall to Richmond Palace, the original palace of Sheen, which Richard II had destroyed in his grief when his queen, Anne of Bohemia, died there. No site could have been more appropriate for the performance of Shakespeare's latest play, and that Christmas the Chamberlain's gave five Court performances to the Admiral's four.

The year 1596 was to be an eventful and tragic one for Shakespeare. It began auspiciously enough, however, with a wedding, that of Thomas Berkeley and Elizabeth Carey at Blackfriars towards the end of February. As the bride was the granddaughter of Lord Chamberlain Hunsdon, the patron of Shakespeare's company, it would be only natural that they should be called upon to present a wedding play, perhaps a modified version of *Love's Labour Lost* with another title and another ending. Then there was another wedding to be celebrated in November, when the two daughters of the Earl of Worcester were to be married, and it is possible that Shakespeare was commissioned to write a play in honour of this double ceremony. The summer of 1596 was a repetition of that of 1594, a cold season of rain and floods, of young corn rotting in the fields, of rheumatic diseases, and even of plague, severe enough to close the theatres for a time. While in Stratford, therefore, when the crimson rose was nipped and blanched with frost, and perhaps with fading memories of that summer twenty years before when Leicester entertained Elizabeth at Kenilworth, Shakespeare invented the fairy story of *A Midsummer Night's Dream* with its marriage of two pairs of lovers, one of the happiest and loveliest plays he ever wrote.

It was a depressing summer in which to create such silvery enchantment. The triumph of Essex's successful raid on Cadiz was sullied by the news that the greatest of all Elizabethan seamen, Drake, had died in attempting to repeat his classic raids on the Spanish Main. Then in July Lord Hunsdon died, and though Shakespeare's company secured his son, the second Lord Hunsdon, as their new patron, he was not the new Lord Chamberlain, and the man who now became responsible for the conduct of the theatres was William Brooke, Lord Cobham, one who had little sympathy with plays and players. A month later Shakespeare suffered the heaviest loss that Fortune could have inflicted on him, for at the beginning of August his only son, Hamnet, died. He was only eleven, the child on whom all his hopes were centred and of whom he must have been partly thinking when writing his early sonnets:

> And nothing 'gainst Time's scythe can make defence
> Save breed, to brave him when he takes thee hence.

He would be present at the melancholy ceremony in Stratford churchyard when the little body was lifted and lowered into the grave. 'How easy dost thou take all England up!' he wrote of the dead Prince Arthur in *King John*, the play on which he was then engaged. For him Hamnet was all England, and his grief found expression in the lament of Constance for her son:

> Grief fills the room up of my absent child,
> Lies in his bed, walks up and down with me,
> Puts on his pretty looks, repeats his words,
> Remembers me of all his gracious parts,
> Stuffs out his vacant garments with his form.

It must have seemed a mockery to Shakespeare that he was at this very moment engaged in correspondence with the Heralds' College about a grant of arms; he had repaired the fortunes of his family, and at his instigation his father had renewed his application for a coat of arms and the status of gentility which he had made twenty years before. But there was now no son to carry on his line; and yet, though Anne was forty, there might be another child, and there were his two daughters to consider, and his younger brothers, all of whom might marry and have sons; and he himself was only thirty-two, the world before him, and in the hierarchical society of that age the rank of gentleman was not to be despised. The application, therefore, went through, and in October the grant was made. According to the polite and agreeable fiction of Sir William Dethick, Garter King of Arms, John Shakespeare's grandfather had done faithful and valiant service for Henry VII, who had rewarded him with land in Warwickshire, while John himself was said to be worth £500 and, less extravagantly, to have married one of the heirs of Robert Arden, Esquire, of Wilmcote. He was, therefore, assigned and granted a shield or coat of arms: 'Gould, on a Bend Sables, a Speare of the first steeled argent. And for his creast or cognizaunce a falcon, his winges displayed Argent standing on a wreath of his coullers.' A few years later the grant was challenged by Ralph Broke, York Herald, who had quarrelled with the arrogant Dethick and accused him of granting arms to base persons, among them John Shakespeare. Dethick's colleague was William Camden, Clarenceux King of Arms, the great antiquary and former headmaster of Westminster School, and the two defended the grant on the grounds that 'the man was a magistrate in Stratford-upon-Avon. A justice of peace, he married a daughter and heir of Arden, and was of good substance and habelité'. The controversy was not really about Shakespeare, only a pretext for a squabble of heralds, and there the matter rested.

Shakespeare returned to his lodgings in the parish of St Helen's, Bishopsgate, a gentleman, but only to find the theatrical world in a state of distress and confusion, the players so persecuted by the Lord Mayor that all was unsettled and uncertain. The new Lord Chamberlain, Cobham, had given way to the Corporation's puritanical importunities and agreed to the expulsion of the players from the City and the closing of the inn-theatres. Shakespeare's company, therefore, Lord Hunsdon's as it now was, who made their winter quarters at the Cross Keys, would have had to stay at the remote and antiquated Theatre if by great good fortune an alternative had not offered itself.

This was Francis Langley's recently completed Swan Theatre on Bankside. Langley was a London goldsmith who had bought the manor of Paris Garden as a speculation, and in 1594 began to build a fine new playhouse not far from the river landing-stage of Paris Garden Stairs, an attractive situation in every sense of the word, for, to the dismay of Henslowe, it would draw those who crossed the Thames by water and were not prepared to walk another half-mile to the Rose. There was the usual outcry from the City Corporation, and in November the Lord Mayor wrote to Burghley: 'I vnderstand that one Francis Langley intendeth to erect a niew stage or Theater (as they call it) for thexercising of playes vpon the Banck side', which plays contain 'nothing ells but vnchast fables, lascivious divises, shifts of cozenage, and matters of lyke sort', attract 'theeues, horsestealers, whoremoongers, coozeners, conny-catching persones, practizers of treason and such other lyke', and draw all manner of people from 'their resort vnto sermons and other Christian exercise, to the great sclaunder of the ghospell'. It had all been said before, and Langley, encouraged no doubt by Hunsdon, went ahead, and by 1596 the Swan was ready.

Fortunately the theatre was visited soon after its opening by a young Dutchman, Johannes de Witt, who described it:

Of all the theatres the finest and biggest is that whose sign is a Swan, for it will seat 3,000 people, is built of a concrete of flints, and is supported by wooden columns so painted that they would deceive the most acute observer into thinking that they were marble. As it appears to resemble a Roman building, I have drawn it.

Obviously de Witt's sketch was made from memory, as he could not have seen the view that he depicts, which is taken from a height some feet above the gallery roof, a mistake he would not have made had he worked in the theatre. Unhappily the original drawing has been lost, and although it was copied by one of de Witt's friends, who, however, may not himself have seen the Swan and understood what he was reproducing, our only illustration of the interior of an Elizabethan theatre is a copy of a sketch made from memory by a visiting foreigner. It is unlikely, therefore, to be accurate in all its details.

It depicts a circular building with three rows of seats in each of its three galleries, the bottom one being marked 'orchestra'. The stage, which is not boarded in at the sides, projects into the yard, where it is supported by two stout posts, and half-way back are two classical columns supporting the shadow. The 'mimorum aedes' or 'actors' building' is at the back, and there is no recess forming an inner stage between the two doors, above which are six boxes apparently occupied by spectators. Above the roof of the shadow is the hut or loft from which a flag is flying and a man appears to be sounding a trumpet, although the play is in progress. There are no curtains, no scenery, no 'above', no 'within', and the only property is a bench.

This was the theatre where Shakespeare's company found refuge in November 1596 when they were deprived of the Cross Keys stage, and it is possible that de Witt's sketch illustrates one of their performances. Shakespeare himself, to be near his work, moved to Bankside from his lodgings in Bishopsgate, where in October he was assessed at 5s. on goods valued at £5.

It happened that earlier in the year Langley had quarrelled violently with a rapacious and rascally Surrey justice, William Gardiner, whom he publicly denounced as a 'false, forsworn and perjured knave', apparently with every justification, for Gardiner did not dare to risk a trial for slander. However, he had not long to wait for his revenge, for the Swan lay within the area of his authority, and when Cobham succeeded Hunsdon as Lord Chamberlain and the City Corporation began to press their advantage, he was eager to support them in their attempt to suppress the theatres on the Surrey side of the river. In this he was seconded by his stepson, William Wayte, 'a loose person of no reckoning or value', and their threats became so ferocious that on 3 November Langley craved sureties of the peace against the pair, 'for fear of death': the same defensive action that John Shakespeare had taken against Ralph Cawdrey in Stratford twelve years before. It must be remembered that in those roistering times fear of death from an adversary was more than a fiction: Marlowe was charged with murder before he himself was murdered, the actor Gabriel Spencer had killed his man before he fell to Ben Jonson's sword, and John Day's rapier found the heart of his fellow dramatist Henry Porter. It was now that Shakespeare appeared on the Bankside scene, and within a month the position had been reversed, for on the 29th it was Wayte who was craving sureties of the peace – against 'William Shakspere, Francis Langley, Dorothy Soer, wife of John Soer, and Anne Lee, for fear of death'. Evidently Gardiner had left the swaggering and bullying to his stepson, who had threatened to close the Swan as well as the Cross Keys to

Lord Hunsdon's company, and Shakespeare had acted so vigorously that it was now Wayte's turn to go in fear of his life. Nothing is known of the two women involved, though no doubt they had an interest in the Swan, and the main importance of the episode is its revelation of Shakespeare as a man with whom it was by no means safe to trifle.

It may be that he satirized Justice Gardiner and his stepson Wayte in *The Merry Wives of Windsor*, though the fussy little Justice Shallow and his pathetically ineffectual cousin Slender are scarcely the men to have made Langley walk in fear of death or to have been threatened by Shakespeare. At the moment, however, he was writing *The Merchant of Venice*, another play that would make Henslowe almost despair, for the Chamberlain's had all the advantages. It is true that he had Alleyn and the plays of Marlowe, but the Chamberlain's had a living genius, not a dead one, as their principal dramatist; they also had Burbage and Kempe, and now the finest and best-situated theatre in London. As a result the Chamberlain's had been commanded to give six Court performances at the Revels, while the Admiral's had been completely ignored.

The Chamberlain's, however, had their own difficulties. The original lease of the land on which the Theatre stood had been for twenty-one years, and was therefore due for renewal in 1597; but the landlord, Giles Allen, was not an easy man to deal with and was demanding almost double the rent. If the playhouse had not been so antiquated and far from the City centre some arrangement might have been made, but negotiations broke down and Burbage engaged in another venture. In 1596 he bought part of the Blackfriars priory, where the Chapel Children used to play, and converted it into a private theatre complete with stage, galleries, and seats. It would make an ideal winter theatre for the Chamberlain's, but it was an unfortunate time for such a speculation. Encouraged by the closing of the inn-theatres and banishing of players from the City, some of the inhabitants of the Blackfriars Liberty petitioned the Privy Council that no playhouse should be allowed there, as it would spoil the amenities of that fashionable precinct, encourage lawlessness and breed plague, while the noise of drums and trumpets would disturb divine service and sermons. Cobham sympathized with the petitioners, and Burbage was forbidden to open his new theatre.

So matters stood in February 1597 when James Burbage died, leaving the Blackfriars playhouse to his younger son Richard and the lease of the Theatre to Cuthbert, the two brothers now becoming joint owners of the building itself. But a private winter theatre which they were not allowed to open and a public summer theatre to which they were denied access were of little use to Lord Hunsdon's Men. Meanwhile, however, they had the Theatre for a season, and they might be able to book the Swan again if they were expelled from their old home.

A month later they had a stroke of luck. Lord Cobham died in March and was succeeded by his son Henry Brooke, 8th Lord Cobham, though not of course as Lord Chamberlain, and within a few days that coveted post had been given to Lord Hunsdon, so that once again, after seven unfortunate months, Shakespeare's company was the Lord Chamberlain's, under the patronage of the man who for them was the most important officer of the kingdom.

There was soon further cause for rejoicing. On 23 April, St George's Day and Shakespeare's thirty-third birthday, Lord Hunsdon was elected a Knight of the Garter, and on 24 May was installed along with three others in the Chapel of St George in Windsor Castle. On the afternoon of the 23rd, according to a herald's report, he rode into Windsor 'with a brave company of men and gentlemen, his servants and retainers, in blue coats faced with orange-coloured taffeta, and orange-coloured plumes in their hats, most part having chains of gold, besides a great number of knights and others'. There were 300 of them altogether, and among them would be Shakespeare, both a gentleman and a servant of the Lord Chamberlain, his Garter-blue coat lined with orange taffeta and a plume of orange ostrich feathers in his hat. He was at this time writing the first part of his history of *Henry IV*, and the pageantry and the herald's account of Lord Mountjoy's men, 'every one a plume of purple estridge feathers in their hats', so impressed him that in the play he himself described the spectacle when portraying Prince Hal and his followers:

> All plumed like estridges . . .
> Glittering in golden coats like images;
> As full of spirit as the month of May,
> And gorgeous as the sun at midsummer.

In his triumph Shakespeare could not resist a sly hit at the new Lord Cobham, an unattractive man and the son of the Lord Chamberlain who had been largely responsible for the difficulties with which he and his company were now faced. In the old play, *The Famous Victories of Henry V*, which he used as a source and in which he may himself have had a reviser's hand at the beginning of his career, for it was a Queen's play in which Tarlton acted in 1588, the name of the boon companion of Prince Henry is Sir John Oldcastle, a historical character who really was a friend of the Prince and died a martyr's death as a Lollard. As Oldcastle was an ancestor of the Cobhams, Shakespeare mischievously retained the name and made him into the fat, witty, debauched, and cowardly Sir John of *Henry IV*. Cobham not unnaturally protested, and Shakespeare changed Oldcastle to Falstaff. But by thus asserting his dignity Cobham laid himself open to ridicule, and from this time was known to his enemies, and they were many, including Essex and Southampton, as Falstaff. Thus, at the beginning of 1598 Essex wrote jestingly to Sir Robert Cecil: 'I pray you commend me allso to Alex. Ratcliff and tell him for newes his sister is maryed to Sir Jo. Falstaff.' The news was nonsense, but it is the first known Falstaffian allusion. Then in the following year the Countess of Southampton wrote to her husband, Shakespeare's friend, to tell him of the arrival of a counterfeit Cobham, an illegitimate little Falstaff:

Al the nues I can send you that I thinke will make you mery is that I reade in a letter from London that Sir John Falstaf is by his Mrs Dame Pintpot made father of a goodly milers thum, a boye thats all heade and veri litel body, but this is a secrit.

'Peace, good pintpot; peace, good ticklebrain,' says Falstaff to Mistress Quickly in *Henry IV*. Who was Cobham's Quickly is unknown, but, as we should expect, the Countess of Southampton knew her Shakespeare as well as the Earl.

Shortly before the installation of Lord Hunsdon Shakespeare had made a journey to Stratford. His wild and eccentric uncle Henry had died since his last visit and his aunt survived her husband by little more than a month, both of them being buried at Snitterfield where the Shakespeares came from. All the Arden property in Snitterfield was now in the hands of his cousin Robert Webbe, to whom John and Mary Shakespeare had sold their interest in 1579, but he too was dying. He made his will on 1 June, providing for his wife, four young daughters, and newborn son, and left the rest of his estate to his elder son William, a boy of ten. A few days later he too was buried at Snitterfield.

Shakespeare saw none of these funerals. He had come to Stratford on business at the beginning of May, and on the 4th he bought New Place, the 'pretty house of brick and timber', the finest house in the town, all but one, College House down by the church, where the wealthy Thomas Combe lived with his three young children. For the last thirty years New Place had been the property of William Underhill, a Catholic recusant described as 'a subtle, covetous and crafty man', who had bought it for £40. As he had other houses in Warwickshire, New Place had been unoccupied for much of the time and was in a bad state of repair, but the recent fires in Stratford had so driven up the price of property that Shakespeare had to pay £60 for the house, two barns, and two gardens at the crossroads in the middle of the town, opposite the Gild Chapel and his old school. Underhill died two months after the transaction; he had been poisoned by his eldest son Fulke, a crazy boy of eighteen, who was tried, found guilty, and executed at Warwick.

And so at the age of thirty-three we find Shakespeare one of the most important and wealthy men in Stratford, a gentleman and the owner of the house that he must have passed with awe almost every day of the long years when he was a schoolboy.

But there was much work to be done to the property, and after moving his wife and two daughters from Henley Street – Susanna was now fourteen and Judith twelve – he began putting the house and garden in order. He sold a load of stone to the Corporation for the repair of Clopton Bridge, possibly the remains of one of his dilapidated barns, and the second part of *Henry IV* is a mirror of his activities in the summer of 1597. Here he is superintending alterations and rebuilding:

> When we mean to build,
> We first survey the plot, then draw the model;
> And when we see the figure of the house,
> Then must we rate the cost of the erection;
> Which if we find outweighs ability,
> What do we then but draw anew the model
> In fewer offices?

Here weeding the neglected flower-beds, for he could not bear to see an overgrown, untended garden:

> He cannot so precisely weed this land . . .
> His foes are so enrooted with his friends
> That, plucking to unfix an enemy,
> He doth unfasten so and shake a friend.

Here observing the strange behaviour of his bees:

> When, like the bee, culling from every flower
> The virtuous sweets,
> Our thighs pack'd with wax, our mouths with honey,
> We bring it to the hive; and, like the bees,
> Are murder'd for our pains.

And here watching the boys pouring out of school and scattering at the crossroads by his door:

> Like youthful steers unyoked, they take their courses
> East, west, north, south; or, like a school broke up,
> Each hurries toward his home and sporting-place.

His nearness to the school must at times have been almost unbearable, for if Hamnet had been alive he would have run into the house with a shout to tell of the day's doings under Alexander Aspinall.

It must have been at about this time that his sister Joan was married, and Shakespeare, who obviously had a great affection for her, would attend the wedding if he could. But it was not in Stratford, possibly because her husband, William Hart, was not a Stratford man. He is a shadowy character about whom very little is known except that he was a hatter, but it seems probable that he and Joan moved into the rooms vacated by the poet and his family in the Henley Street house. It was the beginning of a long occupation, for their descendants were to remain there for more than two hundred years.

As the Harts were moving in the Shakespeares were moving out. The poet's family was now at New Place; his brother Richard, aged twenty-three, had probably taken over his father's business and still lived with his parents, but the thirty-one-year-old Gilbert was working in London, for in this year one of the sureties of William Sampson, a Stratford cloakmaker, was 'Gilbert Shackspere de parochia sancte Brigitte, London, Haberdasher'. His youngest brother Edmund, who was only seventeen, may have taken Hamnet's place in his affection. The boy's ambition was to be an actor and to repeat his eldest brother's success, and it may well be that when Shakespeare returned to London he took Edmund with him to become a hireling in his own company. Perhaps Richard Quiney accompanied him as well, for in October he went to London with a petition from the Stratford Corporation to the Exchequer concerning the making of malt and the enlargement of certain articles in the town charter. If so, Shakespeare left him at the Bell in Carter Lane, near Richard Field's Sign of the White Greyhound, before crossing the river to his lodgings on Bankside.

CHAPTER 6

1597–1600

THE GLOBE

*

THE man of property who rode back to London in the autumn of 1597 was very different from the light-hearted lover who had ridden up to Stratford in the summer of the previous year. The death of Hamnet was a blow that seems for a time to have unsettled the delicate balance of his nature, so that after expressing his first grief in *King John* he turned to themes that matched the temporary cynicism of his outlook. Perhaps it was now that he wrote a hurried first draft of *All's Well that Ends Well*, in which the heroine encourages the obscenities of Parolles (a first sketch of Falstaff) and resorts to a bed trick to win a worthless husband. If so, he soon abandoned it in favour of *The Merchant of Venice*, a heartless comedy of revenge about a vindictive Jew and a company of Christian adventurers whose main object is to marry money and whose pastime is Jew-baiting. The priggish Portia is the least attractive of all Shakespeare's heroines, and Jessica, whatever else she may be, is a turncoat and a thief.

There are signs, however, that while he was writing, Shakespeare recovered his poise. Shylock, originally intended to be a mere figure of fun to amuse an audience that delighted in baiting any lonely and helpless creature, becomes a tragic character after he has been robbed of his daughter and his ducats, and in the trial scene his stature grows with the slow realization of his defeat at the hands of his tormentors, for he is the only one who has any dignity or depth of feeling. 'I pray you, give me leave to go from hence; I am not well,' he says, and the play is over – except for the beautiful and bawdy nonsense of the rings. There follows the moonlight and music and poetry of Belmont:

> The moon shines bright: in such a night as this,
> When the sweet wind did gently kiss the trees

Merchant of Venice a turning point;
Shakespeare becomes more
The Life of Shakespeare understanding

> And they did make no noise, in such a night
> Troilus methinks mounted the Troyan walls,
> And sighed his soul toward the Grecian tents,
> Where Cressid lay that night.

The harmony of internal rhyme and assonance throughout this wonderful duet of Lorenzo and Jessica makes a formal rhyme-scheme appear almost a clumsy and mechanical contrivance. It is the culmination of Shakespeare's early lyrical style, and it is also his farewell:

> Peace, ho! the moon sleeps with Endymion,
> And would not be awaked.

And the music ceases.

The Merchant of Venice is a turning-point in Shakespeare's career. Until this time he was a proud young lover and poet identifying himself primarily with the young lovers and poets whom he created, often careless of and sometimes mocking his other characters, but after Hamnet's death and his recovery from the blow there is an extension of sympathy to people of every age and class, a greater understanding and compassion, a mellowness that is reflected in his style as well as in his characterization. The young poet and lover had written almost entirely in verse, often in rhyme after the earliest plays; prose he had used only for broad comedy, and as there is virtually no comedy in any of the histories from *Henry VI* to *King John*, there is no prose. Yet prose was the medium out of which he had made most of the memorable characters of his lyrical plays, for neither the rhetorical verse of his first period nor the rhyming poetry of the next is the stuff out of which character is easily created, and though we remember the poetry of Proteus, Romeo, and Theseus, the people we remember are Launce, Juliet's nurse, and Bottom. Then came *The Merchant of Venice*, and Shylock, the comic character, the butt, begins in prose, and though he speaks verse as well, it is his prose that we chiefly remember: 'If you prick us, do we not bleed? if you tickle us, do we not laugh? if you poison us, do we not die? and if you wrong us, shall we not revenge?' And: 'Thou torturest me, Tubal: it was my turquoise; I had it of Leah when I was a bachelor: I would not have given it for a wilderness of monkeys.' The Jew fired Shakespeare's imagination and roused his sympathy as he wrote, and the importance of Shylock is that he is the first hero, or first protagonist, the first serious character to be created largely out of prose. Although he was almost an accident, a by-product of the comedy, Shakespeare had learned a lesson, and in the next half-dozen plays, from *Henry IV* to *Twelfth Night*, there is far more prose than verse, and it is no longer only the minor comic characters who speak it: Viola and Olivia speak prose, Orlando and Rosalind make love in prose, Benedick and Beatrice skirmish in prose, Falstaff speaks only a dozen lines or so of verse altogether, Prince Hal speaks Falstaff's language as often as not, and even when king woos his wife in prose.

It was, then, largely out of prose that Shakespeare was to create the teeming characters of his middle period – Falstaff, Prince Henry, Mistress Quickly, Pistol, Fluellen, Shallow, Benedick, Beatrice, Dogberry, Rosalind, Touchstone, Malvolio, Sir Toby, Maria, Viola – for prose does not invite a cumulative rhetoric, lyrical digression and merely ornamental detail, and from the restraint of this functional, and therefore dramatic, prose Shakespeare learned to write functional, dramatic verse. It was not that the lyric vein was exhausted, but lyric was now confined virtually to the songs, rhyming dialogue almost disappeared, and blank verse assumed some of the characteristics of prose dialogue, becoming more natural, free, colloquial, more concentrated than the former poetry, a much closer approximation to the language really spoken by men. The development – or better, the transition, so sudden was it – can easily be illustrated. Here is Bolingbroke in *Richard II* when the king surrenders to him at Flint Castle:

> See, see, King Richard doth himself appear,
> As doth the blushing discontented sun
> From out the fiery portal of the east,
> When he perceives the envious clouds are bent

> To dim his glory and to stain the track
> Of his bright passage to the occident.

It is the language of the sonnets, of sonnets seven and thirty-three in particular, the pursuit of an image through a series of subordinate clauses and qualifying phrases, to which Shakespeare sacrifices both action and character, almost indeed falsifying that of the ruthless and bustling Bolingbroke who has nothing but contempt for Richard and his poetry. Compare this with Hotspur's description of Bolingbroke in 1 *Henry IV*:

> Why, look you, I am whipp'd and scourged with rods,
> Nettled, and stung with pismires, when I hear
> Of this vile politician, Bolingbroke.
> In Richard's time – what do you call the place? –
> A plague upon it, it is in Gloucestershire;
> 'Twas where the madcap duke his uncle kept,
> His uncle York; where I first bow'd my knee
> Unto this king of smiles, this Bolingbroke, –
> 'Sblood! –
> When you and he came back from Ravenspurgh.

This is dramatic poetry, verse that advances the action and is creative of character, both of the rash, intemperate Hotspur and of the calculating schemer he so vividly reveals in a four-word image, 'this king of smiles'; and this is the kind of verse that Shakespeare was to use in his histories and comedies of character when he reached maturity after Hamnet's death and the writing of *The Merchant of Venice*.

While he was moving into New Place and writing *Henry IV* in the summer of 1597, in the greater world there had been much ado about islands. Essex, accompanied by his friend Southampton, his rival Raleigh, and the young poet John Donne, who described the adventure, sailed on the so-called Islands Voyage to the Azores in an attempt to seize the Spanish treasure ships on their way back from America. The expedition was not only a failure, but the long absence of the fleet might well have allowed Philip of Spain to land troops in England had not his third Armada been caught and scattered by autumn gales off the Cornish coast: the scare and fiasco to which Shakespeare returned in October.

Of more immediate concern to him, however, were the fortunes of Francis Langley. The proprietor of the Swan had persuaded a number of actors, including three hirelings from the Chamberlain's and two sharers from the Admiral's, to form a new company under his management and the patronage of the Earl of Pembroke and to play exclusively at his theatre for the next twelve months. In July, when Essex was setting out on his futile Islands Voyage, Pembroke's presented a new comedy at the Swan, *The Jeylle of Dooges* as Henslowe so enchantingly spelled it. *The Isle of Dogs* is a lost play, but we may take it that the Isle was England and the Dogs were Englishmen, a satire keen and critical therefore, in which the Privy Council scented 'very seditious and sclanderous matter' and immediately ordered the closing of all the theatres and imprisonment of some of the actors and the author. This was the irrepressible Nashe, who, however, escaped to Yarmouth, where he protested that there was no deep politic meaning in his lines and that in any event he was responsible only for the induction and first act, the remainder having been written by another hand. Perhaps this was not quite the whole story, but there seems to be little doubt that a part-author of the play was an ambitious and tetchy young man eight years Shakespeare's junior, Benjamin Jonson, who was one of those thrown into the Marshalsea. Henslowe lent him £4 to pay for his keep in prison and another 5s. when he was released in October, a small price to pay for getting a promising new dramatist into his play-making concern, and on the 11th, three weeks before he should have done, reopened the Rose. Langley, however, was not allowed to reopen the Swan as Tilney refused to renew his licence for a time. The new Pembroke's, like the old, were broken, and Langley, unable to form another company, was eventually reduced to letting his theatre for various kinds of non-dramatic entertainment such as fencing and feats of activity. The Swan was now closed to the Chamberlain's, as was the Theatre, the lease of which had not been renewed, and it was at the inferior and antiquated Curtain that

Shakespeare for the next two years or so had to put on his plays.

Richard Quiney spent Christmas in London and apparently saw something of Shakespeare when he was not too busy taking part in the Court Revels – *Love's Labour's Lost* was one of the plays presented at Whitehall – for on 24 January his friend and fellow councillor, Abraham Sturley, wrote to him from Stratford:

This is one special remembrance from your father's motion: It seemeth by him that our countryman, Master Shakespeare, is willing to disburse some money upon some odd yard-land or other at Shottery or near about us. He thinketh it a very fit pattern to move him to deal in the matter of our tithes. By the instructions you can give him thereof, and by the friends he can make therefor, we think it a fair mark for him to shoot at, and not unpossible to hit. It obtained would advance him indeed, and would do us much good.

It looks as though Shakespeare may have been considering buying his wife's old home at Shottery, her stepmother having recently died, but Sturley, contemptuously dismissing this as 'some odd yard-land', and prompted by old Adrian Quiney, had a better suggestion to make: that Shakespeare should invest his money in Stratford Corporation tithes, which would certainly be profitable to him, while the Corporation could rely on him to pay his rent, unlike the late William Underhill from whom Shakespeare had bought New Place and whom Sturley had recently prosecuted for non-payment. More precisely, the tithes that Sturley was pushing, 'our tithes', were probably those held by himself and Adrian. Shakespeare, however, had another investment in mind and it was some years before he bought a substantial portion of Stratford tithes.

Sturley goes on to tell Quiney of the growing discontent in Stratford. The country as a whole was by now thoroughly tired of the long inglorious war of attrition with Spain, the consequent high taxation and rising prices, evils that were aggravated by the cost of trying to smother the flame of rebellion that had flared up in Ireland. Then Warwickshire had been particularly badly hit by the wet summers and bad harvests of

1594-5-6, while Stratford itself had suffered severely from the two fires that had gutted a large part of the town, and to make matters even more depressing there had been an outbreak of plague in 1597. There was a shortage of wheat and barley, and though, acting on Privy Council orders, the local magistrates forbade the making of barley into malt for beer instead of into flour for bread, those who could afford to bought and stored corn and malt, partly as a safeguard against dearth, partly in the hope of profiting from a rise in price. In December 1597 a return of cornholders was made in Stratford, and Sturley and Quiney were among those reported as being 'great corn-buyers', Quiney holding 47 quarters of barley and 32 quarters of malt of his own as well as stocks belonging to other men. No wonder Sturley wrote fearfully to his friend of how Thomas West, a shoemaker, had said 'he hoped within a week to lead some of the maltsters in a halter', and John Grannams, a weaver, had hoped 'to see them hanged on gibbets at their own doors'. On 4 February 1598, a fortnight after Sturley wrote, there was another corn inquiry. There was little wheat and practically no barley hoarded in the town, but there were considerable stocks of malt: Sturley held 5 quarters of his own and $12\frac{1}{2}$ for Sir Thomas Lucy; Quiney 14 of his own and 7 for Sir John Huband; Alexander Aspinall, the schoolmaster, had 11, Richard Byfield, the vicar, 10, and William Shakespeare of New Place had 10 quarters in his barn. In short, everybody in Stratford was hoarding malt, from the magistrates and parson to Sir Fulke Greville's cook, and in this matter Shakespeare was no better than his fellow townsmen.

In this year, 1598, Shakespeare probably finished the second part of *Henry IV* and wrote *Much Ado about Nothing*, having discovered the original of Dogberry, if we are to believe Aubrey, at Grendon on the road between London and Stratford. He was back in London by September to play in Ben Jonson's *Every Man in His Humour*, for when the comedy was published it gave the list of actors or 'principall Comoedians' who first performed it: 'Will. Shakespeare, Ric. Burbage, Aug. Philips, Ioh Hemings, Hen. Condel, Tho. Pope, Will. Slye, Chr.

Beeston, Will. Kempe, Ioh. Duke.' William Sly had succeeded George Bryan as a sharer in the company, but Christopher Beeston and John Duke seem never to have been more than hirelings.

According to Rowe it was Shakespeare who recommended Jonson and his writings to the public when he was a struggling playwright altogether unknown to the world. It is not improbable, and it may well have been Shakespeare who persuaded the Chamberlain's to buy and produce Jonson's first great comedy at the Curtain in the autumn of 1598, as it may be a token of Jonson's gratitude that Shakespeare was one of the few dramatists with whom he never quarrelled, at least in print. Yet the two had little in common but their genius. Shakespeare was a romantic, tolerant and easy-going, a rapid and careless writer, caring little for scholarship and nothing for rules when they conflicted with the way in which he wanted to express himself. Jonson, on the other hand, was arrogant and irascible, a slow, painstaking writer with a passion for exact scholarship and the classics that William Camden, his master at Westminster School had instilled in him. With a reverence for the 'rules' of Aristotle's *Poetics* and Horace's *Art of Poetry*, he was also a realist, convinced that Marlowe and Shakespeare had set the drama on the wrong, the romantic course. Contemporary tragedy was chaotic, too loosely constructed and comprehensive, where all should be concentrated, unified, and ordered; and comedy was even worse, sentimental romances, improbable fictions of fairies and girls masquerading as boys. Jonson had a mission: to purge the world of its follies, and to do this comedy should be realistic, a reflection of the absurd antics of humanity, by beholding which it would be shamed into behaving more like men than monsters. If Shakespeare chose to write comedies for the world's delight, he would write them to reform the world, or at least to make it a more tolerable place to live in. Because Jonson was so critical of Shakespeare's art it is all the more important to remember that he wrote:

> I confess thy writings to be such
> As neither Man nor Muse can praise too much;

and, 'I loved the man and do honour his memory, on this side idolatry, as much as any. He was, indeed, honest, and of an open and free nature; had an excellent fancy, brave notions and gentle expressions.'

Jonson wrote this after Shakespeare's death, but by 1598 the commendations of his contemporaries were beginning to appear in print. John Marston, another quarrelsome young satirist like Jonson, paid tribute to *Romeo and Juliet* and the applause that greeted Shakespeare's plays at the Curtain, and young Richard Barnfield, a devout imitator of his work, expressed his admiration in the *Venus and Adonis* stanza:

> And Shakespeare thou, whose honey-flowing vein,
> Pleasing the world, thy praises doth obtain,
> Whose *Venus* and whose *Lucrece,* sweet and chaste,
> Thy name in Fame's immortal book have plac'd,
>   Live ever you, at least in Fame live ever:
>   Well may the body die, but Fame dies never.

John Weever, just down from Cambridge, followed with a halting sonnet to 'Honie-tong'd Shakespeare', in which he protested that Adonis, Lucrece, and Tarquin were, like Venus, more than mortal, so sweet their sugared tongues, the offspring of a Goddess and of the God of Poetry himself, and, more confusedly, that Romeo and Richard and 'more whose names I know not' must be saints, 'for thousands bow to them subjective duty'. It was the poems that had made Shakespeare famous – *Venus and Adonis* was going into its fifth impression – but Weever was at least acquainted with two of the plays and ranked them equally highly.

The most remarkable panegyric, however, came from the pen of a thirty-year-old parson-schoolmaster, Francis Meres, whose *Palladis Tamia: Wits Treasury* was published at about the same time as the first production of *Every Man in His Humour,* in September 1598. The book is a quite worthless piece of edifying pedantry apart from a short section in which the author tries to equate his contemporaries with the Greek, Latin, and Italian poets. Thus:

As the Greeke tongue is made famous and eloquent by Homer, and the Latine tongue by Virgill, so that English tongue is mightily enriched, and gorgeouslie inuested in rare ornaments and resplendent abiliments by Sir Philip Sidney, Spencer, Daniel, Drayton, Warner, Shakespeare, Marlow and Chapman.

After this introduction Meres begins his elaboration: Sidney is our rarest poet, Spenser our divinest, and Drayton, Shakespeare's friend, is particularly commended as 'a man of vertuous disposition, honest conuersation, and wel gouerned cariage, which is almost miraculous among good wits in these declining and corrupt times, when there is nothing but rogery in villanous man'. The last phrase is a quotation from 1 *Henry IV*: 'Here's lime in this sack too,' Falstaff complains, 'there is nothing but roguery to be found in villanous man.' Then follows the famous passage:

As the soule of *Euphorbus* was thought to liue in *Pythagoras*: so the sweete wittie soule of Ouid liues in mellifluous & honytongued *Shakespeare,* witnes his *Venus* and *Adonis,* his *Lucrece,* his sugred Sonnets among his priuate friends, &c.

As *Plautus* and *Seneca* are accounted the best for Comedy and Tragedy among the Latines: so *Shakespeare* among the English is the most excellent in both kinds for the stage; for Comedy, witnes his *Gentlemen of Verona,* his *Errors,* his *Loue labors lost,* his *Loue labours wonne,* his *Midsummers night dreame,* & his *Merchant of Venice*: for Tragedy his *Richard the* 2. *Richard the* 3. *Henry the* 4. *King Iohn, Titus Andronicus* and his *Romeo* and *Iuliet.*

As *Epius Stolo* said, that the Muses would speake with *Plautus* tongue, if they would speak Latin: so I say that the Muses would speake with *Shakespeares* fine filed phrase, if they would speake English.

Not only does Shakespeare surpass all his countrymen as a writer both of comedy and tragedy, but he is also in the first flight of English lyric poets and, more curiously, among those 'the most passionate to bewaile and bemoane the perplexities of Loue'.

As criticism, of course, the conventional sugared and honied compliments of Meres are nothing, though it is good to hear that an intelligent contemporary considered Shakespeare the greatest writer of his day, and biographically his information is invaluable. His sonnets, we learn, were circulating in manuscript among his friends, though Meres does not mention that one of these, his patron Southampton, perhaps the 'lovely boy' who had inspired the poems but now a man of twenty-five, had at last, precipitately, answered his appeal, and was in the same sort of trouble that Shakespeare himself had been in almost twenty years before. He had fallen in love with Essex's cousin, Elizabeth Vernon, one of the Queen's Maids of Honour, and when in 1598 it became apparent that she was with child he secretly married her. Fortunately the marriage was a singularly happy one, but it was almost treason to seduce one of the virgins who girdled the citadel of the Queen's virginity, and after a period of penance in the Fleet prison Southampton found what it meant to incur a prince's displeasure. So long as Elizabeth was Queen his career was ruined.

More immediately important is Meres's list of the plays that Shakespeare had written by the middle of 1598, some of which it would be difficult to date with any certainty without this guide. Meres affected a euphuistic balance in his prose, setting six comedies against six tragedies, which may account for the omission of *Henry VI*, though it does not account for the mysterious 'Love's Labour's Won'. We should, of course, expect this to be an alternative title for *The Taming of the Shrew*, the only other early play, as far as we know, that Meres fails to mention, but this simple solution has been ruled out by a recent discovery. This is a list drawn up by the Exeter stationer Christopher Hunt of the books that he had in stock in August 1603. Among the 'interludes & tragedyes' are *marchant of vennis, taming of a shrew, loves labor lost, loves labor won*. Evidently, therefore, 'Love's Labour's Won' is not another name for *The Taming of the Shrew*, and Meres is referring to some other comedy, either one that has been lost and is otherwise unknown, or much more probably one that was later included in the Folio but had been published in quarto by 1598 under another title. Perhaps the reference is to an early version of *All's Well that Ends Well*, a play for which the alternative title of 'Love's

Labour's Won' would be particularly appropriate, but whatever the solution, a copy of this unknown quarto would, if discovered, be among the most valuable books in the world.

As a footnote it is worth remarking that Hunt was no more scrupulous than some of the London publishers. Ten years before, 'it was his good hap to get into his hands' five cantos of Richard Carew's *Godfrey of Bulloigne*, which he piratically published in Exeter in 1594. Carew, a country gentleman who lived on the Cornish side of the Tamar, was an admirer of Shakespeare, at least of his poems, for apparently he did not know his plays, and in a letter to Camden, extolling the excellency of the English tongue, coupled him with Marlowe and compared him to Catullus.

Only eighteen, exactly half, of Shakespeare's plays were published separately in quarto in his lifetime, and if it had not been for the collected edition of the Folio the other eighteen, including *Twelfth Night*, *Julius Caesar*, *Macbeth*, *Antony and Cleopatra*, and *The Tempest*, might have perished, an almost inconceivable loss. By 1596, although there were garbled, pirated editions of *Henry VI*, Parts 2 and 3, as far as we know only one good quarto of a play had been published, *Titus Andronicus*, though this had inspired a drawing by the young artist Henry Peacham, much the earliest of the innumerable illustrations to Shakespeare. It is interesting, depicting an episode from the first scene of the play, 'Tamora pleadinge for her sonnes going to execution', and shows that the Elizabethans conceived Aaron the Moor, and presumably, therefore, Othello as well, as a coal-black Negro, and that, though minor characters wore Elizabethan, that is 'modern' dress, there was some attempt at historical accuracy in the costumes of the principal characters, at least of Roman times. Then in 1597, after a pirated 'bad' quarto of *Romeo and Juliet*, came good authorized quartos of *Richard III* and *Richard II*, the first of which was reprinted in the following year, while *Richard II*, one of Shakespeare's most popular plays, was twice reissued. Neither of these plays bore Shakespeare's name on the title-page, nor did 1 *Henry IV* published early in 1598, but when *Love's Labour's Lost* appeared in the same year it was as 'A pleasant Conceited Comedie . . . As it was presented before her Highness this last Christmas. Newly corrected and augmented By W. Shakespere', and from this time all quartos, with two exceptions, were issued with his name. Publishers rarely bothered to print the names of the authors of such unconsidered trifles as plays, but Shakespeare's name was now a guarantee of quality, enough in itself to sell a book, as the enterprising printer William Jaggard very well knew when he collected a little miscellany of twenty-one poems and published them in 1599 as 'The Passionate Pilgrime: By W. Shakespeare', even though only five of them were his, and three of these filched from *Love's Labour's Lost*.

Soon after the publication of *Palladis Tamia* Richard Quiney rode up to London again, partly on private business but mainly to petition the Privy Council for some relief for Stratford from the heavy taxes levied by the last Parliament to pay for the Spanish war and Irish rebellion: 4s. in the £ on land, 2s. 8d. on goods, and six-fifteenths on personal property. Early in October he received a letter in Latin from his eleven-year-old son, another Richard, asking for copy-books for himself and his younger brother Thomas, the boy who was to marry Shakespeare's daughter Judith. No doubt the good Aspinall had something to do with the Ciceronian composition, which began, 'Patri suo amantissimo, Magistro Richardo Quinye, Richardus Quinye filius Salutem Plurimam Dicit,' and ended, 'Filiolus tuus tibi obedientissimus.' A few days later came a letter from his old father Adrian, addressed to 'my loving son at the Bell in Carter Lane', and a parcel containing cheeses and 'tobecker'. Sturley also wrote with business-like piety, wishing him luck and informing him that he stood 'in some present need the while'. Then early on 25 October, before setting off for Richmond to present his case to the Privy Council, Quiney wrote a hurried letter to Shakespeare. As this is the only relic of Shakespeare's correspondence it is worth transcribing in full:

Haste. To my Loveinge good ffrend & countreymann Mr Wm. Shackespere deliver thees. Loveinge Countreyman, I am bolde of yowe as of a ffrende, craveinge yowre helpe with xxx*ll* vponn M*r* Bushells & my securytee or M*r* Myttons with me. M*r* Rosswell is nott come to London as yeate & I have especiall cawse. Yowe shall ffrende me muche in helpeinge me out of all the debettes I owe in London, I thancke god, & muche quiet my mynde which wolde nott be indebeted. I am nowe towardes the Cowrte in hope of answer for the dispatche of my Buysenes. Yowe shall neither loase creddytt nor monney by me, the Lorde wyllinge, & nowe butt perswade yowre selfe soe as I hope & yowe shall nott need to feare butt with all hartie thanckefullenes I will holde my tyme & content yowre ffrende, & yf we Bargaine farther yowe shalbe the paiemaster yowre self. My tyme biddes me hasten to an ende & soe I commit thys to yowre care & hope of yowre helpe. I feare I shall nott be backe thys night ffrom the Cowrte. Haste. The Lorde be with yowe & with vs all Amen.

ffrom the Bell in Carter Lane the 25 October 1598.

Quiney wanted a loan of £30 (£1,000 today) from his friend, and offered as security his, and presumably Shakespeare's, acquaintances, Thomas Bushell, eldest son of a wealthy squire of Long Marston near Stratford, and Richard Mytton, like Peter Rosswell, a gentleman in the service of Sir Edward Greville, lord of the manor of Stratford. Apparently Shakespeare readily agreed, for that same night Quiney wrote to Sturley, who in his reply acknowledged his letter 'of the 25 of October, which imported that our countriman Mr. Wm. Shak. would procure vs monej'. A few days earlier Adrian had written: 'Yff yow bargen with Mr Sha. or receve money therfor, brynge your money home yf yow maye. I see howe knite stockynges be sold, ther ys gret byinge of them at Evysshome. Edward Wheat and Harrye, your brother[-in-law's] man, were both at Evyshome thys daye senet, and, as I harde, bestow 20*ll* ther in knyt hosseyngs, wherefore I thynke yow maye doo good yff yow can have money.' It looks, therefore, as though Quiney's main object was to interest Shakespeare in hosiery and to persuade him to finance a deal for the Quiney–Sturley firm of mercers. It is to be hoped that Shakespeare's flutter in Evesham knitwear was as successful as Quiney's official mission, for shortly before Christmas the Chancellor of the Exchequer wrote that he thought it very reasonable to grant relief to Stratford, 'twice afflicted and almost wasted by fire'.

As was now the custom, the Chamberlain's opened the play-season of the Court Revels with a performance on 26 December. Presumably Elizabeth had seen the first part of *Henry IV*, 'with the humorous conceits of Sir John Falstaff', the previous Christmas, and it would be only natural for the Master of the Revels to select its sequel to entertain the Queen at the beginning of the merry-making in 1598. In the Epilogue, it will be remembered, Shakespeare wrote: 'If you be not too much cloyed with fat meat, our humble author will continue the story, with Sir John in it, and make you merry with fair Katharine of France: where for anything I know, Falstaff shall die of a sweat.' If there is any truth in Rowe's story that the Queen was so enchanted with Falstaff that she commanded Shakespeare to write a play showing him in love, this may well have been the occasion, for it would never do for Sir John to die before exhausting all the possibilities of his humorous conceits. Again, if a late seventeenth-century tradition is to be trusted, Shakespeare took only a fortnight to fulfil the Queen's command, and even if he took twice as long there would be time to rehearse this comedy of 'Falstaff in Love', *The Merry Wives of Windsor*, before presenting it at Richmond, the last play of the season, on 20 February.

Under normal conditions there would have been ample time for rehearsal, but for the Chamberlain's in that winter of 1598–9 conditions were far from normal. For more than a year they had been exiled from the Burbage Theatre, which, from the adjacent Curtain they could see decaying 'in dark silence and vast solitude', and now Cuthbert Burbage's negotiations with Giles Allen over renewal of the ground rent finally broke down. Availing himself, therefore, of a clause in the original lease and supported by his brother Richard, shortly after Christmas he began to dismantle the building, and at the beginning of 1599 sent his carpenter Peter Street and a dozen men, 'armed', according to Allen, who 'did then alsoe in most forcible and ryotous manner take and carrye away from thence all the wood and timber thereof'. Allen claimed damages for £800, not forgetting to include 40s. for trampling his grass, but he lost his case, and Burbage carried out his scheme of building a new theatre with the timber of the old on another site. This was a river-sodden plot of land on the Bankside within a few yards of the Rose, a deliberate challenge to Henslowe and the Admiral's, and here, as Jonson wrote, 'flanked with a ditch, and forced out of a marish', the theatre with which Shakespeare is imperishably associated, the Globe, 'the glory of the Bank', was reared. It was not merely the old Theatre under another name, but a playhouse embodying the long experience of the fellowship, incorporating all the latest improvements, all the machinery and devices that Shakespeare required for the staging of his plays, a theatre that must have made the fifteen-year-old Rose look shabby and old-fashioned.

The venture was an expensive one, but the cost was borne by a company of seven, composed of Cuthbert Burbage and six full adventurers of the fellowship. The Burbage brothers supplied half the capital, mainly in the form of timber, the other half being subscribed in equal amounts by Shakespeare, Heminge, Phillips, Kempe, and Pope, each of whom held one of the ten shares into which the capital was divided. To help them in the legal formalities of this share distribution they employed two men, both of whom were neighbours of Heminge in St Mary Aldermanbury: William Leveson, a merchant interested in the colonization of Virginia, on behalf of which he later organized a lottery, and Thomas Savage, a native of Rufford in Lancashire, the home of Sir Thomas Hesketh, who nearly twenty years before had commended 'William Shakeshafte nowe dwellynge with me'. Thus, the Chamberlain's added a theatre to their common stock, and as each member of this syndicate of housekeepers, as they were called, was entitled to his share of half the profits from the galleries, Shakespeare's investment was another, and exceedingly valuable, source of income. For this free association of plays with a common interest in the success of their theatre now had every advantage over their rivals across the way at the Rose, who, in debt to their employer and bound to his service, must have regarded them with envy. But the two companies were not to remain neighbours for long; the competition proved altogether too much for Henslowe and Alleyn, and within a few months they were looking for a site for another theatre as far away from Bankside as possible.

The removal of the Chamberlain's to Bankside admirably suited Shakespeare's arrangements, as the site for the Globe was close to his lodgings in the Liberty of the Clink, where he had at last been traced by the tax collectors. In 1596, when he was living in the parish of St Helen's near Bishopsgate and the Theatre, his goods had been valued at £5, but in the following year the petty collectors of the parish reported that he, like many others, was not to be found, being either 'dead, departed and gone out of the sayde warde', so that they were quite unable to collect the 5s. that he owed. It was the same story in 1598 when he became liable for a further 13s. 4d., but by 1600 the amount owing had been referred to the Bishop of Winchester, who was responsible for tax collection in the Liberty of the Clink, and as no more is heard of the matter presumably Shakespeare paid his arrears to the bishop's agents when they called at his lodgings.

Meanwhile, however, the Chamberlain's were still at the Curtain, and while Peter Street and his men were busily erecting the Globe, Shakespeare was fulfilling the promise he had made in the Epilogue to *Henry IV* of continuing the story of Prince Henry, though breaking his promise to give his expectant audience a further taste of fat meat. Sir John had so stolen the applause that the two plays of *Henry IV* were popularly known as 'Falstaff' or 'Oldcastle', and there was the danger that Falstaff would quite eclipse the glory of the hero-king in the epic drama that he had in mind. Falstaff, therefore, had to go, and in Mistress Quickly's valedictory compound of lyric and prose, bawdiness and pathos, he departed at the turning of the tide. And so, in the flowing, limpid verse of which he was by now the master, having invoked the Muse and appealed to the audience to use their imaginations, to piece out imperfections with their thoughts, to make imaginary puissance, transforming words into horses, men, and ships, Shakespeare began to write his history of *Henry V*. In a way it was a repetition of *Richard III*, for as that play was the last of a tetralogy in which order was restored by Henry VII after the chaos of the Wars of the Roses, so *Henry V* was the play that completed the tetralogy that began with *Richard II*, the legitimate Henry uniting the nation again after the rebellions caused by his father's usurpation and murder of Richard: Lancaster triumphantly succeeding Plantagenet as Tudor succeeded York.

Shakespeare had written the first four acts when, towards the end of March, London poured out her citizens to cheer the Earl of Essex as he set off at the head of nearly 20,000 men to crush the rebellion in Ireland. He had asked for the command, and as nobody else wanted it Elizabeth, after some hesitation, had agreed, and her Secretary, Sir Robert Cecil, son of Lord Burghley who had died in 1597, had no objection to his rival's going to what foreign diplomats called 'the Englishman's grave'. With him, still in disgrace, went the Earl of Southampton whom he intended to make his General of the Horse as soon as he reached Ireland, even though the Queen had expressly forbidden his promotion. When, therefore, in the last act of *Henry V* Shakespeare described his hero's reception in London after the Agincourt campaign, he compared it to the anticipated victorious return of Essex:

> As, by a lower but loving likelihood,
> Were now the general of our gracious empress,
> As in good time he may, from Ireland coming,
> Bringing rebellion broached on his sword,
> How many would the peaceful city quit
> To welcome him!

When the play was put on at the Curtain a few weeks later there can be little doubt that the Prologue who spoke the splendid epic verse of the Chorus was Shakespeare himself.

He must have worked very hard that summer, for it seems that by the end of August he had finished *Julius Caesar*. This again was something new, the first of the Roman tragedies based on his reading of Plutarch, while Brutus, a good man who does the wrong deed for the right reason, was more subtly drawn than any character that he had yet created. He appears to have written with deliberate restraint to match the austere grandeur of his theme, pushing the clear and easy style of this period to the limits of simplicity, so that no other play has fewer images or more monosyllabic lines:

> My heart doth joy that yet in all my life
> I found no man but he was true to me.

Simplicity could scarcely be carried further than that.

If Shakespeare had worked quickly, so had Peter Street, for by the middle of September the Globe was open, and *Julius Caesar* must have been one of the first plays produced there. It happened that a German doctor, Thomas Platter, was in London at the time, staying apparently at the Bull in Bishopsgate Street, and after dinner on the 21st, shortly before two o'clock, he crossed the Thames with his companions and made his way to the 'thatched house' – the thatched galleries of the Globe were to be its undoing – where he saw the tragedy of what he called 'the first Emperor, Julius Caesar'. Apparently he missed the point of the play, and unfortunately he tells us nothing about it except that there were some fifteen characters and that the acting was very good. As his knowledge of English was limited, he was more interested in the jig at the end of the performance, danced by two men and two boys dressed as women, and he obviously enjoyed a farce at the Curtain, where there was much throwing about of shoes by drunkards, more than the tragedy at the Globe. However, we learn that the stage and galleries were so arranged that everybody could see very well, that refreshments could be bought in the theatre, and that the actors were most expensively and elegantly attired.

Exactly a week later Essex returned to London; not however in triumph, bringing rebellion broached on his sword, as Shakespeare had hopefully predicted in the spring, but as a fugitive and suppliant. After futile marchings up and down

Ireland, he had made a truce with the rebel leader, Tyrone, lost his nerve, and fled to England, where he threw himself on the Queen's mercy. She placed him under arrest, but Sir Robert Cecil and Francis Bacon persuaded her not to rouse the passions of the people, for Essex was the most popular man in the country. Eventually he was released, but as a ruined man, no longer the Queen's favourite, though still the people's darling: a dangerous man, ambitious, irresponsible, impulsive, and unpredictable, the cousin of a childless Queen who had made no provision for the succession to her throne.

Ireland was Essex's undoing; it was also Spenser's. He had been driven out of the country by the rebels, who had burned his house, and shortly after his arrival in London he died. He was buried beside Chaucer in Westminster Abbey, his body carried by the poets of the capital, Shakespeare among them no doubt, who threw their elegies and the pens with which they had written them into his grave.

These tragic and disastrous events coincided with the building of the Globe, with the writing and production of *Julius Caesar*; but after tragedy came comedy, for another play produced at the Globe soon after its opening was Ben Jonson's *Every Man out of His Humour*; 'this thronged round', 'this fair-filled Globe', he called the theatre, with characteristic confidence anticipating his audience, but neither Shakespeare nor Kempe was among the actors who presented it. Kempe had already 'danced himself out of the world', or in other words sold his share in the Globe and parted company with the Chamberlain's, and from a remark in Jonson's comedy, 'Would I had one of Kempe's shoes to throw after you', it seems probable that he was still at the Curtain in the slipper-slinging farce that Platter had just seen there. But Kempe was ever a wanderer; a few months later he was dancing his famous morris from London to Norwich, and after the successful publicizing of this exploit he went abroad, where he is said to have repeated his feat over the Alps.

Shortly before the Chamberlain's moved into the Globe, Kempe's place was taken by Robert Armin, for Shakespeare an almost priceless acquisition. Kempe was a dancer, an acrobat, and a clown in the old tradition of Tarlton, but Armin was a singer, a wit rather than a clown, sensitive and imaginative, himself an author and minor playwright. It may, indeed, have been Armin who inspired Shakespeare to write his next play, *As You Like It*, with Touchstone almost a central character, and for Armin he was to create the parts of Feste and the Fool in *Lear*.

As Jonson was a realist and anti-romantic, bent on purging the follies of his age, his plays are far more topical than Shakespeare's, and in *Every Man out of His Humour* there are several allusions to Shakespeare and his latest work, *Henry IV* and *Julius Caesar*. The last words of the play are 'Sir John Falstaff', and the taciturn Fungoso is said to be a kinsman to Justice Silence; 'Et tu, Brute', spoken in jest in the comedy, are the dying words of Caesar, and 'reason long since is fled to animals, you know', is clearly a reference to Antony's 'O judgement, thou art fled to brutish beasts, And men have lost their reason.' There is probably irony in Jonson's paraphrase, for elsewhere he wrote that Shakespeare

many times fell into those things could not escape laughter; as when he said in the person of Caesar, one speaking to him: 'Caesar thou dost me wrong'; he replied: 'Caesar did never wrong, but with just cause' and such like, which were ridiculous.

According to the Folio, however, Shakespeare wrote, 'Know, Caesar doth not wrong, nor without cause Will he be satisfied,' though it looks as though the lines have been altered, probably as a result of Jonson's mockery.

It may be that Jonson had another, and unkinder, cut at Shakespeare in this comedy of humours. John Shakespeare had just made a further application to the Heralds' College for leave to impale the arms of his wife's family, which would mean that he and his descendants would have the right to combine the Arden arms with those of Shakespeare on the same shield. Apparently the application was not granted, for the Shakespeares never made use of the Arden arms, nor for that matter of their own motto, *Non Sans Droit*, 'Not Without Right' or 'Not Without Just Cause', which recalls Jonson's version of Caesar's words, and he may have had Shakespeare's motto in mind when he made one of his characters suggest as a motto for a newly bought coat of arms, 'Not Without Mustard'.

Perhaps Shakespeare's riposte to these bantering thrusts was to put the anti-romantic and 'humorous' Jonson into the most romantic of all his plays as the melancholy Jaques, a character who does not occur in Lodge's romance, *Rosalynde*, from which he took the plot, and a name that would at once suggest Jonson to those who knew any French. In the character of Asper, and without false modesty, Jonson had described himself as 'of an ingenious and free spirit, eager and constant in reproof, without fear controlling the world's abuses', and he added an explanation of what he meant by 'humour':

> As when some one peculiar quality
> Doth so possess a man, that it doth draw
> All his affects, his spirits and his powers,
> In their confluctions, all to run one way,
> This may be truly said to be a humour.

With the possible exception of Nym, Jaques is the only truly 'humorous' character in Shakespeare's plays, and like Asper-Jonson he demands the right

> To speak my mind, and I will through and through
> Cleanse the foul body of the infected world.

Yet if Jaques was a hit at Jonson the bout was a friendly one, and there was no malice in the caricature.

After the Revels at Richmond that Christmas, when the Chamberlain's gave three performances, they were called upon by their patron to give a special performance one afternoon early in March, 1600. The new Flemish ambassador was being entertained by members of the Privy Council, and after the Lord Chamberlain had given him a delicate dinner his players presented 'Sir John Old Castell', no doubt under difficulties in the small space of Hunsdon House, yet 'to his great contentment'. The play, of course, was one of the parts of *Henry IV*, and not the *Sir John Oldcastle* recently written for the Admiral's as a counterblast to Shakespeare's history. Anthony Munday, inspired by the trouble that Shakespeare had got into by burlesquing Lord Cobham's ancestor, had conceived the idea of writing 'the true and honorable historie' of Oldcastle and his martyrdom. In October 1599 Henslowe paid Munday and his team £10 for the play, and when *Henry IV* was put on at the Globe at the beginning of November the Admiral's presented their virtuous version of *Oldcastle* at the Rose, the true, historical Oldcastle, 'no pampered glutton, nor aged counsellor to youthful sin' like the 'forged invention' to be seen across the way. *Sir John Oldcastle* was one of the best plays to come from the Henslowe workshop – Michael Drayton had a main hand in it – so good, indeed, that when republished twenty years later it was, ironically enough, as 'Written by William Shakespeare'.

But neither *Sir John Oldcastle* nor the other products of the Henslowe workshop could compete with the plays at the Globe, with *Henry IV, Henry V, Much Ado about Nothing, Julius Caesar, As You Like It, Twelfth Night*. For this we have the testimony of Leonard Digges, stepson of Shakespeare's friend Thomas Russell:

> So have I seen, when Caesar would appear,
> And on the stage at half-sword parley were
> Brutus and Cassius, oh, how the audience
> Were ravish'd, with what wonder they went thence . . .
> when let but Falstaff come,
> Hal, Poins, the rest, you scarce shall have a room;
> All is so pester'd, let but Beatrice
> And Benedick be seen; lo, in a trice
> The cockpit, galleries, boxes all are full
> To hear Malvolio, that cross-garter'd gull.

On the other hand, sometimes the audience at the Rose would 'scarce defray the seacoal fire and door-keepers'. No wonder, then, that Henslowe and Alleyn looked across the river, and by the end of 1599 had found a site for a new theatre beyond the northern walls of the City, in the Liberty, and rapidly growing suburb of Finsbury. They lost no time, and on 8 January 1600 engaged Peter Street to build another playhouse for them. The contract has been preserved and is important not only because it describes the structure of an Elizabethan theatre but also because the model for the Fortune, as it was to be called, was the Globe, except that it was to be square instead of round, and of course bigger and better. The frame, on the outside eighty feet each way, enclosed a yard fifty-five feet square. The three galleries, in which were four 'gentlemen's rooms' and a number of twopenny rooms, had seating throughout, an innovation perhaps, for the 'stinkards' in the penny galleries used to stand. The stage, forty-three feet broad (leaving an alley six feet wide at each end) and twenty-seven and a half feet deep, paled in below with oaken boards and protected by a shadow or cover, extended into the middle of the yard, and was 'in all other proportions' like that of the Globe. A plan was attached to the contract, but unhappily it has been lost, so that, although we know that the windows of the tiring-house were glazed we do not know where they were, or how they contrived an 'above' and 'within' for the staging of plays. There is no mention, as surely there would be, of an upper or inner stage in the tiring-house wall, though neither is there mention of posts in the stage to form the frames of 'houses'.

Of course there were the usual protests from interested parties, but Henslowe and Alleyn were wealthy enough to overcome opposition, and in the autumn of 1600 the Fortune was opened. The year had seen a complete reversal of the situation. The Chamberlain's had moved from Shoreditch to Bankside and driven the Admiral's from Bankside to Finsbury, and their rivalry had been transferred from the Theatre and Rose to the Globe and Fortune. The Privy Council sought to regularize the situation. Because plays 'yeald hir Maiestie recreacion and delight', the Chamberlain's and Admiral's were confirmed in the tenure of their theatres, but because 'the vse and moderacon' of them must be retained, they were to be the only authorized companies; there was to be no playing in the City inns, and all the other playhouses were to be plucked down. Council orders, however, were not the same thing as their execution. In October Pembroke's were playing at the Rose, their last appearance in London, a few months later the Council complained, not that the Curtain was still open, but that a particularly offensive play was being given there, and in the following year they themselves licensed Worcester's to perform at the Boar's Head, though this may have been the Whitechapel inn outside the City walls, whose owner had just rebuilt the galleries round the yard. Then, although Langley died in 1601, the Swan also remained open, as a sort of variety theatre.

Moreover, despite the Council's decrees, not only did all the old theatres remain, Curtain, Rose, and Swan, but another new one appeared. Although Bankside was said to be 'verie noysome for the resorte of people in the wynter tyme', the Admiral's had played there all the year round, and the Chamberlain's now proposed to do the same. Having no immediate use, therefore, for the private Blackfriars theatre prepared by his father as winter quarters for the company, Richard Burbage let it to a syndicate headed by Henry Evans, a businessman, and Nathaniel Giles, Master of the singing boys of the Chapel Royal, who commissioned Jonson to write for them. Among the boys who sang the odes and lyrics with which Jonson liberally garnished *Cynthia's Revels* were John Underwood and Nathan Field, both of whom were to become sharers in the Chamberlain's, the latter to take the place of Shakespeare himself. At about the same time as the opening of the Fortune and second Blackfriars theatres in 1600, the Paul's boys, who had been silent, dramatically at least, for the last ten years, again began their performances in the cathedral singing-school with plays written for them by Jonson's rival, John Marston. As Jonson had parodied Marston's turgid style in *Cynthia's Revels*, and Marston depicted Jonson as a discontented cuckold in one of his Paul's plays, a lively war of the theatres was rapidly developing.

These theatrical events of 1600 inevitably affected Shake-speare. The first company of the Chapel Children had been disbanded in 1584, the Paul's Boys in 1590, just as he was begin-ning to write for the stage, so that he had never had to meet the competition of children, who were so popular because of the quaintness of their playing men's parts as well as women's, and because they had the big advantage over the adult companies of being able to sing like angels. This, presumably, was why he wrote so many songs for *As You Like It* and *Twelfth Night*, and approached Thomas Morley, one of the greatest composers of that golden age of English music, and one whom he must have known well, for settings to them. 'It was a lover and his lass' and 'O mistress mine' were both set to music by Morley.

Shakespeare was probably writing *Twelfth Night* in Stratford in August 1600 when his first nephew was born, William Hart, the son of his sister Joan. He was called William after his uncle, who acted as his godfather, appropriately enough, for the boy became an actor and is said to have been the father of Charles Hart, one of the leading actors of the Restoration, who, like Betterton, helped to revive the plays of Shakespeare when the theatres reopened in 1660.

When Shakespeare returned to London for the winter season, it was to find competition far fiercer than it had been in the previous year, for the three new theatres on the north bank, Fortune, Blackfriars, and little Paul's playhouse, drew away many of the former frequenters of the Globe, particularly in the winter when the Bankside was so 'noysome for the resorte of people', and, after all, the trip across the Thames cost as much as entry to the theatre. He was himself to say as much in his next play. Although there had been no decline in the stand-ards of the adult companies, he wrote, the children were now so much the fashion that the flag of the Globe, 'Hercules and his load', fluttered over an almost empty playhouse. Burbage must have regretted the lease of 'the great hall or roome' at Blackfriars to the 'eyrie of children' for a term of twenty-one years.

As far as we know, the Chamberlain's were not driven to

travel like 'the tragedians of the city' in *Hamlet*, but to tide over the crisis they had to sell some of their stock, including a number of Shakespeare's plays. On 23 August Andrew Wise and William Aspley registered 'Two bookes, the one called Muche a Doo about nothinge. Thother the seconde parte of the history of Kinge Henry the iiij^th with the humours of Sir John Falstaff: Wrytten by master Shakespeare', the first appearance of Shakespeare's name in the Stationers' Register. A few days later the quartos were on sale in the shops in St Paul's Churchyard, each with the advertisement, 'As it hath been sundrie times publikely acted by the right honourable, the Lord Chamberlaine his seruants. Written by William Shakespeare.' It is worth noting that the *Much Ado* quarto seems to have been set up from Shakespeare's 'foul papers', his original manuscript, for as he wrote rapidly and with little alteration, there was normally no need for him to make a fair copy. 'His mind and hand went together,' Heminge and Condell were later to testify, 'and what he thought, he uttered with that easiness that we have scarce received from him a blot in his papers.' Sometimes the prompter or a professional scribe made a fair copy, but the *Much Ado* manuscript was probably Shakespeare's original, for 'Kempe' and 'Cowley' are sometimes printed instead of 'Dogberry' and 'Verges', presumably because Shakespeare had written the names of the actors whom he had in mind for the parts, which the compositor did not always remember to alter. *A Midsummer Night's Dream* came out in October, and was followed a few weeks later by *The Merchant of Venice*. It is a measure of their financial difficulties in 1600 that four of the fourteen plays that the Chamberlain's sold to the stationers in Shakespeare's lifetime were disposed of in this year. They also lost a play, for some hireling or other who had acted in *Henry V* vamped up a mangled version and sold it to the publisher who had already issued 'bad' quartos of the last two parts of *Henry VI*.

To make up for their losses, however, Shakespeare had two new plays for the Revels that bridged the sixteenth and seventeenth centuries: *As You Like It* and *Twelfth Night*.

CHAPTER 7

1601–3

THE MAN OF PROPERTY

*

THE Revels that were to see out the old century and bring in the new were held at Whitehall. They began as usual on 26 December with a play by the Chamberlain's, possibly *As You Like It*, and two days later came a performance by the Admiral's under the leadership of Alleyn, an actor whom the Queen greatly admired. On 1 January the Paul's boys made their first Court appearance since 1590, and on the same evening a provincial company of the Earl of Derby presented some sort of entertainment, probably one of the comedies that their patron, the fifth Earl, was said to be 'busy penning for the common players'. Then, on 6 January, Twelfth Night and the climax of the Revels, there were four performances at the palace, where two very important foreign visitors had to be entertained. At midday the Queen dined in state in the Great Chamber with the Russian ambassador, or rather, near that formidable diplomat – 'a man of tall Stature, very fatte with a great face and a blacke bearde cutt rownde, of a swarfye Colour his face, and his gate very maiesticall' – for he was given a separate table at the side of the Chamber. It was during this feast that Nathaniel Giles presented his newly formed company of Chapel Children, not in a play, but in 'a showe with musycke and speciall songes prepared for the purpose'. Meanwhile, her other guest dined in the adjoining Council Chamber with a number of great officers of the Crown. This was Don Virginio Orsino, Duke of Bracciano, a handsome, elegant young man of twenty-eight, much more to the liking of the sixty-eight-year-old Queen than the pompous, uncouth Muscovite, and moreover a nephew of the Grand Duke of Tuscany, a valuable friend in time of war with Spain. After supper came the plays; in one chamber

Derby's gave their second performance, and in the other the Admiral's presented *Phaethon*, a play by the improvident Dekker, newly done up for the occasion; but the play of the evening was that graced by the Queen in the great Hall, almost certainly the one presented by the servants of the Lord Chamberlain, who was himself responsible for the entertainment, and almost certainly *Twelfth Night*.*

The vast banqueting-hall built by Wolsey in his pride, a hundred feet long and almost half as wide, was richly hung with tapestry and surrounded by wooden tiers of seats along the walls, set up by the Office of Works for the occasion, and at the dais end was a platform for the Queen's state, or canopied throne. All, or almost all, the chivalry and nobility of England were there: Whitgift, Archbishop of Canterbury, the Lord Keeper, the Lord Treasurer, the Lord Admiral, the Earl of Derby, the Earl of Worcester, the Countess of Derby, the Countess of Worcester . . . all but the Earls of Essex and Southampton. 'The Musitions of the Citty' were in a gallery under the direction of John Bull, the Chapel organist, and Robert Hales, the Queen's lutenist and 'Orpheus of the Court', was 'to have one place expresly to shewe his owne voyce'. Perhaps he sang 'Come away, death', instead of Armin that night.

It was after ten o'clock when Elizabeth, accompanied by her great nobles and Don Virginio, left her Chamber and, to a flourish of trumpets, entered the Queen's door into the Hall.

Her Majesty mounted the stairs [Orsino wrote to his wife] amid such sounding of trumpets that methought I was on the field of war, and entered a public hall, where all round about were rising steps with ladies, and diverse consorts of music. As soon as her Majesty was seated in her state, many ladies and knights began a Grand Ball.

The dancing done, all withdrew to their seats round the walls, and the comedy was played in the middle of the dancing-floor, without a stage, but probably with two silk-hung houses, one for Olivia, the other for the Duke of Illyria.

* See Leslie Hotson, *The First Night of 'Twelfth Night'*.

What was the original name that Shakespeare gave to the Duke of Illyria we may never know, but it seems probable that when he learned, about a week before the performance, that the Duke of Bracciano was to be present, he changed it to Orsino as a compliment to the Queen's guest, adding perhaps a few topical allusions. Dr Hotson suggests, for example, that Malvolio means 'Mal voglio', 'I want Moll', and that Olivia's steward is a caricature of Sir William Knollys, Comptroller of the Household, an elderly man with puritanical pretensions and notorious for his pursuit of Mary Fitton, another of the Queen's much molested Maids of Honour. It may be so, and it may be that the aged Queen identified herself with Olivia as, with Don Virginio standing beside her, where once had stood the Earl of Leicester and the Earl of Essex, she watched Shakespeare and his fellows perform the last and loveliest of his romantic comedies on that first Twelfth Night of the seventeenth century.

Never before had Shakespeare written a play with such a wealth of good parts for his company: Orsino, Malvolio, Sir Toby, Sir Andrew, Feste, Olivia, Maria, and, above all, Viola. She is the last of the heroines of the middle comedies and at the same time the first of those of the romances – Marina, Perdita, Miranda – who, like Viola, cast up on the Illyrian coast, are all associated with the sea. And she is also the first of the heroines whom Shakespeare brought fully to life in verse. Beatrice and Rosalind are creatures of prose, but Viola is of another and rarer element, created out of the perfected poetry of this period, a poetry less obvious than the earlier lyricism, because no longer dependent on the beauty of the single line, more natural, therefore, and for that reason more dramatic. Consider, for example, what the following five lines tell us about the two women, as Olivia unveils and Viola exclaims:

> 'Tis beauty truly blent, whose red and white
> Nature's own sweet and cunning hand laid on:
> Lady, you are the cruellest she alive,
> If you will lead these graces to the grave
> And leave the world no copy.

And consider the music of the words, so harmoniously related throughout the whole passage, many of them disyllables imposing a reversed and falling rhythm on the basic rising measure: *nature, laid on, lady, lead, alive, grave, graces, cruel, truly*. . . . It is the music of the nightingale, with whose swelling liquids one always associates Viola, and that is why one might hazard the guess that Shakespeare's original name for Orsino was Alonso. As Shylock had taught Shakespeare to write dramatic verse, so Viola taught him to write dramatic poetry, how to restore the lyric element, so sparingly used since *The Merchant of Venice*, to the flexible and open-textured verse of comedy and history, and, having perfected his medium, he turned to themes profounder than any hitherto attempted.

About a fortnight after the Court performance of *Twelfth Night*, Bankside was invaded by a number of Shakespeare's Stratford friends and neighbours. The death of Sir Thomas Lucy in the previous summer had deprived the Corporation of a good friend and defender of their privileges against the high-handed and officious Sir Edward Greville, who had recently inherited the manor of Stratford. It is true that the lord of the manor had certain rights of appointment and veto – Greville had tried to prevent the election of Richard Quiney as bailiff, and in 1599 had succeeded in preventing that of William Parsons – but he certainly had no right to enclose the common pasture of the Bankcroft, which he did at the beginning of January 1601. Passive resistance broke out into open warfare, and on 21 January the bailiff, Henry Wilson, and a number of leading townsmen, including Shakespeare's friends, Richard Quiney, John Sadler, and Henry Walker, armed with spades and mattocks, broke into the Bankcroft enclosure, cut down the newly planted hedges, levelled the ground, drove in horses, cattle, swine, and 'hoggerels', lopped forty willows, carried away the wood and committed other 'enormities', to the damage, according to Greville, of £40. As a result they were arrested for riot and taken to the Marshalsea on Bankside, where, however, they were released on bail. Quiney consulted Thomas Greene of the Middle Temple, a Warwick man who had just been appointed solicitor to the Stratford Corporation, and 'three days together' they waited on the Attorney-General, Sir Edward Coke, but 'could not have him at leisure by the reason of these troubles'.

'These troubles' were troubles indeed, and Coke had far more urgent business on his hands than listening to petitions from riotous Stratfordians. At the beginning of February the disgraced and discontented Essex made his desperate attempt to overthrow the government and force 'the crooked old woman', as in his ravings he called the Queen, to nominate him as her successor, a venture in which Shakespeare and his company were unwittingly involved. Essex, a student of Shakespeare's *Henry IV*, had come to identify himself with Bolingbroke, and Elizabeth, despite her sex, in his imagination played Richard II to his Henry IV. There was precedent for the dethroning, and even killing, of an English monarch, and it was possible to prepare the London citizens for an insurrection by reminding them of it. On Friday, 6 February, therefore, half a dozen of his supporters went to the Globe where they spoke to some of the players, Augustine Phillips among them, and asked them to play Shakespeare's *Richard II* the next day, Saturday; but the Chamberlain's protested that the play was 'so old and so long out of use' that very few would come to see it. The excuse was a thin one, for if the play, now in its third edition, really had been so out of fashion, it would have been almost impossible to revive it at such short notice. However, when they were offered 40s. for their pains they agreed, and on the following afternoon, having dined on the north bank, the conspirators crossed the Thames by water and made their way to the Globe. No doubt they took the best seats, stools on the stage where all could see them, and loudly applauded the speeches of Bolingbroke as Shakespeare and his company performed to an astonished and bewildered audience, instead of the play that had been advertised, that 'of the deposyng and kyllyng of Kyng Rychard the second'.

Elizabeth and Cecil were well aware of what was afoot, and when on the next morning, Sunday, 8 February, the infatuated

Essex, seconded by the Earl of Southampton, dashed out of Essex House at the head of 300 desperate men and rushed up the Strand towards the City, brandishing his sword and calling on the Londoners to join him in 'liberating' the Queen from her evil counsellors, a herald was already proclaiming him a traitor. He had hopelessly miscalculated, for although he was still the hero of the people, their loyalty to the almost legendary Queen was unshakable, and not a man joined him. Even his original followers slipped away down alleys when they found all the doors in Cheapside shut against them, and he turned desperately for home. Now a fugitive, he managed to reach the river and slip into Essex House by the water-gate, where, after destroying his papers, he surrendered.

Ten days later Essex and Southampton were brought to trial before their peers, the business that prevented Quiney and his friends from obtaining an interview with the Attorney-General, and they returned to Stratford with the news of what had happened in London. Coke made the most of the *Richard II* affair and of Essex's notorious admiration for Bolingbroke and Shakespeare's *Henry IV*: 'I protest upon my soul and conscience,' he shouted, 'I do believe she should not have long lived after she had been in your power. Note but the precedents of former ages; how long lived Richard the Second after he was surprised in the same manner? The pretence was alike for the removing of certain counsellors, but yet shortly after it cost him his life.' The two earls were found guilty and condemned to the traitor's death of hanging, drawing, and quartering. After the trial Essex broke down, confessed all, and denounced both himself and his friends, but Elizabeth would do no more than change the form of his execution to beheading, though Cecil persuaded her to commute Southampton's sentence to life imprisonment, as 'the poor young earl, merely for the love of Essex, had been driven into this action'.

The Chamberlain's were closely cross-questioned, for the affair at the Globe was taken very seriously, and if there had been any evidence of complicity and incitement to revolt it would have gone very hard with them indeed. However,

Augustine Phillips made a deposition which apparently satisfied their examiners, for on Shrove Tuesday, 24 February, they
presented the last play of the Court season before the Queen
at Whitehall. On the following morning Essex went to the
block.

The effect of the Essex rebellion on Shakespeare appears to
have been profound. He had written plays on the subject of the
dethroning and killing of kings, and described the confusion
that followed the forcible upsetting of the divinely established
order, but that was history, events that had happened two
centuries before. Now he was confronted with an attempt to
overthrow the settled government of his own day, perhaps not
the last, for the succession to the throne was still undecided,
the Queen beginning to fail, and after almost twenty years of
war with Spain the people had become disillusioned, restless,
and unstable. And then, the man who had led this abortive
rebellion had been inspired by what he himself had written and
the figure of Bolingbroke that he had created, so sympatheti-
cally drawn at the beginning of *Richard II*. Essex and his followers were not slow to draw a parallel between his outcast
condition when the Queen dismissed him from Court after the
disastrous outcome of his Irish expedition and Richard's ban-
ishment of Bolingbroke, for whom he had written:

> Nay, rather, every tedious stride I make
> Will but remember me what a deal of world
> I wander from the jewels that I love.
> Must I not serve a long apprenticehood
> To foreign passages, and in the end,
> Having my freedom, boast of nothing else
> But that I was a journeyman to grief?

And these words had been spoken, possibly by himself, on that
fateful Saturday afternoon at the Globe. Moreover, like the
Queen and almost everybody who was not jealous of his influence, Cecil and Raleigh, for example, he had admired Essex,
the handsome, generous, impetuous (and therein so unlike his
Bolingbroke), and princely soldier, a man of his own years who,

in return, had greatly admired his work. But it was not only Essex who had failed him. Southampton, the patron and friend to whom he had addressed so many of his sonnets, had been infected and, branded as a traitor, now languished in the Tower, a prisoner for life. It was a tragic overture to the seventeenth century.

The death of Hamnet had been the first major crisis in Shakespeare's life, and, as far as we know, the Essex rebellion was the second. The first had led, after a brief period of cynicism, to an extention of sympathy, symbolized almost by his less discriminating use of prose, the more even distribution of which broke down social barriers and produced the happy histories and carefree comedies of the last years of the sixteenth century. Now, the second led to a profounder perception, a more serious and sombre view of life. There had always been a grain of tragedy in his comedies, Don John in *Much Ado about Nothing*, Oliver in *As You Like It*, but this had withered and been overwhelmed by the happier action; now, however, the emphasis was shifted: the tragic seed forced its way through, and though sometimes arrested, it was enough to darken the comedy. There were to be no more pure comedies such as *Twelfth Night* and *As You Like It*, and Shakespeare embarked on a series of enigmatic plays, *All's Well that Ends Well*, *Hamlet*, *Troilus and Cressida*, *Measure for Measure*, before turning to pure tragedy and the exploration of the themes of jealousy, ingratitude, and ambition. It is not suggested that the Essex rebellion was directly responsible for *Othello*, *King Lear*, and *Macbeth*, but it is clear that after the rebellion, and probably because of it, there was a change of mood, and the period of *Hamlet* and anti-romantic comedy led, naturally enough, into the period of tragedy.

Having perfected a dramatic form, it was never Shakespeare's custom to repeat it; there were other fields to be won, and there are signs of a change in *Twelfth Night*, premonitions perhaps of tragedy: in the dirge-like 'Come away, death', and in the indefinable melancholy of Feste's last bawdy song, 'When that I was and a little tiny boy'. Then there is the strange and beautiful 'Phoenix and Turtle', written at about this time, a threnody or lament for the death of truth and beauty. The Essex rebellion seems to have precipitated the change, and it is probable that the shock made him turn instinctively to the play that he had written so hurriedly after the shock of Hamnet's death, *All's Well that Ends Well*, and begin to revise it, for one cannot read the first scene of this extraordinary play without being struck by its resemblance to *Hamlet*, not only in phrasing but also in the texture of the verse. The very first words, spoken by the Countess of Rousillon, 'In delivering my son from me, I bury a second husband', have their echo in the Player Queen's speech in *Hamlet*, ' A second time I kill my husband dead, When second husband kisses me in bed.' Helena's first words, like Hamlet's, are a riddle concerning a father's death, 'I do affect a sorrow, indeed, but I have it too.' Lafeu's reply is a brief version of Claudius's advice to Hamlet, 'Moderate lamentation is the right of the dead; excessive grief the enemy to the living,' and the Countess summarizes the precepts of Polonius when she gives her blessing to her departing son:

> Love all, trust a few,
> Do wrong to none: be able for thine enemy
> Rather in power than use; and keep thy friend
> Under thy own life's key: be check'd for silence,
> But never tax'd for speech.

But the play was unsatisfactory, and having partly rewritten its opening and added a few other touches, Shakespeare turned to the writing of *Hamlet*.

It may be that after their last Court performance at the beginning of Lent the Chamberlain's went on tour to escape any further consequences of their unfortunate production of *Richard II*, and discreetly to allow it to be forgotten. If so, Shakespeare would return to Stratford earlier than usual that year, and he may have been there in April when Thomas Whittington, the old shepherd of the Hathaways, died. It was a common custom for servants to bank with their masters, and when Whittington made his will he had entrusted £2 of his savings to the daughter of his former employer, whom he remembered as Anne Hathaway:

I geve and bequeth unto the poore people of Stratford 40ˢ that is in the hand of Anne Shaxspere, wyf unto Mr Wyllyam Shaxspere, and is due debt unto me, beyng payd to myne Executor by the sayd Wyllyam Shaxpere or his assigns.

Apart from her marriage, it is the only recorded incident in the life of Shakespeare's wife.

Richard Quiney returned to London in June to present the Stratford Corporation's case against Sir Edward Greville, taking with him a statement drawn up by Thomas Greene in consultation with four of the most respected elderly townsmen, knowledgeable about old customs. One of them was Adrian Quiney and another John Shakespeare, friends of fifty years' standing, both having begun their Stratford careers in Henley Street half a century before. It is the last glimpse we have of Shakespeare's father, in his old age happily restored to prosperity and an honourable position in the town, for, a few days after the election of Richard Quiney to his second bailiwick, he died, and on 8 September was buried in the parish church.

Subject to his mother's dower, the Henley Street property passed to William as the eldest son. The family living there was now a small one: his mother, his sister Joan, and her husband and baby son. Of his brothers, Gilbert and Edmund were probably still in London, the one a haberdasher, the other an actor, but of Richard there is no record, though that he did not carry on his father's business is suggested by the fact that Shakespeare let the eastern wing of the house, the old workshop, to Lewis Hiccox of Welcombe, who converted it into an inn with the sign of the Maidenhead. The remainder he let to his sister Joan at a nominal rent of a shilling. Perhaps he took his mother to live more spaciously at New Place, though she may have preferred to remain with her daughter in her old home.

It was at about this time that Thomas Greene, while still practising as a barrister in London in term-time, came to live in Stratford, where shortly afterwards he was appointed Town

Clerk. He may have been a distant relation of the Shakespeares, for he called the poet 'my cousin Shakespeare', though as he called a number of other men his cousins it may have been no more than a term of familiarity. In any event, Shakespeare must have known him well and liked him, for he offered the young man and his wife rooms in New Place, where their first child was born in 1604. She was called Anne, no doubt after Anne Shakespeare.

Another enterprising young man who arrived in Stratford at this time was John Hall, a physician of puritanical sympathies. Born in Bedfordshire in 1575, he was only fourteen when he entered Queens' College, Cambridge, where he took his M.A. degree in 1597, then, after studying medicine in France, settled in Stratford shortly before John Shakespeare's last illness and death. He built up a fashionable and very extensive practice, sometimes being called to attend the Earl and Countess of Northampton at Ludlow Castle, more than forty miles away, and no doubt soon became a frequent visitor at New Place, where Shakespeare's eighteen-year-old daughter, Susanna, would be an attraction additional to the conversation of the poet. It is, perhaps, not altogether fanciful to find the influence of Hall in the medical references and images of the plays of this period, in *All's Well that Ends Well* and *Hamlet*, where the dominating image is one of disease, symbolizing the rotten state of Denmark and corruption of the Danish court.

One is apt to forget how young Shakespeare was at this time. Now the head of his family, the owner of New Place, with one marriageable daughter and another of sixteen, the author of a score of imperishable plays, from *Richard III* to *Twelfth Night*, he was still only thirty-seven, perhaps only thirty-six when he began to write what must be the most famous of all plays, *Hamlet*. His father's illness and death and the consequent domestic worries, upsets, and responsibilities must have been a sore distraction during this critical stay in Stratford in 1601, and when he returned to London he would find himself involved in a controversy that threatened the welfare of his company and their theatre.

The quarrel of Jonson and Marston had broken out into a regular War of the Theatres, primarily of the children's theatres for which they wrote, Jonson for Blackfriars, Marston for Paul's. In *Cynthia's Revels* Jonson had parodied Marston's inflated style, coupling Dekker with him as an impudent, ignorant, arrogating puff; then, knowing that his opponents were penning a reply, wrote *The Poetaster* with unwonted speed for the Chapel Children, who presented it at Blackfriars in the early autumn. The scene of the play is ancient Rome, and Jonson himself appears as the virtuous poet Horace, who suffers from the attacks of the envious versifiers, or poetasters, Crispinus (Marston) and Demetrius (Dekker). Apparently Jonson knew that the Chamberlain's, as well as the Paul's Boys, were to produce his victim's projected reply, for he introduces the actor Histrio, who says that his company has hired Demetrius 'to abuse Horace, and bring him in, in a play'. Histrio must be one of the Chamberlain's men, and could be Shakespeare, who received the famous 40s. for their notorious production of *Richard II*, for he is to give 'forty – *forty* shillings' to persuade Crispinus to help Demetrius, and Jonson has some good sport at the expense of the company 'on the other side of the Tiber'. 'We have as much ribaldry in our plays as can be,' boasts Histrio, 'all the sinners in the suburb come and applaud our action daily.' Eventually the plot to ridicule Horace on the stage is discovered, and Crispinus and Demetrius are arraigned before Caesar. When they plead guilty and admit that their only motive was envy, Horace generously forgives them, though not without making Crispinus swallow pills to purge his brain and bowels of his windy words. The retching poetaster calls for a basin into which he vomits his astonishing vocabulary – *glibbery, oblatrant, prorumped, obstupefact*, and the rest – and the prisoners are dismissed, having solemnly sworn never again to pester Horace.

It was not long before Dekker and Marston replied in *Satiromastix, or The Untrussing of the Humorous Poet*, staged both by the Paul's Boys and the Chamberlain's at the Globe. Horace is unmercifully baited and at last brought to trial before, of all people, William Rufus. Crispinus acts as judge, but refuses to administer pills because of the stinking arrogance that they would bring up, and orders him to be crowned with nettles instead, to match his stinging wit. Finally, he is made to promise never again to attract attention to himself while watching his plays in a theatre, by grimacing from the gallery or venturing on the stage to talk to the gallants in the lords' room.

This was the end of the War of the Theatres, for Jonson was not allowed to reply: the Privy Council did not like the political implications of *The Poetaster* with its oblique allusions to *Richard II* and the Essex rebellion. But that Christmas the undergraduates of St John's College, Cambridge, performed an anonymous play, *The Return from Parnassus*, in which there was an echo of the controversy. Burbage and Kempe are introduced as characters, and Kempe exclaims: 'Few of the university men pen plays well. ... Why, here's our fellow Shakespeare puts them all down, ay, and Ben Jonson too. O that Ben Jonson is a pestilent fellow; he brought up Horace giving the poets a pill, but our fellow Shakespeare hath given him a purge that made him bewray his credit.' The purge that Shakespeare gave Jonson is a mystery, for though Jaques in *As You Like It* may be a sly hit at Jonson, it could scarcely be called a purge of any drastic consequence. Perhaps the author of *Parnassus* had heard of the recently produced *Satiromastix* and, knowing that the Chamberlain's had been ridiculed in *The Poetaster*, assumed that Shakespeare was the author. Cambridge followed the fortunes of the Chamberlain's, for the town lay within the province of their summer tours, though the academic world was sadly behind the times if it thought that Kempe was still with the company.

As a footnote, it is worth remarking that the author of *Parnassus*, one of the 'university men' whom Kempe is made to depreciate, was as envious of the professional players' success as the University Wits had been, and as the learned Jonson and the Oxfordian Marston now were:

> But is't not strange these mimic apes should prize
> Unhappy scholars at a hireling rate? ...

England affords those glorious vagabonds,
That carried erst their fardels on their backs,
Coursers to ride on through the gazing streets,
And pages to attend their masterships.
With mouthing words that better wits have framed,
They purchase lands, and now esquires are made.

It is the old gibe of Greene, himself a John's man, at upstart
crows beautified with poets' feathers, but if the last lines were
directed at Shakespeare, the man of property and newly made
gentleman, they were a little unfair, for after all most of the
finest feathers were his. The prejudice against players died very
hard.

The war waged in the private theatres of the boys meant a
serious loss to the Chamberlain's. Histrio explains why they
are hiring Demetrius to write against Horace: 'It will get us a
huge deal of money, and we have need on't; for this winter has
made us all poorer than so many starved snakes; nobody comes
at us.' And he hopes that the success of *Satiromastix* will mean
that they will not be driven to go on tour, their shoes full of
gravel, following 'a blind jade and a hamper, and stalk upon
boards and barrel heads to an old cracked trumpet' – a vivid
sketch, or caricature, of the hardships endured by a travelling
company, and the makeshift stages on which they had to act.
Shakespeare added his comment in *Hamlet*: the children 'are
now the fashion, and so berattle the common stages – so they
call them – that many wearing rapiers are afraid of goose-quills,
and dare scarce come thither'.

Although the wordy warfare, so lucrative to the boys and
their poets, so impoverishing to the adult players, was over by
the end of 1601, the competition of the boys remained, and that
Christmas the Chapel Children gave three of the nine performances at the Revels. These were all after the Queen had paid a
visit to Lord Hunsdon at his Blackfriars house, where she
dined and saw a play, possibly by the children in their theatre.
The Admiral's, apparently, were even more seriously hit, for
they appeared only once at Court, in some sort of tumbling
show. Henslowe, however, had another string to his bow.

Despite the Privy Council regulations, he had let the Rose to another company, the Earl of Worcester's, and after entertaining them to supper at the Mermaid he agreed to finance them after the manner of the Admiral's, which meant, of course, that they were soon in his debt and bound to him like his other company at the Fortune. They were a strong combination, including Kempe, just back from Italy, young John Lowin, soon to become one of Shakespeare's fellows, and Thomas Heywood, like Shakespeare, a playwright as well as a player. The Chamberlain's, therefore, had to meet not only the competition of the boys, but also that of another and formidable company on Bankside, only a few yards away from the Globe. However, they gave four performances at the Revels, one of which was probably *Hamlet*.

Driven by the competition of the boys to sell part of their most valuable stock, four of the comedies of Shakespeare, the Chamberlain's must have pressed him to write a really popular play, something like *The Spanish Tragedy*, which a few years before had drawn all London. They had Kyd's old tragedy of revenge, *Hamlet*, which they had revived as recently as 1596 both at the Theatre and Swan, just the thing, if Shakespeare would rewrite it and give it a new lease of life. Fortunately Shakespeare, having finished *Twelfth Night*, was ready for a new venture, and after the Essex rebellion needed no further prompting, for the theme of *Hamlet* was, or could be made into, that of the confusion that follows the murder of a monarch, a confusion that England had so narrowly escaped that year and which still threatened. That he fulfilled the confidence and hopes of his company is clear from the testimony of his contemporaries: the poet Anthony Scoloker, writing of 'friendly Shakespeare's tragedies', described *Prince Hamlet* as one that 'pleases all', and even the disagreeable and cantankerous Gabriel Harvey admitted that 'his *Lucrece* and his tragedy of *Hamlet* have it in them to please the wiser sort'. Harvey may have seen the play at Cambridge, Scoloker at Oxford, to both of which towns it was soon taken, but it was seen much farther afield than at the universities, for Captain William Keeling of the East India Company had it performed at least twice on board his ship on his passages to India, not perhaps for the highest aesthetic reasons, though for the very laudable object of keeping his 'people from idlenes and unlawful games, or sleepe'. Then, if the touchstone of popularity is quotation, from no other book, apart from the Bible, have so many phrases passed into common speech: 'more in sorrow than in anger', 'to the manner born', 'more honoured in the breach than the observance', 'brevity is the soul of wit', 'caviare to the general' to mention only a few.

Hamlet is the great landmark in Shakespeare's progress, standing like a rock, conspicuous and unmistakably defined, exactly in the middle of his career and exactly at the turning of the centuries. In sheer bulk it is much the biggest of the plays; its hero is the most famous in all literature, for we all tend to identify ourselves with Hamlet, to see in him the shadow of our aspirations and reflection of our failures, and the style is so distinctive that it cannot be mistaken for the poetry of any other period, its most obvious characteristic being the pairing of adjectives and coupling of nouns, often the Latin with the Saxon, abstract with the concrete, to form an image: 'ponderous and marble jaws', 'black and grained spots', 'shot and danger of desire', 'whips and scorns of time', 'expectancy and rose of the fair state'.

We can imagine the elementary melodrama of the lost *Hamlet* that was the source of Shakespeare's play: the Ghost crying miserably like a fish-wife, 'Hamlet revenge!', and the rant of the dispossessed hero, mad as old Jeronimo in *The Spanish Tragedy*, tearing passions to tatters. It was this sort of crude stuff that Shakespeare had to refine, adding subtler motives for Hamlet's revenge, and for a simple physical obstacle substituting a psychological one. Not madness, however, for Hamlet is not mad, and much of the excitement and satisfaction lies in our knowledge that he is not, that he is outwitting his opponents by pretending to be mad. Shakespeare is at pains to tell us this: Hamlet warns his friends that he may put an antic disposition on, assures his mother that he is only 'mad in craft', and always speaks prose in his feigned insanity, never in his soliloquies. Moreover, it was not Shakespeare's way to put two mad people into a play, and as Edgar's pretended madness finally drives Lear over the threshold of insanity, so Hamlet's pretence drives Ophelia into real madness and a muddy death. In this lies much of the pathos and tragedy.

The Ghost really is that of Hamlet's father, no devil in a pleasing shape – 'It is an honest ghost,' 'I'll take the ghost's word for a thousand pound,' says Hamlet – and that the story it tells is true is made clear to him by the success of the Mousetrap play, and to the audience by the confession of Claudius in his attempted prayer. Hamlet, therefore, has motives enough for his revenge:

> He that hath kill'd my king, and whored my mother,
> Popp'd in between the election and my hopes,
> Thrown out his angle for my proper life . . .

In that order: the main, overwhelming motives being his uncle's murder of his father and seduction of his mother; the others are comparatively minor considerations, for as the throne of Denmark is elective, Claudius is guilty of nothing worse than corrupting the electors, and Hamlet sets no more value on his life than a pin's fee.

Convinced, then, of his uncle's guilt, and having motives for his revenge, he also has the means: 'cause and will and strength and means to do't'. There is no physical impediment either within or without, and we witness one perfect opportunity when he finds Claudius alone, unarmed and on his knees with his back to him. And yet he does nothing. He himself does not know why – 'I do not know Why yet I live to say "this thing's to do"' – and his inaction has led to the writing of more words than any other comparable topic in literature.

Yet there is no great mystery. Although Shakespeare lived long before the age of the scientific exploration of the mind, he was well aware of the duality of man's nature, of the two levels of his thought and action: half angel, half beast, half reason, half passion, half judgement, half blood, or as we should say today, half conscious, half unconscious. Hamlet's frailty is a propensity to passion, and passion is the mark of the beast – 'a beast that wants discourse of reason', 'fair judgement without the which we are mere beasts' – while reason is the prerogative of man: 'that noble and most sovereign reason', 'that capability and god-like reason'. And so on the one hand he can say, 'What a piece of work is a man! how noble in reason! how infinite in faculty! the paragon of animals!', and on the other, 'What should such fellows as I do crawling between heaven and earth?' It is because Horatio's blood and judgement are so well commingled that he is not passion's slave that Hamlet prizes him above all other friends; yet Horatio never encourages him in his purposed vengeance, never even admits that a private vengeance is justified. Thus, when Hamlet asks, 'Is't not perfect conscience to quit him with this arm?' Horatio turns the question with the warning that Claudius will soon learn the fate of Rosencrantz and Guildenstern. And anybody who asks if it is not perfect conscience to commit a murder is very far from being sure of himself.

The theme of *Hamlet* is ostensibly the simple and popular one of revenge, the appeal to the beast in man, but fundamentally it is the conflict of reason and passion, of man's higher nature with his lower, of his god-like reason with his baser instincts. Horatio would not have killed Claudius in Hamlet's place, nor would Hamlet if his reason had been in control of his passion. He knows that murder in any form is wrong; *the Ghost itself had told him so* even as it called for vengeance:

> Revenge his foul and most unnatural murder.
> Murder most foul, *as in the best it is*.

Hamlet, therefore, both wants and does not want to murder his uncle; passion urges him on, but reason holds him back, and he can act only peripherally, on the circumference, by organizing plays and feigning madness; at the centre all action is neutralized. Neutralized except when passion gets the better of reason: and in passion he kills Polonius, sends Rosencrantz and Guildenstern to their deaths, kills Laertes, and finally kills

Claudius. Here is the confusion that follows the murder of a king, and this is not all, for his vengeance costs him his own life and is also responsible for the madness and drowning of Ophelia and the poisoning of his mother. No wonder he cries after the first visitation of the Ghost: 'O cursed spite, That ever I was born to set it right!'

Set it right! Perhaps he does so after a fashion, but eight lives is a heavy price to pay, and the tragedy of Hamlet is his failure to find a rational solution. Although Shakespeare identified himself and sympathized with his hero, he cannot have approved of his conduct, but, he seems to say, given such a situation and such a man, this is the way events would work out, and this, or something like this, might have been the result of Essex's failure to control his blood and passion earlier in the year. The moral, no doubt, was little more than a by-product of the play, for Shakespeare was more concerned with Hamlet than with Essex and Southampton, and perhaps there is more of himself than of the earls in his creation, or rather of the impulsive young man he had been when he was Hamlet's age. And this is another reason for the perennial popularity and fascination of *Hamlet*: that in this play we seem to come so close to Shakespeare himself. We certainly hear him speaking, as naturally and informally as he spoke to his friends, in the person of Hamlet when he gives his instructions to the players, advice that he must have given his company when rehearsing on the stage of the Globe, explaining his own conception of acting, and ridiculing the old-fashioned rant practised by Alleyn and the Admiral's: 'Speak the speech, I pray you, as I pronounced it to you, trippingly on the tongue: but if you mouth it, as many of your players do, I had as lief the town-crier spoke my lines. . . .' Then, we hear the mature Shakespeare, more concerned now with the wrongs and injustices of the world, in Hamlet's most famous soliloquy:

> The oppressor's wrong, the proud man's contumely,
> The pangs of despised love, the law's delay,
> The insolence of office, and the spurns
> That patient merit of the unworthy takes.

It is the theme of Sonnet 66, 'Tired with all these', but the poem lacks the conviction of the soliloquy, which is evidence of Shakespeare's deeper concern at man's predicament, his indifference and inhumanity, a concern that was to underlie all his later work and find such impassioned expression in *King Lear*. And then there is the pervading mystery of *Hamlet*: not so much the mystery of Hamlet himself, his melancholy and indecision, as Shakespeare's meditations on the mysteries of life and death, nowhere more powerfully suggested than in this play. When Hamlet compares himself to a recorder it is Shakespeare speaking of the mystery of man: 'You would pluck out the heart of my mystery; you would sound me from the lowest note to the top of my compass: and there is much music, excellent voice in this little organ; yet cannot you make it speak.' And in the profounder medium of verse there is the ever-present mystery of

> The undiscover'd country from whose bourn
> No traveller returns.

Hamlet may not be Shakespeare's greatest play, but it is not difficult to understand why it is the one that everybody knows, or at least knows of.

It may be that *Hamlet* was the last play to be given at the Revels of 1601–2, on Shrove Tuesday, before the beginning of Lent. Twelve days earlier, on 2 February, the barrister John Manningham of the Middle Temple made a note in his diary, that to celebrate their Candlemas Revel, their Grand Day, they had 'a play called Twelue Night, or What You Will'. Perhaps Thomas Greene, another Middle Temple man, had something to do with the choice. It would be presented in the great hall of the inn, with its magnificent, recently completed hammer-beam roof, and the performance so impressed the young lawyer that he described Malvolio's part and compared the play to *The Comedy of Errors* and the old Italian comedy of *Gl'Ingannati*, which was indeed, at two or three removes, Shakespeare's source for the more serious themes. Evidently Shakespeare himself impressed Manningham, for a few weeks later he made another entry in his curious scrapbook of a diary, an anecdote related by a fellow lawyer of the Middle Temple, Edward Curle. According to Curle, a citizen's wife fell so much in love with Burbage when he was playing Richard III that she invited him to visit her one night by that name. Shakespeare, however, having overheard their conversation, anticipated his friend and 'was entertained and at his game' before Burbage arrived. Then when the message was brought that Richard III was at the door, Shakespeare sent the reply that William the Conqueror came before Richard III. There is probably no truth in the anecdote, which is just the sort of story that one young man has told another throughout the centuries, but that such a fable should have been invented is evidence of the popularity of Shakespeare and his work among the young men of the inns of court.

It was probably Richard Martin, wit, friend of poets, patron of the Mermaid Tavern, and Prince d'Amour, the mock sovereign of the revels at the Middle Temple, who invited the Chamberlain's to present *Twelfth Night* at their Candlemas frolics, and it may have been he who asked Shakespeare to write another comedy of love for the following year. If so, it was a strange play that Shakespeare wrote for them in 1602, for *Troilus and Cressida* is what Polonius might have called 'tragical-comical-satirical', though just the play to tickle the Templars, stuffed full, as it was, of topical allusions, wit, legal jargon, and love: the theme taken from the bitter words of Hamlet to his mother, 'Reason pandars will.' There was something to suit all tastes: the mincing light-of-love Cressida, the greasy talk of her uncle Pandarus, the obscenities of Thersites, the lyrical love-making of Troilus, the elephantine bombast of Ajax, and the high debate of Ulysses, who gave classic expression to Shakespeare's philosophy of degree, or established order, so vital at that critical time when the Queen was visibly failing:

> The heavens themselves, the planets and this centre,
> Observe degree, priority and place,
> Insisture, course, proportion, season, form,
> Office and custom, in all line of order. . . .

Take but degree away, untune that string,
And hark, what discord follows. . . .

Troilus and Cressida seems to have been the only play that Shakespeare wrote in 1602, and from now on, instead of writing an average of two plays a year, as had been his practice for more than a decade, he wrote only one. He could afford to take things more easily.

He must have begun negotiations about the purchase of an estate on the outskirts of Stratford when he was at New Place in the previous summer. It lay just to the north of the town, west of the hamlet of Welcombe, and consisted of 107 acres of arable land and 20 acres of common pasture. The owners were William Combe, a wealthy Warwick lawyer, incidentally another Middle Temple man, and his nephew John, and from them 'William Shakespere of Stratford vppon Avon, gentleman', bought the property and 'thappertenaunces' on 1 May 1602, for the sum of £320, a big investment, equal to about £10,000 today. As Shakespeare was not in Stratford at the time, the conveyance was delivered to his brother Gilbert, who seems to have returned to his native town. There was probably no disturbance of the existing tenants, one of whom was Lewis Hiccox, tenant also of part of Shakespeare's Henley Street property, now the Maidenhead Inn, a somewhat embarrassing tenant, for in the following year his wife handled her next-door neighbour of the Bell so roughly that she was bound over to keep the peace. It must have been a profitable investment, or Shakespeare, always a good businessman, would not have made it, but it would have been far more profitable had the land been enclosed instead of lying in an open field. In the Stratford area there had been little enclosure, a movement strenuously opposed by the conservative Corporation, and Shakespeare's property was divided in the medieval manner into small strips or allotments, in every way a wasteful system that virtually prevented improved methods of cultivation, while the custom of common pasturage made it equally difficult to improve the breed of sheep and cattle.

The conveyance was made in Stratford on 1 May. Two days

later Shakespeare's friend, Richard Quiney, was mortally hurt. The Corporation was still at loggerheads with Sir Edward Greville, who claimed the toll-corn of the town, and matters came to a head when the May Fair was held at the beginning of the month. On Monday, the 3rd, the first day of the Fair, Greville sent his men into the town to seize the toll-corn, and that night they gathered in a house where heavy drinking was followed by a brawl. As bailiff, Quiney with his officers patrolled the streets to see that the peace was kept, but when he got involved with Greville's followers he was accidentally struck on the head by one of his own men and severely wound-ed. After lingering for nearly four weeks he died, and on 31 May was buried in the parish church. Never before had a bailiff died in office, and after the funeral the Corporation met to elect his successor. Old Adrian Quiney, Richard's father, was there, and Abraham Sturley kept the minutes.

In this year, 1602, Shakespeare went to a good deal of trouble to consolidate his position. Prudent man that he now was, he seems to have felt that his title to New Place was not altogether secure after the murder of William Underhill, from whom he had bought it, and the execution of his crazy elder son Fulke for the crime, for the estate had been forfeited before being re-granted to Fulke's brother Hercules. When, therefore, Hercules came of age in the summer of 1602, Shakespeare sent his agent to see him in Northamptonshire and get another conveyance of the house, with its two barns, two gardens, and – an addition to the original deed – two orchards. Evidently Shakespeare had been planting fruit trees, and perhaps it was for his gardener that, in September, he bought a cottage in Chapel Lane, just below the Gild Chapel and opposite the gardens of New Place. He may have been in Stratford at the time, for though he bought it from Walter Getley, the tenure was copyhold as it lay within the estate of the Countess of Warwick, to whom he had to swear fealty and pay an annual rent of 2s. 6d.

Despite the competition of the boys' companies, the Chamberlain's were prospering, thanks largely to the success of *Hamlet*, which must have drawn crowded houses to the Globe throughout 1602. Their prosperity is mirrored not only in the fortunes of Shakespeare, but also in those of his fellows; Burbage, Heminge, Phillips, and Pope had all achieved, or were about to achieve, the rank of gentleman, all of them were buying property in London, while Phillips had a house at Mortlake and Condell a 'country house' at Fulham. They were certainly doing better than the Admiral's, with the exception of Alleyn, who, in partnership with Henslowe was amassing a huge estate. Joint owner of the Fortune and the Admiral's stock, joint Master of the Game in Paris Garden, he had large and lucrative investments in London and Sussex, and was on the point of retiring and buying the manor of Dulwich, where he was to found his famous school.

Shortly before Shakespeare bought the Chapel Lane cottage, Elizabeth celebrated her sixty-ninth birthday, and two months later, on 17 November, there was the traditional tilt on Queen's Day, the forty-fourth anniversary of her accession. But she was failing rapidly, suffering apparently from cancer, and when her godson, Sir John Harington, arrived at Court for the Revels, he wrote sadly to his wife,

Our dear Queen doth now bear show of human infirmity; too fast for that evil which we shall get by her death, and too slow for that good which she shall get by her releasement from pains and misery.

Yet the Revels that Christmas began with exceptional gaiety. The first play was given by the Chamberlain's at Whitehall on 26 December, but a month later the Court moved to Richmond, and on 2 February, in bitterly cold weather, Shakespeare and his company made the ten-mile journey up the river to entertain the Queen. It was Candlemas, the Middle Temple Grand Day, and, though *Troilus and Cressida* was written – it was registered five days later – if Richard Martin and his friends had hoped to see it that night they were disappointed. Perhaps it was the play that the Chamberlain's presented before the Queen. If so, it was the last play that she saw. The indomitable woman was broken at last; no longer able to stand, but refusing all help from her assembled physicians, she lay listlessly on cushions with her finger in her mouth. At length Cecil persuaded her to go to bed, where she lay with her face to the wall, speaking to no one. On 19 March the Privy Council issued an order forbidding all stage-plays until further notice, and on the following day Cecil wrote to James VI of Scotland to tell him that the Queen had named him her successor. Then, having left the affairs of her country in order and listened to the prayers of her aged Archbishop, early in the morning of 24 March she died.

CHAPTER 8

1603–7

THE KING'S SERVANT

*

THE new king was a man of thirty-seven, about the same age as Shakespeare, though far less fortunate in his parentage. His father was the vicious youth Lord Darnley, who had been murdered by his mother's lover, and his mother, Mary Queen of Scots, after a captivity of twenty years, had died a traitor's death. It was an unpromising background, and education had done little for James but fill him with a mass of knowledge and an exaggerated opinion of his own capacity and importance. Yet obstinate, prejudiced, superstitious, and narrow-minded though he was, he had a warm and generous heart, and was bent on extravagantly enjoying himself in his new and far more wealthy kingdom. Physically he was feeble and weak in the legs, a disability that he compensated by forcing himself to become a fearless rider and hunter, and after the chase his great delight was drink and the company of handsome young men. His wife, Anne of Denmark, was only twenty-eight, young enough to be carried away by the prospect of endless revels, masquerades, and entertainments after the austerities and restraints of Scotland, though she was no mere featherhead, but intelligent, loyal, and a devoted mother to her beautiful and gifted children, Prince Henry, aged nine, and his sister Elizabeth, aged seven. Prince Charles was only two.

Sir Robert Cecil had been primarily responsible for the peaceful but perilous transition from the house of Tudor to that of Stuart, and James gratefully acknowledged his indebtedness by creating him Viscount Cranborne and, shortly afterwards, Earl of Salisbury. Raleigh, however, was in disgrace. Arrogant, brilliant, and therefore unpopular, he was the leader of the party that favoured the Spanish war, an extravagance that

James was determined to end as soon as possible, and when he was found to be implicated in a plot to overthrow the King he was committed to the Tower, where he was to spend the next thirteen years writing his *History of the World*. Raleigh entered the Tower shortly after Southampton left it, for one of the first acts of James was to free Shakespeare's patron after the two years' imprisonment that followed the Essex rebellion. If Southampton really was the young man who had inspired Shakespeare to write his sonnets, it was probably now, in the early spring of 1603, that he wrote number 107:

> Not mine own fears, nor the prophetic soul
> Of the wide world dreaming on things to come,
> Can yet the lease of my true love control,
> Supposed as forfeit to a confined doom.
> The mortal moon hath her eclipse endured,
> And the sad augurs mock their own presage;
> Incertainties now crown themselves assured,
> And peace proclaims olives of endless age.
> Now with the drops of this most balmy time
> My love looks fresh, and Death to me subscribes,
> Since, spite of him, I'll live in this poor rhyme,
> While he insults o'er dull and speechless tribes:
>> And thou in this shalt find thy monument,
>> When tyrants' crests and tombs of brass are spent.

Dr Hotson thinks that the eclipse of the mortal moon refers to the defeat of the deadly crescent-shaped Spanish Armada of fifteen years before, but if the reference is to the death of Elizabeth, who for all the poets of the period was Cynthia, the virgin goddess of the moon, 'my love' is almost certainly the confined Southampton, released at 'this most balmy time' of spring, when James, proclaiming his determination to make peace with Spain, had confounded the prophets by succeeding to the throne without the disorders, and even civil war, that had been so gloomily predicted and so greatly feared.

For the dramatists and players of the time the attitude of James to the Puritans was all-important, for if he sympathized with their demand to close the theatres their careers were virtually finished. But James had had some experience in Presbyterian Scotland. When Prince Henry had been born he had invited Lawrence Fletcher and a company of English actors to come to Edinburgh to celebrate his christening with a series of plays, and in spite of the horrified protests of the Kirk had forced the General Assembly to permit public performances and even to acquiesce in the building of a theatre. Then, when within a few months, old Archbishop Whitgift followed Elizabeth to the grave, James appointed as his successor Richard Bancroft, an implacable opponent of the Puritans, who was supported by his ex-chaplain, Samuel Harsnet, author of *A Declaration of Egregious Popish Impostures*, the book in which Shakespeare found Flibbertigibbet and the other foul fiends that plagued Edgar in *King Lear*.

Shakespeare had every reason to be satisfied with the events of that critical spring of 1603, and even the one mischance proved to be only a further stroke of fortune. Lord Hunsdon, who had been ill for some time, resigned his office of Lord Chamberlain at the beginning of April, and shortly afterwards died, leaving without a patron the company which, in the course of the last ten years, had achieved immortality under his and his father's protection. But they were not long without a patron. After a slow and triumphant progress from Scotland, James arrived in London on 11 May, and on the 19th issued letters patent appointing the late Lord Chamberlain's Men his own servants:

Knowe yee that Wee ... haue licenced ... theise our Servauntes. Lawrence Fletcher, William Shakespeare, Richard Burbage, Augustyne Phillippes, Iohn Heninges, Henrie Condell, William Sly, Robert Armyn, Richard Cowly, and the rest of theire Assosiates freely to vse and exercise the Arte and faculty of playinge ... as well for the recreation of our lovinge Subjectes as for our Solace and pleasure when wee shall thincke good to see them.

Lawrence Fletcher had come from Scotland with James, and was, therefore, already a King's Man, but his position in the company appears to have been merely honorary, for there is no record of his ever acting with them. The name of Thomas Pope, one of the original members of the fellowship is missing; he was confined to his Southwark house, where, after making his will in July, he died.

Their elevation from Chamberlain's to King's Servants did not necessarily mean any change of fortune, for players were paid by their patron only when they performed before him. But James was to prove a far better patron to players than Elizabeth had been. In her reign an average of about seven plays had been given during the season of the Revels, most of them within the Twelve Days of Christmas, but James considerably extended the period, which now began as early as 1 November and sometimes lasted until well after Easter, so that in January 1605 a bewildered Elizabethan wondered if Christmas was to be with them all the year. Rarely were there fewer than twenty performances, though it is true that the King did not always see them; horses were a more powerful magnet than *Hamlet*, and he would slip away to his stables, leaving the Queen and Prince Henry to enjoy their entertainment, and sometimes pay for it too. Since their formation ten years before, the Chamberlain's had given thirty-two Court performances; in the next ten, as the King's, they were to give four times as many. As the reward for a Court performance was £10, this meant an increase in their joint income of something like £3,000 of our money, or about £300 for each sharer.

Like the Queen's Men of the eighties, the company with which Shakespeare had probably served his apprenticeship, the King's were sworn in by the new Lord Chamberlain as Grooms of the Chamber, taking rank between the Gentlemen and Yeomen. They were thus a part of the household establishment, though their Court duties were nominal, and the Master of the Great Wardrobe supplied each of them – 'William Shakespeare, Augustine Phillipps, Lawrence Fletcher, John Hemminges, Richard Burbidge, William Slye, Robert Armyn, Henry Cundell, Richard Cowley' – with four and a half yards of scarlet cloth for their royal liveries. Before the end of the year the other two London companies had been taken under royal patronage, the Admiral's becoming Prince Henry's, and

Worcester's, who had moved from the Rose to the Curtain, Queen Anne's. There was a vast difference between the actors of the old days, at one remove only from rogues and vagabonds, and the royal companies whom James protected by ordering all justices, mayors, sheriffs, and other officers 'to be aidinge and assistinge to them, yf anie wronge be to them offered'.

It was at about this time that Shakespeare moved from South-wark to the fashionable parish of St Olave's, near Cripplegate, in the north-west corner of the City. Probably he wanted to be near his friends Heminge and Condell, who lived in the next parish of St Mary Aldermanbury, and perhaps they recom-mended him to the house of their neighbour Christopher Mountjoy, a Huguenot who had left France because of the per-secution of Protestants, and set up business in Silver Street as a tire-maker. Tires, or attires, were the beautiful and often extravagantly expensive head-dresses worn by Elizabethan and Jacobean ladies, nets of gold thread into which were sewn pearls, diamonds, emeralds, rubies, and other precious stones to adorn their hair. 'Alas,' says poor Julia in *The Two Gentlemen of Verona* as she looks at the portrait of her rival,

> If I had such a tire, this face of mine
> Were full as lovely as is this of hers.

And, according to Falstaff, Mistress Ford had a brow worthy of 'the ship-tire, the tire valiant, or any tire of Venetian admit-tance', evidence of the fantastic shapes sometimes devised to set off a woman's beauty. Mountjoy, then, was a practiser of this art of working 'Venice gold and silver thread', and his wife assisted him in the mystery, in 1604 furnishing Queen Anne with tires to the value of £59, or £2,000 of our money. Shakespeare was lodging with no common shopkeeper, but with an artist-craftsman who dealt in the most precious of all materials and supplied the Queen herself with head-dresses. The Mountjoys had an only child, Mary, brought up in the craft, and Shakespeare must often have watched her weaving webs of golden tissue. They also had an apprentice, Stephen Belott, a Huguenot like themselves. Apparently Shakespeare took a liking to his hosts, and when the romantic Mrs Mountjoy sounded him about the possible marriage of Mary and Stephen he willingly agreed to talk to the young man and act as an intermediary in the matter of a suitable marriage portion. He succeeded in his match-making, and in November 1604 the young couple were married.

It is possible that Shakespeare was responsible for making another match. In Philip Lane, just across the way from his Silver Street lodgings, was the handsome house of Anne Digges, the wealthy widow of Thomas Digges, the famous astronomer and mathematician, and mother of Dudley and Leonard Digges, the one a graduate, the other still an undergraduate at Oxford. Anne was an extremely eligible lady in search of a second husband, and it may well have been Shakespeare who introduced her to his friend Thomas Russell, whose wife and children had all tragically died within the last few years. In any event the match was made, though much against the will of Dudley Digges, the heir, and in August 1603 the couple were married, and went to live on Russell's Cotswold manor at Alderminster, only a few miles from Stratford.

Up till this time Shakespeare had always lived near his work: first in Shoreditch near the Theatre and then on Bankside within a few minutes of the Globe. Now that he could afford to take things more easily and live at some distance from the playhouse, Silver Street had advantages besides the companionship of his colleagues: only a quarter of a mile away was the Fortune, which he must frequently have visited to keep an eye on his rivals, and even nearer, just off Cheapside in Bread Street, was the Mermaid Tavern. The host was William Williamson, to whom in 1591 William Johnson, a boy of about sixteen, had been apprenticed. After nine years as Williamson's servant, Johnson was admitted as freeman of the Company of Vintners, and in the spring of 1603, when the Chamberlain's became the King's Servants, Williamson retired and sold him the lease of the tavern. It must have been soon after this that the Mermaid became the regular meeting-place of the poets and wits of London, or as one of its frequenters, Thomas Coryat, put it, of 'the worshipful fraternity of sirenaical gentlemen that meet the first Friday of every month at the sign of the Mermaid'. Johnson valued their patronage and looked after them well, too well, for a few years later he was heavily fined for serving them with meat at their Friday suppers, Friday being by law a 'fish day', an offence of which he had been guilty at least thirty times.

Among the members of the Mermaid Club were Ben Jonson and Inigo Jones, both of an age, thirty in 1603, who were already making plans for collaborating in the provision of spectacular entertainment at Court. There was John Donne, aged thirty-one, author of a number of unpublished but revolutionary and dazzling poems, much admired by Jonson and no doubt by Shakespeare as well. There was Shakespeare's Warwickshire neighbour, Michael Drayton, who sometimes stayed with Sir Henry Rainsford at Clifford Chambers on the outskirts of Stratford, and was now engaged on his interminable verse gazeteer of England, *Polyolbion*, and Thomas Campion, lawyer and doctor, poet and musician, who composed the settings for his own graceful lyrics, and of course the irrepressible Richard Martin of the Middle Temple. Then there were two new men who were yet to make their names: John Fletcher, son of a former Bishop of London, and young Francis Beaumont of the Inner Temple. It was Beaumont who was to write to Jonson of these happy days at the beginning of the century when all were young:

> What things have we seen
> Done at the Mermaid! heard words that have been
> So nimble, and so full of subtle flame,
> As if that every one from whence they came
> Had meant to put his whole wit in a jest,
> And had resolved to live a fool the rest
> Of his dull life.

There is no record of Shakespeare's being a member of the club, but it is scarcely conceivable that he was not, the leading poet and dramatist of the age with lodgings only five minutes' walk from the Mermaid, and probably Fuller was thinking of these Mermaid meetings when he wrote, fifty years later, 'Many were the wit-combats between him and Ben Jonson', and compared Jonson to a heavily built and armoured Spanish galleon, Shakespeare to a nimble English man-of-war, able to take advantage of wind and tide 'by the quickness of his wit and invention'.

Any meetings at the Mermaid, however, would be sadly reduced in the early summer of 1603. London was full of visitors come to see the coronation pageantry and spectacle, adding greatly to the anxiety of the Privy Council who were watching the weekly returns of deaths in the City. There had been plague deaths as early as April, and when James issued his warrant to the King's Men on 19 May he licensed them to play at 'their vsual howse called the Globe when the infection of the plague shall decrease'. Evidently the theatres had not been reopened since their closure when Elizabeth died two months before. There were thirty plague deaths in the last week of May, forty in the following week, and soon they were running into hundreds and even thousands. More than 30,000 people were to die of plague that year. In June the Court moved to Windsor, in July to Hampton Court, whence James and Anne hurried to Westminster to be crowned in the Abbey, before going on a progress which eventually took them to Wilton House, near Salisbury, the home of the young Earl of Pembroke, where they stayed until the middle of December. All who could left London; the theatres remained closed; the King's Men were forced to travel unprofitably in the provinces, though James generously gave them £30 for their 'mayntenaunce and releife, being prohibited to presente any playes publiquelie in or neere London by reason of the plague', and Shakespeare, presumably, returned to Stratford to get on with the writing of his next play, *Measure for Measure*.

It is a strange play, or rather an unexpected one, very different from any other that he had yet written, a romantic comedy in which romance approaches and even marches with the frontier of tragedy; the frigid Angelo has at least one quality of the tragic hero, over-confidence, and all the elements of tragedy are there when he finds that virtue is not proof against the assaults of virtue. Up till this time Shakespeare had written partly, and of necessity, to please a popular audience, his treatment of moral problems had been comparatively superficial and conventional, his comments rarely more disturbing than the easy aphorisms that so pleased Juliet's nurse; but now, secure in his position and no longer so dependent upon popular favour, he abandoned such themes as Much Ado about Nothing, As You Like It, What You Will, and plunged for the heart of the mystery. The theme is retribution, death for death, Measure for Measure; the key-words strike and strike again: *authority, law, justice, death, hope, pity, mercy, pardon*; and the atmosphere is one of confinement, with a corresponding darkness of background, that of 'the fantastical duke of dark corners' and 'dark deeds darkly answered', as Lucio, the Chorus, puts it.

On the other hand, the comedy of Elbow, Froth, and Pompey Bum is as good as anything that Shakespeare ever wrote, and there is no need to imagine any physical or spiritual crisis to account for his serious treatment of a serious theme: that, because allusions to and images from the body and its ailments become more frequent, he was suffering from some disease, that because the Duke speaks of the moral corruption of Vienna boiling and bubbling till it overran the stew, Shakespeare was himself revolted by what he saw in London. He *may* have been both physically and spiritually ill, but there is nothing in his outward circumstances, so far as we know them, to suggest that he was. What *is* certain is that the evolution was inevitable: the application of his fully developed dramatic poetry to more serious themes and to the highest form of drama, tragedy, to which *Measure for Measure* is in the nature of an overture. We do Shakespeare an injustice if we assume that he turned to tragedy as a vehicle for the outpouring of his own unhappiness, that the denunciations of women, denunciations that flow over into the last romances, are evidence of a spiritual insurrection occasioned by the conduct of some woman. There are singularly few unchaste women in his plays: nearly all his heroines are heavenly true, as the suspicious fathers, lovers, and husbands eventually discover, and he seems to have had a greater admiration for women than for men. But when he wrote of jealousy or ingratitude or ambition he was no longer Shakespeare, but Othello or Leontes, Timon or Lear, Macbeth or Lady Macbeth, so passionately did he identify himself with his characters and theme. Then, we know that the disaster of Hamnet's death had been the prelude to his most radiant plays, and he had written misanthropic and misogynous dramatic verse long before the writing of the great tragedies:

> Let heaven kiss earth! now let not Nature's hand
> Keep the wild flood confined! let order die!
> And let this world no longer be a stage
> To feed contention in a lingering act;
> But let one spirit of the first-born Cain
> Reign in all bosoms, that, each heart being set
> On bloody courses, the rude scene may end,
> And darkness be the burier of the dead!
>
> You seem to me as Dian in her orb,
> As chaste as is the bud ere it be blown;
> But you are more intemperate in your blood
> Than Venus, or those pamper'd animals
> That rage in savage sensuality.

The first, which might be Lear, Timon or the world-weary Macbeth, is Northumberland in 2 *Henry IV*; the second, which might almost be Othello, is Claudio in *Much Ado about Nothing*.

The accession of James, then, coincided with a change in Shakespeare's work, a change not only of matter, but of manner as well, of the dramatic medium and vehicle of his thought, for the one demanded, necessitated, the other, and it is possible to make a broad distinction between his Elizabethan and his Jacobean poetry. The essential characteristics of the former are definition and expansion: a definition, or clarity, imparted by the concrete vocabulary, the comparative regularity of the metre and the conspicuous rhetorical framework that contains the illustrative elaborations and images, so often in the extended form of simile:

How like a younker or a prodigal
The scarfed bark puts from her native bay,
Hugg'd and embraced by the strumpet wind!
How like the prodigal doth she return,
With over-weather'd ribs and ragged sails,
Lean, rent and beggar'd by the strumpet wind!

The Jacobean poetry, on the other hand, is one of compression and lacks the definition of the Elizabethan; thought is packed tight and imagery reduced to the single word of metaphor; diction becomes more personal, syntax more elliptical, and the structural outline loses its precision because of the greater metrical freedom and disappearance of rhetoric. Moreover, the treatment of moral problems demanded a more philosophical vocabulary, so that there are far more abstract latinisms, reducing the concreteness and increasing the complexity of the verse, both in texture and its music:

perpetual durance, a restraint,
Though all the world's vastidity you had,
To a determined scope.

In terms of music, the Elizabethan poetry is one of the purity of virginal, viol, and recorder, of the higher registers, the Jacobean is symphonic, sonorous with all the instruments of the orchestra, and with a far wider range. In terms of the visual arts, the one has the brightness and linear beauty of medieval architecture and painting, the other the depth, plasticity, and chiaroscuro of the Renaissance; or the earlier poetry might be compared to the painting of Botticelli, the later to that of Rembrandt. It is not that the one is more beautiful than the other, but the latter was essential for the expression of the full compass of Shakespeare's experience and the creation of his titanic characters. And in this enrichment and extension of his medium Shakespeare was among the pioneers of European artists, for all the arts of the seventeenth century were to move in this direction of a greater depth and volume.

One cannot help wondering if Shakespeare was writing *Measure for Measure* in the garden of New Place in the summer

of that plague year of 1603, and described it when Isabella tells
the Duke that Angelo

> . . . hath a garden circummur'd with brick,
> Whose western side is with a vineyard back'd;
> And to that vineyard is a planched gate
> That makes his opening with this bigger key:
> This other doth command a little door
> Which from the vineyard to the garden leads.

The plague reached its mortal climax in London in the last week
of August, when there were 3,000 deaths in the City and
suburbs, and by the middle of October the worst was over. On
the 21st Joan Alleyn wrote from Bankside to her husband,
Edward, who was hawking in Sussex:

About us the Sickness doth cease, and is likely more and more, by
God's help, to cease. All the companies be come home, and are well,
for aught we know; but that Browne of the Boar's Head is dead, and
died very poor: he went not into the country at all. And all of your
own company are well, at their own houses. My father is at the
Court: but where the Court is, I know not.

Browne was one of Queen Anne's (formerly Worcester's) company, licensed to act at the Curtain and Boar's Head Inn, and
recently joined by Will Kempe, who was probably another
victim of the plague if he was the 'Kempe a man' buried on
Bankside, at St Saviour's, on 2 November. But the plague was
not yet gone, even on Bankside: there were thirty burials at
St Saviour's in the first week of November, and the Court
remained at Wilton.

Wilton was the house to which Sir Philip Sidney had retired
after incurring Queen Elizabeth's displeasure, and where he
wrote his *Arcadia* to his 'most dear lady and sister' Mary, who
had married Henry Herbert, second Earl of Pembroke. Under
Mary, Countess of Pembroke, Wilton House was, in the words
of Aubrey, 'like a college, there were so many learned and ingenious persons. She was the greatest patroness of wit and
learning of any lady of her time'. Spenser was often there, and
Samuel Daniel was the tutor of her son, William Herbert, who

is thought by some to have been the youth to whom Shakespeare wrote his sonnets, though the evidence is slight, depending mainly on the fact that his initials were W. H. By the time he came of age in 1601, the year in which he succeeded to the earldom on the death of his father, Shakespeare was no doubt well acquainted with him, his mother, and the Wilton House circle, but if, as is most probable, his first sonnets were written ten years earlier, William Herbert was much too young to have been the youth whom he implored to marry and beget children.

In November the King's Men were at Mortlake, not far from Hampton Court, where they were rehearsing for the Revels, possibly in the house of Augustine Phillips, and Shakespeare must have been with them at the end of the month when they received a summons to go to Wilton to give a Court performance. There is some evidence that the Countess of Pembroke wrote to her son, who had accompanied the King on a visit to Salisbury, telling them to return to see *As You Like It*, and adding, 'we have the man Shakespeare with us'. The King's Men gave their performance on 2 December, so far as we know their first appearance before the King, who seems to have been well pleased, for they were paid £30 for their 'paynes and expences in comming from Mortlake unto the courte and there presenting before his majestie one playe'. Perhaps the players, as Grooms of the Chamber, accompanied the King when he left Wilton a few days later, leaving the royal retinue at Hampton Court, where the Revels were held that Christmas.

They began with five plays by the King's Men, one of them apparently *A Midsummer Night's Dream*, and there can be little doubt that the Queen, Anne of Denmark, would insist on seeing the new play about the Prince of Denmark. *Hamlet* was so popular that some actor or other had reproduced it as best he could from memory and sold his mutilated version to a stationer who had published it at the height of the plague that summer, as

The Tragicall Historie of Hamlet Prince of Denmarke. By William Shake-speare. As it hath beene diuerse times acted by his Highnesse seruants in the Cittie of London: as also in the Vniuersities of Cambridge and Oxford, and else-where.

In the following year a corrected quarto was issued, 'enlarged to almost as much againe', though Hamlet's unfortunate reference to Denmark as a prison was omitted, as no doubt it had been when Queen Anne saw the play at Court. It may have been now, for it was sometime in 1603, that the King's Men gave the first performance of Jonson's new tragedy, *Sejanus*, the work that had occupied him since writing *The Poetaster*. If so, it made a nice foil to *Hamlet*, which was precisely what Jonson intended, for his tragedy obeyed all the rules of the ancients, climbing to the height of Seneca's style, while Shakespeare's quite ignored them. Unfortunately for him both Court and people preferred Shakespeare to Seneca, and while *Hamlet* continued to fill the Globe, 'well-laboured' *Sejanus* left it almost empty.

Shakespeare was one of the principal actors in its first performance, the others being Burbage, Phillips, Heminge, Sly, Condell, Lowin, and Cooke. The last two were new members of the company, Alexander Cooke having been taught his acting as a boy by Heminge before becoming a hireling and finally a sharer. John Lowin was a young man from Worcester's, who was to remain with the company until the closing of the theatres forty years later, and to link the Elizabethan with the Restoration age, for he seems to have survived well into the reign of Charles II and outlived Davenant. His playing of Falstaff was received 'with mighty applause', and there is a stage tradition that Shakespeare taught him how to play the part of Henry VIII. It is very probable, for the list of players in *Sejanus* is the last record of Shakespeare as an actor, and this, together with his removal from St Saviour's to St Olave's, from Bankside to Mountjoy's house, and the increase in the number of sharers, suggests that he now virtually retired from acting to concentrate on the writing of plays for his company and the coaching of his fellows in their parts: 'Speak the speech as I pronounced it to you. . . . Do not saw the air too much with your hand, thus, but use all gently. . . . Be not too tame neither, but suit the action to the word, the word to the action, with this special observance, that you o'erstep not the modesty of nature.'

The Court moved to Whitehall in February 1604, for the

plague was almost over, and in the following month James, accompanied by the Queen and Prince Henry, made his long-delayed official entry through London, from the Tower to Whitehall Palace, a long, elaborate business of triumphal arches, tableaux, and speeches devised by Jonson, Dekker, and Thomas Middleton. Shakespeare, as a Groom of the Chamber, was in attendance in his scarlet livery.

It was just a year since Queen Elizabeth had died, and for all that time the theatres had been closed, but on 9 April the Privy Council wrote to the Lord Mayor and Justices of Middlesex and Surrey informing them that, as the King's Players had given good service in their quality of playing, and as Lent was now over (Lent had made no difference to the revelling at Court), they thought it fit to

suffer the three Companies of Plaiers to the King, Queene, and Prince publicklie to Exercise ther Plaies in ther vsuall howses, and noe other, viz. The Globe scituate in Maiden Lane on the Banckside, the Fortun in Golding Lane, and the Curtaine in Hollywell, except there shall happen weeklie to die of the Plague Aboue the Number of thirtie within the Cittie of London and the Liberties thereof.

It was the month of Shakespeare's fortieth birthday, and no doubt he stayed in London to see the opening of the first season of Jacobean public playing, and to work at his tragedy of *Othello* in Mountjoy's house, for that summer he was reserved for special duty as a Groom of the Chamber. The twenty years war with Spain was over, and in August the Spanish envoys arrived in London to arrange the terms of peace. On the 10th the Spanish Ambassador, the Constable of Castile, took up his lodgings in Somerset House, where Shakespeare and the other eleven Grooms were appointed to attend him, though they were not called upon to present a play. Perhaps the Spaniards' English was not good enough, for even after the great dinner celebrating the signing of the treaty on the 19th the entertainment provided was bear-baiting and acrobatics. The Ambassador should have gone the next day, but an attack of gout confined him to his bed, where James visited him to say farewell before going off for a holiday in Hertfordshire. He had recovered sufficiently to leave London on the 25th, and for this waste of almost three weeks' precious time – for as the Ambassador had brought 300 attendants of his own there can have been little to do – Shakespeare received £2.

We can imagine the relief with which he would escape from the inanities of the Court and take horse for Stratford to spend a month or so in the quiet of the country where he could finish *Othello*. The urge to write had never been stronger, he was at the summit of his powers, and now indeed it was true to say, as his colleagues knew so well, that his mind and hand went together, that what he thought he wrote with such ease that there was rarely any need of revision and alteration. The wonder is that any man could create such men and women out of words, and write the poetry both of Iago and Othello, the hypnotic incantations of the one and the oceanic utterance of the other, his speech rising like a fountain on the solid column of its monosyllables, and falling in the dazzling polysyllabic splendour of its latinisms.

Shakespeare, however, was not a man to forget the ordinary pleasures of living in the pursuit of his art, and it was from his zest for life that he drew so much of his power. Physically as well as mentally he was in his prime, and might almost have been the elder brother of his two daughters – it was the year of Susanna's coming of age – who must always have looked forward to his return to New Place and the companionship, had they known it, of the most brilliant man in England. Nor did he forget the ordinary business of life, even while writing *Othello*. In High Street lived the apothecary and tobacconist Philip Rogers, who had bought several bushels of malt from New Place earlier in the year, but had failed to pay the £2 that he owed. Shakespeare, therefore, put the matter into the hands of his solicitor and it was settled in the Stratford Court of Record, the usual means of extracting payment in those casual times. In a litigious age, Shakespeare was exceptional in so very rarely taking cases to court; there is no record of his ever being sued for debt himself, but it is clear that he had a head for business as well as for poetry and the theatre.

He would be back in London by the beginning of October for the rehearsal of *Othello*, for the Revels that year were to begin on 1 November. Fortunately the Revels Accounts for the year 1604–5 have been preserved, or, to put it the other way round, unfortunately the only extant Revels Accounts for the whole period when Shakespeare was writing are those for the years 1604–5 and 1611–12. We have the Chamber Accounts giving date of performance, the name of the company, and sometimes of the payee, but the Revels Accounts generally give the title of the play as well, and those for Elizabeth's reign infuriatingly finish in Armada year, probably the very year in which Shakespeare began to write for the stage. If we had the complete Accounts for this critical period of the dramatic revolution we should know the first plays of Shakespeare performed at Court and the company of which he was probably a member. However, it is something to have two sets of Jacobean Revels Accounts, and they give us an idea of Shakespeare's popularity. There were twenty-two performances at Whitehall in the winter of 1604–5, and of these the King's gave eleven, the Prince's (Admiral's) eight, the Queen's (Worcester's) one, and the Queen's Revels (the new name of the Chapel Children) two. Of the eleven performances by the King's, eight were plays by Shakespeare, or 'Shaxberd' as the scribe preferred to call him, some of them old ones that the new King and Queen had not seen. Even if Shakespeare was no longer acting he would be present at these Court performances of his plays, both as a Groom of the Chamber and as their author and producer.

The Revels began with what may have been the first performance of *Othello*, given, experimentally perhaps, in the old wooden Banqueting House at Whitehall, a temporary structure set up by Elizabeth more than twenty years before, spacious, but with its canvas roof, cold at the beginning of November. *Othello* was strong meat for James and his frivolous Court, and on the 4th they moved into the cosier quarters of the dining-hall to see a performance of *The Merry Wives of Windsor*. Then there was a three weeks' lull, during which, on the 19th, Shakespeare probably attended the wedding of Stephen Belott and Mary Mountjoy in St Olave's church. Meanwhile at the Globe the King's were playing a new tragedy of *Gowrie*, based on an attempt to assassinate James in Scotland four years before. No doubt it was complimentary, as befitted the King's Servants, and it was certainly popular, 'with exceeding concourse of all sorts of people', but it was a dangerous precedent to represent a reigning monarch on the stage, particularly one so easy to caricature as James, with his peculiar mannerisms and broad Scottish accent, and apparently the Privy Council ordered it to be taken off. Perhaps James's displeasure is reflected in the run of four plays allotted to the Prince's before the King's resumed their place at Court after Christmas.

On 26 December they gave the first recorded performance of *Measure for Measure*, a play in which James would find it easy to identify himself with the meddling Duke, followed early in January by *The Comedy of Errors* and *Henry V*, shortly after which the Chamberlain of the Exchequer wrote to Robert Cecil, Lord Cranborne:

I have sent and bene all thys morning huntyng for players Juglers & Such kinde of Creaturs, but fynde them harde to finde, wherfore Leavinge notes for them to seeke me, Burbage ys come, & Sayes ther ys no new playe that the quene hath not seene, but they have Revyved an olde one, Cawled *Loves Labore lost,* which for wytt & mirthe he sayes will please her excedingly. And Thys ys appointed to be playd to Morowe night at my Lord of Sowthamptons, unless yow send a wrytt to Remove the Corpus Cum Causa to your howse in Strande. Burbage ys my messenger Ready attendyng your pleasure.

It is an interesting and informative letter: the Queen had made up for time lost in Scotland by exhausting the plays of England; actors were still dismissed by some at least of the aristocracy as 'Such kinde of Creaturs', and the Revels and Shakespeare's plays not only flowed over Twelfth Night but also into the houses of the nobility, for on 14 January the courtier Dudley Carleton wrote:

The last nights revels were kept at my Lord of Cranbornes, where the Q. with the D. of Holst and a great part of the Court were feasted, and the like two nights before at my Lord of Southamptons.

In fact the Revels went on for another month and even into Lent. On Shrove Sunday the King's presented *The Merchant of Venice*, which was so much to the liking of James that he called for a repeat performance on the following Tuesday, and the Revels ended a week later with a performance by the Prince's.

With eight performances out of a total of twenty-two the Revels had been a triumph for Shakespeare; but they were also a triumph for Jonson. Two of the other three plays given by the King's had been *Every Man in His Humour* and *Every Man out of His Humour*, while on Twelfth Night, when Prince Charles was created Duke of York, he presented the first of his famous masques. The Elizabethan masque had been a relatively simple affair of dressing up, tableaux, and mime, a sort of elaborate amateur charade, after the presentation of which the masquers mingled with the spectators in dance and revel. Jonson's conception of the masque, however, was very different: for him it was a form of drama set off by music, song, splendid costume, and lavish spectacle, and though the performers were amateurs, lords and ladies of the Court, and even queens and princes, the author of the lines they spoke was a professional poet. The conception of his architect collaborator, Inigo Jones, was similar, though the emphasis was different; for him the words and music were merely a background to the spectacle, and at one end of the Banqueting House he set up a stage, beneath which was machinery for his effects, and in front a proscenium arch and curtain in the latest Italian manner. In this way their joint *Masque of Blackness* was performed on Twelfth Night 1605, the Queen herself, wearing a fabulous amount of jewellery, leading the troupe of twelve aristocratic blackamoors, and in the course of the next ten years Jonson and Inigo Jones collaborated in the making of almost as many masques.

It was the beginning of the degeneracy of the drama. It was only fifteen years since Marlowe and Shakespeare had raised the drama from a kind of variety show to the plane of poetry, and now words were to be lost again in mere prettiness and spectacle, for it was not long before Court and commoners alike demanded an element of masque in all their dramatic entertainment. It is ironical, or perhaps it was inevitable, that degeneration should set in when Shakespeare was writing his greatest plays, and even in what was probably his next play, *Timon of Athens*, he himself introduced a 'Maske of Amazons, with Lutes in their hands, dauncing and playing', unless it is a later interpolation.

Although we know few details of Shakespeare's doings, we can feel fairly sure about the major rhythm of his life at this time: that he generally spent winter and spring with his company in London, summer in Stratford, and returned to London in autumn for the Revels' rehearsals and winter season at the Globe. If, therefore, *Timon* was his next play, he probably wrote most of it at the Mountjoys, and it may be that when he wrote,

> As we do turn our backs
> From our companion thrown into his grave,
> So his familiars to his buried fortunes
> Slink all away,

he was thinking of the funeral of Augustine Phillips and the shame he felt at leaving a friend alone in the grave. Phillips died at Mortlake at the beginning of May, a great loss to his fellows, to most of whom he left legacies: to Shakespeare, Condell, Lawrence Fletcher, Armin, Cowley, Cooke, and Nicholas Tooley, a newcomer, as well as to his 'servant' Christopher Beeston and his apprentices Samuel Gilburne and James Sands, to whom he left gifts of clothing and his musical instruments, viol, cittern, bandore, and lute. Heminge, Burbage, and Sly were his executors, each of whom was to have a silver bowl.

It was at about this time that Stephen Belott began to quarrel with his father-in-law, and left the Mountjoy house with his wife for the parish of St Sepulchre's, where they lodged with the dramatist George Wilkins. Wilkins wrote for the King's Men, and is suspected by some of having had a hand in both *Timon* and *Pericles*, and perhaps Shakespeare introduced the young couple to his house. And again at about the same time, he would welcome to London the daughter of his Stratford neighbour Thomas Rogers, for in April Katherine Rogers married Robert Harvard, a butcher of Southwark, where, in 1607, their famous son was born, John Harvard, who was to give his name to Harvard University.

By the end of July he was in Stratford, where he made another big investment. The Corporation owned the corn and hay tithes in Old Stratford, Welcombe, and Bishopton, though they had long ago been leased to private investors, and it was in 'our tithes' that Adrian Quiney and Abraham Sturley had advised Shakespeare to put his money when he was considering buying 'some odd yardland or other at Shottery'. That was in 1598, when Shakespeare needed his money to finance the building of the Globe, but in 1605 the proposition was attractive, and on 24 July – the day on which his second nephew, Thomas Hart was christened – he agreed to pay Ralph Huband £440 for the lease of the tithes that he held, about one fifth of the total. It is true that he had to pay a rent of £17 to the Corporation and another £5 to John Barker, owner of the original lease, but as the income from the tithes was £60 he made a profit of £38, or nearly nine per cent. Shakespeare, however, was not thinking only in terms of profit; if that had been his main consideration he would have bought property in London like his colleagues, for the rapidly expanding capital was a far better field for investment than a stagnant provincial town. His one London investment was his share in the Globe, but in Stratford he owned his father's Henley Street property, New Place, the Chapel Lane cottage, an estate of more than a hundred acres, and now a substantial part of the tithes. It is clear that he loved his native town and intended to retire there when he felt that his work in London was finished. What the natives thought about it all we do not know, but many of them, if ever they gave a thought to the matter, cannot have approved of his source of prosperity, for the town was becoming increasingly Puritan, and the Council had recently decreed that plays were no longer to be acted in the Gild Hall and that any member who licensed their performance should be fined. No doubt Shakespeare, genial and tolerant, smiled at his neighbours' absurdities, and when at New Place made a point of appearing to lead the life of a country gentleman, more interested in his garden and the price of bullocks than in poetry and plays.

Yet he was probably wrestling in his study with the intractable *Timon*. The trouble was that Timon was not a tragic hero, but merely a foolish man susceptible to flattery, who thought that he could buy friendship and gratitude with gold, and on discovering his mistake fell into an insane misanthropy – 'I am misanthropos, and hate mankind' – out-cursing the professional misanthropist Apemantus. There is a school of criticism that prefers to find personifications instead of people in Shakespeare's plays, symbols in place of men and women; for which Timon is a Christ-like figure, 'a choice soul crucified', 'a principle of the human soul, a possibility, a symbol of mankind's aspiration', while through the play runs 'a mighty rhythm of a race's longing, of human destiny unalterable and uncomplained'. This is the very ecstasy of criticism; Shakespeare did not write moralities, but plays about people, like ourselves involved in the human predicament, and though there is magnificent poetry in *Timon*, dramatically it would not do, and he put it aside for a play on the same theme of ingratitude, but with a hero who had some cause for misanthropy, and began the writing of *King Lear*.

At the beginning of October there was plague about in London, not very serious, but as plague deaths rose to more than thirty a week the theatres were closed, and on the 9th the King's Men were at Oxford, where Shakespeare may have gone to see them. If this new visitation of the sickness delayed his return to London, he would see something of the new tenant of Clopton House, the grounds of which bordered his Welcombe estate. The house belonged to George Lord Carew and his wife Joyce Clopton, but towards the end of September it was rented as a hunting lodge by a wealthy young man from Suffolk, Ambrose Rookwood. There was much coming and going, much riding of horses, and on the Sunday after Michaelmas

Day a great dinner attended by a host of strangers. It was all very mysterious, and an eclipse of the moon followed by an eclipse of the sun on 2 October seemed to portend no good. No good indeed. One of Rookwood's visitors was his friend, Robert Catesby, a tall, athletic man with estates in Warwickshire, by whose direction thirty-six barrels of gunpowder had been hidden in a cellar under the House of Lords, where James was to open his second Parliament on 5 November. Clopton House was to be a base for the great Catholic rising when the King and his Parliament had been blown at the moon.

In London Catesby and his fellow conspirators were trying to find a meeting-place in the Blackfriars Gatehouse, the home of the Catholic Fortescues, dining at the Mermaid and the rival Mitre on the other side of Bread Street, and supping in one another's houses, where on one occasion the unsuspecting Ben Jonson, a temporary Catholic, formed one of the company. On 26 October the plot was betrayed, and at midnight on 4 November Guy Fawkes was arrested in the cellar where he was guarding the powder that he was to fire on the following day. When the conspirators heard that their plot had miscarried they leaped to horse and rode into Warwickshire to raise the now hopeless insurrection. On Wednesday, the 6th, the bailiff of Stratford armed the constables with calivers, cleared the gaol and raided Clopton House, only to find that all but the servants had fled, leaving little but a cloakbag full of copes, vestments, crucifixes, chalices, and 'other massing relics'. On the 8th the little band of desperate men was trapped at Holbeche House in Staffordshire, where Catesby was killed and the rest taken prisoner. A few weeks later Guy Fawkes and Ambrose Rookwood were executed in Old Palace Yard overlooking the Parliament House they had planned to blow up, and Shakespeare, engaged on *King Lear* wrote:

These late eclipses in the sun and moon portend no good to us: though the wisdom of nature can reason it thus and thus, yet nature finds itself scourged by the sequent effects: love cools, friendship falls off, brothers divide: in cities, mutinies; in countries, discord; in palaces, treason.

Although the words are those of the superstitious Gloucester, Shakespeare was being by no means altogether ironical. We are apt to forget how dangerous were the times in which he lived, not at all the olive age that he had hoped for; since coming to London he had experienced attempted invasion, an attempt to overthrow Elizabeth's government, and now an attempt to blow sky-high the King and all the leaders of the country. If the plot had succeeded, as so nearly it did, what would have happened staggers the imagination. No wonder he insisted on order and degree, and that the key-word of his tragedies is 'unnatural': 'unnatural murder', 'unnatural daughters', 'unnatural deeds do breed unnatural troubles'.

That Christmas the King's Men gave ten of the nineteen plays performed at Whitehall, and though we do not know their names there can be little doubt that most of them were Shakespeare's, though one would almost certainly be Jonson's recently finished masterpiece *Volpone*, in which, incidentally, Shakespeare did not act. Among these Revels plays there must have been at least one of his histories, and James would see no reason why his dramatist Groom of the Chamber should confine himself to the reigns of English kings. Perhaps he ordered, perhaps he cajoled, or perhaps 'the amicable letter to Mr Shakespeare' that he is said to have written with his own hand hinted that a play about Scottish history would be welcome: nothing too topical, of course, like the ill-fated *Gowrie*, and certainly not like the recent *Eastward Ho!* in which he and his light-hearted creation of 'Scotch knights' – for a consideration, of course – had been ridiculed, and for which two of the authors, Chapman and Jonson, had been thrown into prison, but something perhaps about one of his remote and more reputable ancestors. It would also be appreciated if the play could be finished by midsummer. So Shakespeare, exhausted after the agony of *King Lear*, but still on the crest of creation, turned to the Scottish section of Holinshed's *Chronicles* and read the story of Macbeth and Banquo, and how they met 'three women in straunge and ferly apparell, resembling creatures of an elder worlde', who hailed Macbeth 'that hereafter shall be king of Scotland' and

Banquo as the progenitor of those 'whiche shall gouerne the Scottische kingdome by long order of continuall discent'. It was just the thing, for James prided himself on his knowledge of witches and had even written a book on the subject, and Banquo was his ancestor, or so Holinshed said.

If this is the correct, or approximately correct, reconstruction of events, Shakespeare had four or five months in which to write *Macbeth*, no impossible feat for such a rapid writer at the height of his powers, and the tragedy, at least as we have it, is one of the shortest of his plays. He would, therefore, have time to ride to Oxford to act as godfather at the christening of William Davenant on 3 March, if he really was his godfather, as he very well may have been. William's father was John Davenant, host of the Crown Tavern in Oxford, where Shakespeare is said to have lodged on his journeys between London and Stratford. Oxford, just half-way between the two, was the obvious place at which to break his journey, and by 1607 he probably knew John Davenant and his wife Jane very well, certainly well enough to agree to be godfather to their fourth child. When he grew up, however, William Davenant seems to have encouraged, or done nothing to discourage the rumour that he was in a more literal sense the son of Shakespeare, 'in which way', added Aubrey, 'his mother had a very light report, whereby she was called a whore'. Certainly Davenant had a quite filial regard for Shakespeare, to whose memory he wrote an ode and whose plays he revived on the London stage when they had long been almost forgotten. On the other hand, it is only fair to the memory of Jane Davenant to remember that she was elsewhere described as 'a vertuous wife'. The story is probably no more than a tasty morsel of Restoration gossip encouraged by Davenant's vanity, but it is not impossible, and it seems likely that Shakespeare passed through Oxford shortly before buying the Stratford tithes, nine months before William's birth.

On 3 May Henry Garnet, alias Farmer, head of the Jesuit mission in England, was hanged for complicity in the Gunpowder Plot. James himself had heard his equivocating defence in March, when he had been present at the trial in disguise, and Shakespeare could not resist inserting a note of congratulation in *Macbeth* by making the drunken porter of hell-gate admit 'a farmer that hanged himself' and 'an equivocator that could swear in both scales against either scale'. He also added a complimentary reference to James's power of curing scrofula by prayer and a touch of the hand, and a prophetic view of himself in Banquo's mirror as king of both Scotland and England, and by the beginning of July the play was finished and ready for rehearsal.

In at least one respect *Macbeth* may be said to be Shakespeare's greatest triumph: the creation of a tragic hero out of a murderer, a regicide and killer of his friends, their wives and children. For in spite of what he does, Macbeth retains our sympathy to the last – by what he says, his poetry; the man who speaks the lines beginning 'She should have died hereafter' can never completely forfeit our compassion. Yet in his twilight world, language, like everything else, has lost its innocence, for all is deceptive and equivocal, false as water, ambiguous as the multiplying images, and 'nothing is but what is not'.

There are those who question the authenticity of the first two scenes, and even Coleridge boggled at the Porter. But this, surely, is a failure to appreciate the unifying atmosphere of the play; the delusive quality of which is invoked at once by the first words of Macbeth and Banquo:

MACBETH: So *foul and fair* a day I have not seen.
BANQUO: How far is't called to Forres? What are these . . .
That *look not like* th' inhabitants o' th' earth,
And yet are on't? Live you? *or* are you aught
That man may *question*? You *seem* to understand me. . . .
And yet . . .

Then: 'seem to fear', 'will grow . . . will not', 'favours . . . hate', 'lesser . . . greater', 'not so happy . . . happier', 'what seemed corporal', 'thine or his', 'whether . . . or . . . I know not', 'ill . . . good', 'present fears . . . horrible imaginings'. These uncertainties and oppositions all come in the last hundred lines of the third scene, and the same riddling doubts and antitheses run throughout the play.

Thus, in the twelve lines of the first scene we have: 'lost and won', 'fair is foul ... foul is fair'; in the second: 'seemth', 'doubtful', 'seemed', 'except ... or ... I cannot tell', 'seems', 'lost ... won'. And the Porter: 'provokes ... unprovokes', 'makes ... mars', 'sets him on ... takes him off', 'persuades ... disheartens', 'stand to ... not stand to'; and one of the imaginary sinners whom he lets into an imaginary hell is the 'equivocator that could swear in both the scales against either scale'. The witches of the first scene, the bleeding sergeant of the second, and the Porter are all integral parts of the tragic pattern, of the web of ambiguity and equivocation that entangles Macbeth. And, as William Empson puts it, 'the machinations of ambiguity are among the very roots of poetry'.

It was unfortunate that plague returned just at this time; in the week ending 17 July there were fifty deaths, and this was the very day on which Christian IV of Denmark arrived to stay a month with his sister Anne and his brother-in-law James. The Court was at Greenwich, and here James entertained his guest with two plays given by his own company, performances at which Shakespeare must have been present as a Groom of the Chamber if not as an actor, and there can be little doubt that one of them was *Hamlet*, for there could be no more appropriate play for presentation before the King of Denmark. It was appropriate in more ways than one. 'We'll teach you to drink deep ere you depart,' says Hamlet bitterly to Horatio, and it was just that that the Danes taught the fast-degenerating English Court before they departed. Sir John Harington, by no means a Puritan, but with memories of his godmother Elizabeth's Court, ironically described the debauch at a masque of *Solomon and the Queen of Sheba* given at Salisbury's Hertfordshire house, Theobalds. The lady who played the Queen was so drunk that she spilt her presents of wine and custard in Solomon-Christian's lap, while Christian himself, in attempting to dance with her fell down and had to be carried away to bed. But the show went on: Charity was able to deliver a flattering little speech to James, but Hope and Faith were quite incapable, sick and spewing in the lower hall.

I think the Dane [Harington concluded] hath strangely wrought on our good English nobles, for those whom I could never get to taste good liquor now follow the fashion and wallow in beastly delights. The ladies abandon their sobriety, and are seen to roll about in intoxication. The Gunpowder fright is got out of all our heads, and we are going on as if the Devil was contriving every man should blow up himself by riot, excess and devastation of time and temperance.

We can understand why the heroic drama of the eighties was changing into one of satire, masque, and a gloomier form of tragedy.

There were other entertainments: a play by the Children of Paul's, their last appearance at Court, a Triumph through London, a tilt, running at the ring, and, of course, any amount of hunting, and then on 7 August a play by the King's Men at Hampton Court. There was little love lost between the two kings, who were jealous of each other, and it seems probable that James kept his trump card until the last moment, and entertained his rival at Hampton Court with the first performance of his dramatist's latest play, a Scottish one to cap the Danish, *Macbeth*. Four days later Christian sailed for Denmark, and Shakespeare was free to return to Stratford for a well-earned holiday. He would be back in London for the Revels, which began later this year with a performance on St Stephens' night of *King Lear*.

Shakespeare had been fortunate in the first half of his career, or rather as a Lord Chamberlain's Man in the last decade of Elizabeth's reign, in that his work had scarcely been interrupted by plague. After the disastrous year of 1593–4, when 15,000 had died of the sickness, London had been little affected and the theatres had rarely been closed. But during the next eight years with his company, as a King's Man from 1603 to 1610, London was rarely quite clear. Thirty-three thousand had perished in 1603, the year of James's accession, and though 1604 and 1605 had been comparatively free from infection there were more than 2,000 deaths each year from 1606 to 1610, and double that number in 1609, an average of nearly fifty a week for the whole period of five years. As the theatres were automatically closed when plague deaths reached thirty a week, they were very rarely open in the summer and autumn, the hot season that favoured the sickness, and the London companies, to their great loss, were forced to travel in the provinces. Thus, in the 'vntymely heate' of early April 1607, the Lord Mayor wrote to the Lord Chamberlain asking him to restrain 'comon Stage Plaies' as the sickness was ominously increasing in the suburbs, though it was July before plague deaths regularly passed thirty, the theatres were closed, and the King's Men went on tour, ranging from Suffolk to Devonshire, from Dunwich on the east coast to Barnstaple on the west, and calling at both Cambridge and Oxford, where they received 20s. from the mayor on 7 September.

But some time before the theatres were closed Shakespeare was in Stratford for the wedding of his elder daughter Susanna and John Hall on 5 June. Susanna was just twenty-four, her husband eight years older. Hall had been seven years in Stratford, where he had built up a highly successful practice and bought a house near the church, to which he made additions. He kept a case-book, written in Latin, which was translated and published after his death with the curious title, *Select Observations on English Bodies*. Among the English bodies upon which he performed his 'Empericall' cures were his own, Susanna's, his daughter's, and Michael Drayton's, but – again infuriatingly – there is no reference to his father-in-law, for his records begin in the year after the death of Shakespeare, whom he must have treated in his last illness, and whose end, with the best intentions, he may have hastened. For his remedies were ferocious, a compound of sympathetic magic and old wives' simples, his main object being to evacuate everything from the patient's stomach and bowels both by vomiting and excretion. Thus, Michael Drayton, 'an excellent poet', was cured of a fever by an emetic that 'wrought very well both upward and down-wards' – no wonder, when frog's spawn, earthworms, hen's dung, and dog's turd were favourite ingredients – the Countess of Northampton was cured of a dropsy by a decoction that gave her forty-one stools in three days, and Susanna was treated for colic in much the same way. It is scarcely surprising that she bore only one child.

Thomas Greene and his wife were still living at New Place, though, like Shakespeare, Greene himself was generally in London, where he practised as a barrister. There seems to have been an understanding, however, that he and his young family would leave New Place when Shakespeare retired, a course that he must have been already considering, for soon after Susanna's wedding the Greenes bought a small house, St Mary's, adjoining the churchyard, to which they could move when the time came.

After the writing of *Othello*, *Timon*, *Lear*, and *Macbeth* Shakespeare certainly needed a rest, and he probably stayed in Strat-ford as long as he could writing *Coriolanus* at his leisure, not the same thing as writing slowly. There are signs of what may be exhaustion in the play. In *Julius Caesar* and *Timon* he had already made use of North's translation of Plutarch, but in those plays North's prose had been merely the source of his plot, whereas in *Coriolanus* it was often the source of his verse as well. Here, for example, is North's account of how Coriolanus put himself at the mercy of his old enemy Aufidius with the object of mak-ing an alliance against Rome:

I am Caius Marcius, who hath done to thy self particularly, and to all the Volsces generally, great hurte and mischief, which I cannot denie for my name of Coriolanus that I beare. For I never had other benefit nor recompence, of all the true and paynefull service I have done and the extreme daunger I have bene in, but this only surname; a good memorie and witnes, of the malice and displeasure thou showldest beare me.

It is the turning-point of the tragedy and the central speech of the play, yet Shakespeare merely adds a phrase about the drops of blood that Coriolanus had shed for his thankless country, and turns the remainder into verse with the minimum of effort:

> My name is Caius Marcius, who hath done
> To thee particularly, and to all the Volsces,
> Great hurt and mischief; thereto witness may
> My surname Coriolanus: the painful service,
> The extreme dangers, and the drops of blood
> Shed for my thankless country, are requited
> But with that surname; a good memory,
> And witness of the malice and displeasure
> Which thou shouldst bear me.

Shakespeare was often careless and lazy, though very rarely in his great tragedies, and this mechanical following of his original may be the result of the strain of the last few years.

In one detail, however, he did not follow North. In Plutarch the initial grievance of the Roman people was against the oppression of usurers, but this Shakespeare changed into an outcry against famine and the high price of corn. Now, in the early summer of 1607, there was a serious revolt in the Midlands against the enclosure of open fields and common pasture, and 'the Diggers of Warwickshire' issued a manifesto urging all other Diggers 'to level and lay open' the enclosures that threatened them with unemployment and famine. Shakespeare had no direct interest in the matter, as he was not enclosing his own estate at Welcombe, but he had a horror of insurrection and as a landowner could not approve of the peasants' taking the law into their own hands, and perhaps that is why, in the character of Menenius, he developed Plutarch's fable of the belly in defence of a well-ordered body politic, and incidentally of the gentry – the word 'gentry' is oddly insistent in this Roman play – of which he was a member.

If he stayed in Stratford as late as the middle of October, he would attend the wedding of his wife's nephew Richard Hathaway, son of his brother-in-law Bartholomew Hathaway, but he must have returned to London soon afterwards, though where he lodged we do not know. Perhaps it was still in Silver

Street, but Mrs Mountjoy had died in the previous year, and though Mary Belott had returned to look after her father and, presumably, his lodger, Stephen did not get on with Christopher Mountjoy, and while Shakespeare was in Stratford they moved again.

It was a bitterly cold winter. Even before Christmas ice was piling up against the piers of London Bridge, and soon the whole river was frozen over as far upstream as Westminster. The great stretch of ice became a highway, a playground, and a fair, with temporary taverns, booths of every description, and even two barber's shops.

> You are no surer, no,
> Than is the coal of fire upon the ice,

Shakespeare wrote in *Coriolanus*. It was no weather for sitting in open theatres or standing in their yards under a freezing sky. Although the frost checked the plague for a time, it was bad luck on the actors to have empty theatres after a season of closure, but the King's Men fared far better than the other companies, for they gave thirteen performances at Whitehall to four by the Prince's and none at all by the Queen's. Their first plays were on 26, 27, and 28 December, though it is improbable that Shakespeare was there, for his youngest brother Edmund was dying. Nothing is known about Edmund's career, except that he was an actor and father of an illegitimate son, who had been buried at St Giles, Cripplegate, in the previous August. Edmund himself was buried in St Saviour's on Bankside on 31 December, and the sexton made the note: 'Edmund Shakespeare, a player, buried in the Church with a forenoone knell of the great bell, xxs.' The fee for burial in the churchyard was only 2s. and that for ringing the lesser bell 1s. The funeral, therefore, was an expensive one, and there can be little doubt that the cost was borne by his brother, the poet. Edmund was only twenty-seven, little older than Hamnet would have been had he lived.

CHAPTER 9

1608–13

A GRANDCHILD

*

SHORTLY after the King's Men had given their last performance at the Revels that Christmas, on 7 February 1608, Shakespeare received news of the birth of his first grandchild. His will makes it clear how ambitious he was to found a family – hence in part the heaviness of Hamnet's loss – and as soon as he heard the news he would ride post-haste to Stratford, where Elizabeth Hall was christened on 21 February. He must have been disappointed that the child was a girl, who could not even perpetuate the name of Hall, which was at least only one remove from that of Shakespeare, but there was no reason to doubt that Susanna would one day be the mother of a son. And then Judith was still unmarried.

He would not linger in Stratford, however, for the great frost had checked the sickness, plague deaths were negligible, the theatres open, and it was important to make the most of the spring season before the heat of high summer threatened another restraint of plays. From the beginning of March, therefore, until the middle of August we may imagine him in London, giving his incomparable advice to his fellows, helping them to select new plays, superintending their rehearsals at the Globe, and occasionally taking a small part himself, possibly Menenius in *Coriolanus*, but mainly engaged in writing the tragedy that has claims to be considered the greatest of all his plays, *Antony and Cleopatra*. Plutarch's *Life of Antonius*, the exotic Egyptian scene, and the vastness of the Roman scale fired his imagination more than anything else he had read in North, and into this golden play he poured all the riches of his poetry. By now it was a poetry as infinitely varied as Cleopatra herself, for in his hands language had become a plastic material, a sculptor's medium, to be modelled into whatever shape he pleased. Every change is rung on the basic springing rhythm of the verse, from a simple reversal of a foot to the back-tolled measure of 'I am dying, Egypt, dying; only . . .'; the speed is anything from the rapid exchanges of the battle scenes to the slow elegiacs of Cleopatra, and the texture may be open as,

> Unarm, Eros; the long day's task is done,
> And we must sleep,

or closely woven as,

> When half to half the world opposed, he being
> The mered question: 'twas a shame no less
> Than was his loss, to course your flying flags
> And leave his navy gazing.

Simplicity neighbours complexity, and an autumnal abundance is set off by the wintry spareness of verse stripped to its elemental structure of noun and verb. The huge scope of the imperial theme is amplified by the imagery: Antony is the triple pillar of the world, Cleopatra an empire, the very minutes stretch themselves to linger the pleasures of their love, and the vastness is further emphasized by the kaleidoscopic changes of scene, from Egypt to Rome and back again to Egypt, the despair of later producers aiming at illusion within a picture-frame stage, and taxing perhaps even the resources of the Globe. It was a play in the great heroic tradition of *Tamburlaine*, in the spacious tradition of the open theatres; but it was the last in this line to be written by Shakespeare, or by anyone else.

Earlier in the year the Blackfriars Children had got into serious trouble over two of their plays, one being Chapman's *Tragedy of Byron*, which, much to the fury of the French ambassador, dealt with the recent history of his country, the other a comedy, now lost, in which King James himself was made a figure of fun. A few of the 'children', some of whom were in fact young men, were thrown into prison, the company was disbanded, though re-formed as the Children of Whitefriars, and their manager surrendered the lease of the Blackfriars theatre to Richard Burbage, whose property it was. The King's Men, therefore, now had the opportunity of taking over this small private theatre on the north bank in addition to their large open playhouse on Bankside, and on 9 August a company of seven was formed, each holding an equal share and liable to pay his part of the rent of £40. The 'housekeepers' were Richard Burbage and his brother Cuthbert, Shakespeare, Heminge, Condell, Sly, and Thomas Evans, a representative of the original lessee. It was a profitable investment, for within a year or two receipts from the Blackfriars theatre were more than double those from the Globe, and a winter season in the one was worth £1,000 more than in the other.

It is important to realize what an innovation this was. Up till now their playhouse had been a large open amphitheatre, their audience a cross-section of London society, from courtiers who sat on the stage to penny gallery stinkards and groundlings who stood in the yard, demanding action and noise and passions torn to tatters. Now, however, their second theatre was small, closed, candlelit, with seats, expensive seats, for all members of their select and wealthy audience. Clearly, in these intimate surroundings, they would still further have to modify their style of acting in the direction of a greater naturalness, and as they were the first company of adult players ever to possess a private theatre it would be an advantage to have an actor or two who had been trained in its technique. It happened that there were two vacancies, for shortly after the forming of the company of seven housekeepers Sly and Lawrence Fletcher died, and to make up the number of Grooms to twelve they admitted into their fellowship two young men who, only a few years ago, had satirized them when, as Children of the Chapel, they played in Jonson's *Poetaster*: William Ostler and John Underwood.

More important than playing were the plays. An ideal play for the Globe, with a large cast and violent action, was by no means an ideal one for the small stage of the Blackfriars theatre, whose sophisticated audience would want sophisticated matter.

Tamburlaine was not a Blackfriars play, nor were *Macbeth*, *Lear*, and *Antony and Cleopatra*. Shakespeare had not written for the private theatre, and we can imagine him, when discussing policy with his fellows, recommending that they should engage a man who had; Jonson was the obvious choice, for not only had he written for the Chapel Children, but he was also the undisputed master of masque, with an unparalleled experience of spectacular effects and musical interludes, both of them highly desirable ingredients in the drama of the private theatre, and from now on Jonson wrote almost entirely for the King's Men. Perhaps it was Shakespeare again who, with an eye for talent, suggested that they should also employ two young poets who were just beginning to make a name, Francis Beaumont and John Fletcher, whose *Woman Hater* and *Knight of the Burning Pestle* had been written for the Paul's and Chapel Children. It was an astute move, though not altogether a fortunate one, for though the new dramatic *genre* that Beaumont and Fletcher exploited, romantic tragi-comedy, filled the Blackfriars and added immensely to the fortunes of the King's Men, it marked a further stage in the degeneracy of the great Elizabethan drama that had begun late in the heroic eighties with Marlowe and Shakespeare. It was not altogether their fault, for they were engaged to please their audience, and it was unfortunate that the Jacobean audience at Blackfrairs was so very different from the robust and vigorous public that had thronged the old Rose and Theatre twenty years before. The corruption and laxity of the Court had seeped into the upper strata of society, and it was for such an audience that Beaumont and Fletcher concocted their peculiar blend of tears and laughter, sweetness, softness, and nastiness.

Finally, to give their new venture every chance of success, it was decided that Shakespeare himself should try his hand at writing for the Blackfriars stage, though there was, of course, no reason why the plays should not be produced at the Globe as well. The challenge came at the right moment, for having brought his tragic art to perfection in *Antony and Cleopatra* he was ready to turn again to romance, though with a difference, and he began the dramatizing of a medieval story by Chaucer's friend, John Gower, *Pericles*. The theme of *Pericles* was appropriate, no doubt the reason why he had chosen it, for the birth of the heroine Marina was the shadow of that of his granddaughter, and the prayer of Pericles for the fresh-new seafarer, the poor inch of nature, that of himself for Elizabeth: 'Now, mild may be thy life! Happy what follows!' There can be little doubt that Elizabeth Hall was a main inspirer of the writing of his last romances, and that Marina, Imogen, Perdita, and Miranda are projections, whether conscious or unconscious, of Susanna's daughter.

It was, however, to be some time before the King's Men moved into the Blackfriars theatre. Even while they were forming their company of housekeepers at the beginning of August, plague deaths rose suddenly to fifty, the theatres were closed once more, and must have remained closed with few, if any, intervals until the end of 1609, in which year more than 4,000 perished. The players were driven into the provinces again – in October the King's were at Coventry, the Prince's at Leicester – and Shakespeare returned to Stratford.

The delight of seeing Elizabeth again did not make him forgetful of the ordinary business of life, and on 17 August, soon after his return to New Place, he obtained a writ from the Court of Record against John Addenbrooke, a gentleman of Stratford who for some time had owed him £6. Addenbrooke secured Thomas Hornby, a Henley Street blacksmith, as his surety, and promised to pay, and there for some months the matter rested. Shakespeare was patient, but as the debt was still outstanding at the end of the year he appealed again to the Court, which ordered Addenbrooke's arrest if he failed to pay the £6 and a further 24s. awarded for damages and costs. By this time, however, Addenbrooke was not to be found. Again Shakespeare waited, and it was not until the following June that the Court issued a precept for the appearance of Addenbrooke's surety. It was hard on Hornby if he had to pay and then try to get his money back from Addenbrooke, but Shakespeare cannot be accused of being an oppressive creditor. He himself seems always to have been scrupulous about money matters, and he expected others to be the same.

About a month after his return to Stratford his mother died, and on 9 September 'Mayry Shaxspere, wydowe' was buried. One feels that there was a great love and sympathy between the poet and his mother, that he owed much of his genius to her, and that her death was a heavy loss. Exactly a fortnight later he would attend a happier ceremony in the parish church, when his nephew Michael Hart was christened. The Henley Street house was again lively with children, for Michael was his sister Joan's third son; William was now eight and Thomas three, but Mary, the secondborn, had died in the previous year. Presumably Shakespeare was William's godfather, and in October he acquired yet another godson when he attended the christening of William Walker, the son of his friend Henry Walker, mercer and bailiff of Stratford.

As a Groom of the Chamber Shakespeare would have to go back to London for the Revels' plays, and presumably for their rehearsal when the King's Men returned from their travels. It had been another bad season and the theatres were still closed, but James was generous to his players and paid them £40 by way of reward 'for their private practise in the time of infection, that thereby they might be inhabled to performe their service before his Majestie in Christmas hollidaies'. They received a further £130 for the thirteen plays they presented.

The year 1609 came in without comfort. Plague deaths were over thirty a week at the beginning of January and, with four exceptions, exceeded forty until the end of November, reaching their maximum in September when they were more than 200. The actors were driven back to the road – at the beginning of May the King's can be traced at Ipswich, and shortly afterwards at Hythe and New Romney – and perhaps it was to tide over this difficult period that they sold three of Shakespeare's plays to the publishers, though there is something odd about all three of these quartos. *King Lear*, which was published in 1608, is such a muddle of verse printed as prose and prose as verse that it is suspected of having been put together from memory by the company when on tour without their prompt-book, or it may have been surreptitiously transcribed from Shakespeare's manuscript by two boy actors, the one who played Goneril dictating to 'Regan'. The first two acts of *Pericles* are far more corrupt, and some attribute them to another author, possibly Wilkins. Heminge and Condell omitted the play from the first edition of the Folio, either because they knew that it was not entirely Shakespeare's, or because they could not find a good text to replace the bad one. It was, however, included in the third edition of 1664. *Troilus and Cressida* is another puzzle. First registered in 1603 as a play acted by the Chamberlain's Men, it was registered again in 1609 and twice issued in the same year. The title-page of the first issue says that it was acted by the King's Men at the Globe, but this statement was omitted in the second issue and a preface added, claiming that it had never been performed, at least on the public stage, and implying that it had been published against the wishes of the 'grand possessors', presumably the King's Men.

Eternall reader [writes the anonymous and facetious author] you haue heere a new play, neuer stal'd with the Stage, neuer clapper-clawd with the palmes of the vulger, and yet passing full of the palme comicall. . . . So much and such sauored salt of witte is in his Commedies, that they seeme (tor their height of pleasure) to be borne in that sea that brought forth Venus. Amongst all there is none more witty then this.

It is only a publisher's puff, but it is interesting. Apparently *Troilus and Cressida* was written for private performance, very probably for one of the inns of court, and the author of the preface, possibly Richard Martin of the Middle Temple, wrote more wisely than he knew:

And beleeue this, that when hee is gone, and his Commedies out of sale, you will scramble for them, and set vp a new English Inquisition.

More important than the publication of these three plays was the publication of the *Sonnets* in 1609, for after all we should have the Folio texts of the plays even if the quartos had never been printed, but without the *Sonnets* quarto the poems would have perished, for no manuscript has survived. If, as seems likely, Shakespeare returned to Stratford at the beginning of 1609 when the Revels were over, for there would be little point in his staying in plague-stricken London, it would be a convenient time to sell his manuscript to a stationer, possibly with the idea of correcting proofs later in the year when the plague abated. On 20 May, however, Thomas Thorpe registered 'a Booke called Shakespeares sonnettes', and soon afterwards they were on sale, apparently without Shakespeare's corrections, for there are more misprints than we should expect if he had supervised their printing. Thorpe added a dedication, which is perhaps the most famous of all literary puzzles:

TO. THE. ONLIE. BEGETTER. OF. THESE. INSVING. SONNETS. MR. W. H. ALL. HAPPINESSE. AND. THAT. ETERNITIE. PROMISED. BY. OVR. EVER-LIVING. POET. WISHETH. THE. WELL-WISHING. ADVENTURER. IN. SETTING. FORTH. T.T.

If 'begetter' means 'inspirer' then 'Mr W. H.' would seem to be the young man to whom Shakespeare addressed his sonnets. He could be Henry Wriothesley, Earl of Southampton, with his initials reversed and title suppressed, or William Herbert, Earl of Pembroke, or Henry Willoughby, author of *Avisa,* or some other young patron altogether unknown to us.

But the 'lovely boy' was not the *only* inspirer of Shakespeare's sonnets, many of which were addressed to his mistress, and Thorpe is not above suspicion, for to the *Sonnets* quarto he added *A Lover's Complaint,* 'By William Shake-speare', which was probably no more his than *A Yorkshire Tragedy,* a King's play published in the previous year as 'Written by W. Shake-speare'. It may be, therefore, that Thorpe obtained a manuscript of the *Sonnets* from some source other than Shakespeare, printing them without his knowledge, and that by 'begetter' he meant 'procurer', a normal Elizabethan usage of the word. If so, Mr W. H. could be almost anybody with those initials. There was, for example, a W. H. who wrote a dedication to the

Fourfold Meditation published as Robert Southwell's in 1606, and there was the printer William Hall, who, however, did not print the *Sonnets* for Thorpe. A more likely candidate for the dedication, which after all is a very courteous one, is Sir William Harvey, who married the Earl of Southampton's mother in 1598, for if Southampton was the youth to whom Shakespeare wrote his sonnets, his mother or his stepfather would be likely to have a copy of them. On the other hand Mr W. H. may simply have been a friend of Thorpe's to whom he showed his gratitude by giving him that eternity, albeit anonymous, promised by Shakespeare to his friend. That friend was probably the Earl of Southampton, to whom he had dedicated *Venus and Adonis* and *Lucrece*, and who in return is said to have given him £1,000, but it does not follow that he was also Mr W. H. of the *Sonnets* dedication. We have lost the key to the puzzle, and perhaps it is not very important, for the sonnets themselves remain, and the young man, whoever he may have been, was little more than a pretext for the poetry, without which our literature would be so immeasurably the poorer.

Shakespeare was probably writing *Cymbeline* at New Place for the greater part of 1609. The long succession of plague years must have made him consider retiring to Stratford sooner than he originally intended, for if the theatres remained closed for the greater part of the time there was no reason why he should stay in London, and he certainly had no intention of travelling about the country with his company. He discussed his arrangements with Thomas Greene, who still had not got possession of his house, suggesting that he and his family should move in a year's time, and on 9 September Greene made a note in his diary: 'I perceived I might stay another year at New Place.' He also wrote to the occupying tenant of St Mary's, George Browne, 'I desire I may have the possession at Our Lady Day next, that then I may begin to make it ready against Michaelmas next.' He had timber ready for the alterations he planned to make between the end of March and the end of September 1610, when he would move in. He spent a lot of money, and made the property into 'a pretty, neat, gentleman-like house, with a pretty garden, and a little young orchard standing very sweet and quiet.'

Shakespeare would return to London at the end of October for six weeks of rehearsal for the Revels, for which his company was paid £30, 'being restrayned from publique playinge within the citie of London in the tyme of infection'. One of the thirteen plays that they rehearsed and presented at Whitehall would be *Cymbeline*, as suitable for Court performance as it was for Blackfriars.

The new year, 1610, promised to be a repetition of the old, but by the end of January plague deaths had dropped to fewer than thirty, the theatres were reopened and the King's moved into their snug Blackfriars house. The Master of the Paul's Boys also considered opening their little theatre again, but was bought off by the offer of £20 a year from the two other companies interested in private theatres, the King's and the Whitefriars Children. This, however, was as far as the Whitefriars manager would go in the way of co-operation with his rivals, and he brought an action against the Blackfriars householders, demanding a share in the profits of the theatre, to which, as a partner in the former Blackfriars company, he claimed to have a right. Their profit, he maintained, was at least fifteen hundred pounds, a fantastic sum, for the theatre can scarcely have opened its doors for more than a few weeks before the beginning of 1610, and Keysar had to seek what redress he could from Henry Evans, the former lessee. Ridiculous as Keysar's claim was, the sum mentioned is an indication of the commercial value of the Blackfriars theatre.

With the spring, however, the King's Men moved across the river to the Globe, where, on Monday, 30 April, a German prince on his travels saw a performance of *Othello*. A month later at least two of Shakespeare's company took part in the water-pageant that celebrated the creation of Prince Henry as Prince of Wales, John Rice, one of their boy actors, as Corinea on a whale greeting him as Duke of Cornwall, and Burbage as Amphion on a dolphin's back saluting him by his new title of Prince of Wales. Another month and plague had returned, the

King's once again went on their travels, to Dover, Oxford, Stafford and Shrewsbury, and Shakespeare retired to Stratford.

Retired to Stratford, but not from work. How could he? He was only forty-six – it is easy to forget how young was this astonishing genius, the author of more than thirty plays, from *Richard III* to *Lear*, from *Romeo and Juliet* to *Antony and Cleopatra*, when he returned to Stratford – and as far as we know in good health. No doubt the prodigal expense of spirit on the great tragedies had left its mark, but it had not exhausted nor had it sealed off the creative vein, and the most beautiful of all his plays was yet to be written. He had to write, just as he had to breathe, but there was no reason why he should any longer be involved in the day-to-day activities of his company: in reading, revising and buying new plays for them, in superintending their rehearsals and occasionally taking a part himself. His heart was in the theatre, it is true, but as a dramatist rather than as an actor, for though he enjoyed acting it had always been a means to an end, the writing of plays. For the last five years, owing to the plague, he had spent much of his time in Stratford, and for the next three, owing to its absence, he probably spent almost as much time in London as before, so that retirement involved no violent break in the rhythm of his life. There is no reason to suppose that he sold shares in the Globe and Blackfriars at this time, or his share in the fellowship of the King's Men, for whom he continued to write, though no doubt he received a smaller proportion of their profits, and if still a sharer in the fellowship he was still a Groom of the Chamber, liable for appearance at the Revels or any other Court performance.

We should, then, think of Shakespeare on his return to Stratford as a healthy man in the prime of life, 'a handsome well shap't man', vigorous and happy in the town and countryside that he had always loved; the writer who created the comedy of Autolycus and the romance of Perdita this year was not an unhappy man. We can form some conception of him from the tributes of his contemporaries: for Henry Chettle he was civil in his demeanour and upright in his dealing; for the poet John

Davies of Hereford he was 'Our English Terence', combining wit, courage, and good shape with generosity of mind and mood; Heminge and Condell knew him as a worthy friend, and Jonson as a friend whom he loved as much as any man, sociable, honest, and of an open and free nature. One does not think of him as a great talker, aggressive either in conversation or in action, but rather as quiet, unassuming and observant, for he had a passionate interest in people, with a breadth of sympathy and depth of understanding that enabled him to identify himself with others and restrained him from judging and condemning. No scholar, though widely read, and the very reverse of a pedant, he had a profound natural wisdom, without, however, any pretension to understanding the riddle of life, but with, as Keats put it, a 'negative capability', the capacity 'of being in uncertainties, mysteries, doubts, without any irritable reaching after fact and reason'. Thus, tragedy was as much a matter of circumstance as of character, people suffer out of all proportion to what they do and are, and with Lear he seems to cry, 'Upon such sacrifices the gods themselves throw incense.'

The philosophy of the tragedies is not a Christian one, nor, I think, in spite of modern interpretation, is that of *Measure for Measure*, with its insistence on the horror of death, a repetition of Hamlet's 'dread of something after death', and the meddling Duke's cold comfort about the miseries of life, gout, serpigo and the rheum. The last plays, the romances, with their themes of reconciliation and forgiveness are Christian in outlook, but taking Shakespeare's work as a whole there is little to suggest that he was a devoutly religious man, and certainly he was not a fanatic. 'He dy'd a Papist,' wrote Richard Davies almost a century after his death. It is possible, and more probable than that he died a Puritan, for which sect, and its attempt to close the theatres and destroy the art for which he lived, he can have had little sympathy. The probability is that he supported the established Anglican Church, not from any compelling conviction, but because it was a buttress of the political order that his simple loyalty and conservatism demanded.

Such a man, friendly, easy with all sorts of people and ready to laugh with them, not at them, witty, and like Falstaff, 'the cause that wit is in other men', interested in everybody and every thing, modest, making no attempt to be 'clever', and reserving his creative activity, his poetry, for the solitude of his study and garden, must have been a welcome addition to the provincial society of Stratford. It is true that he took little part in the town's affairs, but then he took little part in the affairs of London; he did not write pageants for Lord Mayor's shows like Anthony Munday, or masques for the Court like Jonson, but preferred to work for his theatre, to write plays for his fellowship, and relax in the Mermaid Tavern. So in Stratford: he had plays to write and a garden to cultivate, and he left the affairs of the town to be managed by those with a taste for such things and little need of books and music to fill their leisure hours.

And then there was the conversation of friends. But first there was his family, from which he had been separated for the greater part of the twenty years of his residence in London. At New Place were his wife Anne, now fifty-four, and his younger daughter Judith, Hamnet's twin, aged twenty-five; the Greenes and their young children, Anne and William – they sound like the godchildren of the poet and his wife – moved to their new house by the churchyard (little Mamillius tells Hermione the story of a man who dwelt by a churchyard), and perhaps Shakespeare's younger bachelor brothers, Gilbert and Richard, moved in. If not, they probably stayed in the old Henley Street house with their sister Joan, her husband William Hart, and their three young sons. Then not far away was the Hall household, his son-in-law Dr John Hall, Susanna, and the two-year-old Elizabeth.

Although some of Shakespeare's friends had gone, there were others in plenty. Richard Quiney and his father Adrian were both dead, but Richard's widow and her elder son still ran the mercery business in High Street, her younger son Thomas kept the tavern next door, and across the road at the Cage was her daughter Elizabeth Chandler, whose husband was also a mercer. Old Abraham Sturley still lived in Wood Street, in somewhat straitened circumstances after the great fire of 1594, though his two sons had gone to Oxford and were now parsons near Stratford. Richard Hathaway, Anne Shakespeare's nephew, was a baker in Bridge Street, where John Lane also lived with his son John, whose sister had just married John Greene, a lawyer like his brother Thomas, the Town Clerk, and an attorney of the Stratford court. Hamnet Sadler, Shakespeare's boyhood friend, and his wife Judith lived in a new house at the corner of High Street and Sheep Street, and his cousin John Sadler, a prosperous former bailiff, within a few yards of New Place. Henry Walker was also a near neighbour, and Juline Shaw's premises bounded Shakespeare's garden. Across the road, in the sunny court on the south side of the Gild Chapel, were the houses of the schoolmaster, Alexander Aspinall, 'Great Philip Macedon' as John Greene called him, and the vicar John Rogers, and farther down the road towards the church lived William Reynolds, still a bachelor at thirty-five, and his Catholic parents. Their neighbours were Mary Combe, whose husband Thomas had died in 1609, and her sons William and Thomas, aged twenty-four and twenty-one. Her brother-in-law, John Combe, from whom Shakespeare had bought his Welcome estate, was of Old Stratford, as were the brothers John and Anthony Nash, whose son Thomas, aged seventeen in 1610, was to become the first husband of Shakespeare's granddaughter. A little further afield, in the manor house of Alderminster on the Cotswolds, was his friend Thomas Russell with his second wife, Anne Digges, her daughters and younger son Leonard, an Oxford graduate now aged twenty-two. Her elder son, Dudley Digges, who was married and a knight, had inherited the great house in Philip Lane, Aldermanbury, and as a leading member of the Council of the Virginia Company was anxiously awaiting news of the lost flagship of the little fleet that had sailed for the colony in May 1609. A 'cruel tempest' had scattered the ships, and when they reached Virginia in August the *Sea Adventure*, carrying their commander, Sir George Somers, and the acting governor, Sir Thomas Gates, was missing.

Meanwhile, in the late summer of 1610, Shakespeare was finishing *The Winter's Tale*, and it may well be that the sheepshearing scene was inspired by a similar festivity that he saw at one of Russell's farms on the Cotswolds. Moreover, if he was in Stratford in November he may have met Sir Dudley Digges at Alderminster, for in the middle of that month Digges came to see his stepfather on business. He also had news. In September Sir Thomas Gates, of whom nothing had been heard for more than a year, arrived in London from Virginia with the story of the *Sea Adventure*. The tempest that scattered the fleet had driven his ship, some of the crew of which were drunk, on to the uninhabited island of Bermuda, popularly known as The Isle of Devils. The devils, however, turned out to be wild hogs, and as there was plenty of water they lived well enough during the temperate though tempestuous winter, building two pinnaces in which they eventually reached Virginia in May. This was the story that Digges had to tell and which Shakespeare may have heard at Russell's house before he went up to London for the Revels. Among the fifteen plays given by the King's Men may have been *The Winter's Tale*, Jonson's latest comedy, *The Alchemist*, and Beaumont and Fletcher's *Maid's Tragedy*. Perhaps the Queen's, now acting at the new Red Bull theatre which specialized in sensation, presented Webster's *White Devil*, full of corruption as a graveyard, but almost as full of poetry as a Shakespearian tragedy. One wonders how many of the Court of King James realized the splendour of the words that were being written at this time. It was the eve of publication of the Authorized Version of the Bible.

Shakespeare would be back in Stratford by the beginning of February, eager to begin work on *The Tempest*, and leaving the King's Men playing profitably at Blackfriars. By April they had moved into the Globe for their spring season, where on the 20th, a Saturday, the noted physician and astrologer, Dr Simon Forman, saw *Macbeth*, a short account of which he added to his *Booke of Plaies*. It is little more than a summary of the plot, though we get at least one vivid glimpse of Burbage and perhaps John Rice as Lady Macbeth: 'And when Mack Beth had murdred the kinge, the blod on his handes could not be washed of by Any meanes, nor from his wiues handes, which handled the bloddi daggers in hiding them.' And we learn that the ghost of Banquo was not a mere figment of the imagination, as some squeamish producers would have it, but a walking, blood-boltered corpse that 'came and sate down in his cheier'. There is a professional note in the doctor's postscript: 'Obserue Also howe Mackbetes quen did Rise in the night in her slepe, & walke and talked and confessed all, & the docter noted her wordes.' A few days later he saw *Cymbeline*, but his attempted synopsis becoming even more involved and confused than the play itself, he abandoned it despairingly with an '&c.' *The Winter's Tale*, which he saw 'at the glob' on 15 May, was more to his liking, particularly Autolycus, 'the Rog that cam in all tottered like coll pixci', and he added the cautionary memorandum: 'Beware of trusting feined beggars or fawninge fellous.' It is exasperating; we are so close to seeing an actual performance at the Globe, yet so tantalizingly shut off. If only Dr Forman had thought about the future to more purpose and described the theatre and the actors, how Burbage played Macbeth, how the masque in *Cymbeline* was staged and how Hermione was discovered, he would have won our gratitude and the fame that eluded him in life and which he tried to achieve in death, for he died, as every good astrologer should, on the day that he had predicted, in the following September.

On the previous day, 11 September 1611, the name of 'Mr William Shackspere' had been added to the list of the principal Stratford residents who had contributed towards the cost of promoting a bill in Parliament for the better repair of the highways. He was also engaged in safeguarding his investments. Some of the Stratford tithe-holders were not paying their full rents and their failure to do so threatened the position of the others, as it gave the owner of the original lease the right to retake possession of all the holdings. Young William Combe of College House was one of the culprits, and as he held a substantial part of the batch of tithes in which Shakespeare had invested, he and the other two holders, Richard Lane and

Thomas Greene, presented a Bill of Complaint to the Lord Chancellor alleging that Combe was not paying his share of the rent, so that they themselves were 'usually dryven to pay the same for preservacion of their estates'. It was a friendly attempt to straighten a muddle caused by vague and badly drawn leases, and was amicably settled, Combe promising to pay a proportional part of the rent in future.

And so, while promoting the improvement of Warwickshire roads and putting his own finances in order, Shakespeare wove the magic of *The Tempest*. It is, one feels, characteristic of the man: perfectly balanced, feeling the earth firm beneath his feet, yet glancing from earth to heaven and sharing the element of Ariel. For of all the poetry that Shakespeare wrote that of *The Tempest* is at once the most earthy and the most celestial, from the simple verse of Caliban to the lyrics of Ariel, but reaching its climax in Prospero's speech when he dismisses the spirits that have performed the Masque of the Three Goddesses and turns to Ferdinand and Miranda:

> Our revels now are ended. These our actors,
> As I foretold you, were all spirits, and
> Are melted into air, into thin air;
> And like the baseless fabric of this vision,
> The cloud-capp'd towers, the gorgeous palaces,
> The solemn temples, the great globe itself,
> Yea, all which it inherit, shall dissolve,
> And, like this insubstantial pageant faded,
> Leave not a rack behind. We are such stuff
> As dreams are made on, and our little life
> Is rounded with a sleep.

The three introductory lines, by the number of words that begin with a vowel, by their fragility and the slight pause necessary before speaking them, express something of the heartache at what time has taken away. Then comes the deeper and more solemn music of the development: what time will take before life is completed, perfected, by the oblivion of sleep. Again, it is not a Christian philosophy, though serene and more consolatory than Claudio's fear of death and Hamlet's dread of that undiscovered country. Then, throughout the speech is woven the counter-rhythm of the chiming and falling trochees – *revels, temples, ended, rounded; spirit, herit; actors, fabric, baseless, faded* – a verbal counterpoint comparable to the harmonized melodies of a fugue. If we compare this mastery with the elementary, though by no means unmusical, verse that Shakespeare had written at the beginning of his career in the *Comedy of Errors*, like *The Tempest* a play in which the action is compressed into a few hours, we have some measure of the distance that he had travelled in twenty years:

> Not know my voice! O time's extremity,
> Hast thou so crack'd and splitted my poor tongue
> In seven short years, that here my only son
> Knows not my feeble key of untuned cares?
> Though now this grained face of mine be hid
> In sap-consuming winter's drizzled snow,
> And all the conduits of my blood froze up,
> Yet hath my night of life some memory,
> My wasting lamps some fading glimmer left,
> My dull deaf ears a little use to hear.

The stage-directions of *The Tempest* are unusually full, as though Shakespeare, working in Stratford, wished to give his company as much help as possible before he arrived to super-vise the final rehearsals. He would have to go up to London early for the Revels that year, for the first play was given by the King's on 31 October, and then, on the following night, 'Hallomas nyght, was presented att Whithall before ye kinges Maiestie a play Called the Tempest'. Fortunate Majesty to be presented with that first performance, and fortunate again if he were there, and not in his stables, four nights later on the anniversary of Gunpowder Plot, to see 'A play Called ye winters nightes Tayle'. The two entries are from the Revels Account, which has been preserved for this year, 1611–12. Unfortunately the names of all the twenty-two plays presented by the King's Men were not recorded; these are the only two of Shake-speare's to be mentioned, and it is significant that Beaumont and Fletcher also had at least two of their plays performed. The facile and unsavoury melodramas of the young Jacobean collaborators were beginning to compete with the plays of the veteran Elizabethan.

The Revels were protracted until the end of April, and if Shakespeare stayed in London all that time he would miss the funeral of his brother Gilbert, who was buried at Stratford on 3 February. He was only forty-five, and apparently died a bachelor. Perhaps, however, Shakespeare was there, for there were long gaps when the King's Men were not required at Court, though he had to be in London at the beginning of May, when he was called as a witness in the case of Belott *v*. Mountjoy. Mountjoy was a difficult man, all the more difficult since the death of his wife and his taking a mistress, and relations with his son-in-law had so deteriorated that he refused to have him in his house and swore he would leave his daughter Mary nothing in his will. Belott, therefore, brought an action in the Court of Requests, alleging that Mountjoy had broken his promise to give a marriage portion of £60 with his daughter and to make a will leaving her another £200. The case was heard at Westminster on 11 May 1612, when a number of witnesses were called on Belott's behalf. There was Joan Johnson, once a servant of the Mountjoys, who said that they urged 'one Mr Shakespeare that laye in the house' to persuade Belott to marry Mary. This was confirmed by Daniel Nicholas, who added that Shakespeare told him that Mountjoy had promised a marriage portion of about £50 in money and certain household stuff. Then 'William Shakespeare of Stratford vpon Aven, gentleman, of the age of forty-eight years' – he was of Stratford, not London, where apparently he had no residence – was called upon to give evidence, and from his deposition we can reconstruct approximately what he replied to the lawyer's questions. It is as near as we can get to his everyday speech:

I have known Stephen Belott and Christopher Mountjoy for the space of ten years or thereabouts.

I knew Belott when he was a servant with Mountjoy, and as far as I know he always behaved well and honestly. No, I never heard

Mountjoy remark that he got any great profit from his employment, though I really think that he was a very good and industrious apprentice.

It was clear to me that all the time that Belott was an apprentice Mountjoy showed great good will and affection towards him, and I often heard him and his wife say that he was a very honest fellow. Moreover, Mountjoy asked him if he would like to marry his daughter, and his wife asked me to persuade him to do so, which I did.

Yes, Mountjoy promised to give Belott a marriage portion, of money and goods – or perhaps only of money – but how much I do not remember, nor when it was to be paid. Nor do I know anything about a promise to make a will leaving £200 to his daughter. All I can say is that when Belott was living with the Mountjoys they all had many conferences about the marriage, which afterwards was solemnized.

No, I do not know what household stuff Mountjoy gave Belott when he married Mary.

Shakespeare signed his deposition, the first of his signatures that we possess, and although there was another hearing of the case a month later, he was not there. His evidence was not very helpful, but then it was nearly eight years since Stephen had married Mary, and he could scarcely be expected to remember details. And perhaps he did not wish to remember, to become too much involved in the case; he had said what he could in favour of Stephen, but Mountjoy was no longer the man he had been when he lodged with him. The elders of the Huguenot church in London agreed, for when the case was referred to them they awarded Belott twenty nobles, which Mountjoy did not pay, and eventually they suspended him because of his licentious life.

It was at about this time that the King's Men lost the services of Francis Beaumont. Aubrey tells us that he and Fletcher were as intimate in their lives as in their work, living 'together on the Banke Side, not far from the Play-house, both batchelors; lay together; had one wench in the house between them, which they did so admire; the same cloathes and cloake, &c., betweene them.' But these happy bachelor days were almost over, for

Beaumont was wooing an heiress, whom soon afterwards he married, and not only did the King's Men lose an author, but Fletcher lost a companion and collaborator. To produce his best work Fletcher needed the stimulus of a partner, and it may be that he approached Shakespeare when he was in London for the Belott–Mountjoy affair and suggested writing a play together; there was an excellent story in the recent translation of *Don Quixote*, the romance of Cardenio and Lucinda, just the thing for the Revels and Blackfriars theatre; if Shakespeare would draft the play and write a few scenes introducing the main characters and themes he would see to the rest. The King's Men would be eager to promote a venture that might lead to a profitable partnership, and perhaps Shakespeare returned to Stratford to sketch a play of *Cardenio* for Fletcher to finish. If so, he probably enjoyed the writing, light work in his semi-retirement, and, after sending off his script to London, began another play, one that he developed more fully, however, leaving only the pathos and adulation for Fletcher, for it rounded off his series of histories – *The Famous History of the Life of King Henry the Eight*.

The theatre companies needed all the new plays they could muster, for on 16 October the young Elector Palatine arrived in London for his marriage with Princess Elizabeth, and the next six months promised to be a period of almost continuous festivity. It was marred, however, at the outset, for on 6 November Prince Henry died, a clever and capable boy of eighteen, universally beloved, who, had he lived, would have retrieved his father's follies and prevented those of his brother Charles, which led him to the block and the country into civil war. The theatres were closed and the Court plunged into mourning, but after a month the Revels were resumed, and on 27 December the Elector and Elizabeth were betrothed. We do not know what play they saw that night, but of all those presented that season the most appropriate to celebrate the betrothal of princes was *The Tempest*, and if that was the play it is probable that Shakespeare himself took the part of Prospero to wish the royal children, for they were no more, the happiness that he had foreseen for Ferdinand and Miranda. Of the twenty-nine performances during the celebrations, twenty were given by the King's Men, and of these, eight were of Shakespeare's plays, for in addition to *The Tempest* there were the two parts of *Henry IV*, *The Winter's Tale*, *Othello*, *Julius Caesar*, and *Much Ado about Nothing*, which was given twice. Beaumont and Fletcher, with five performances, were almost as popular as Shakespeare, relatively far more popular, for their collaboration had lasted only five years, whereas Shakespeare had been writing for twenty-five and had thirty-five plays to choose from. And then there was *Cardenio*, which was never printed and has been lost, though it was registered forty years later as being by 'Mr Fletcher and Shakespeare': not Shakespeare and Fletcher, but Fletcher and Shakespeare.

The wedding took place on 14 February, but it was another two months before the Revels were ended and the young couple set out to meet their misfortunes, leaving King James free to go to Newmarket.

Shakespeare must have been in London for the greater part of these six months, and it is unlikely that he was at home when the last of his brothers died, exactly a year after Gilbert. 'Richard sonne to Mr John Shakspeer' was buried at Stratford on 4 February 1613. Nothing at all is known about him; at least we know that Gilbert was at one time a haberdasher in London, and that Edmund was an actor, but of Richard the only records are those of his birth and death. Apparently he too died a bachelor. They were a short-lived family, these Shakespeare brothers: Gilbert was forty-five when he died, Richard not quite thirty-nine, Edmund twenty-seven, and William had only three more years to live.

He was certainly in London in March, for some time before the 24th he and Richard Burbage designed and made the Earl of Rutland's *impresa* for the tournament held on that day. This was a pasteboard shield bearing a painted emblematic device and motto, which his squire carried for him at the tilt, the interpretation of the allegory being part of the entertainment. Sir Henry Wotton particularly admired those of the Earl of Pem-

broke and his brother the Earl of Montgomery: the one a pearl
'and the word *Solo Candore Valeo*; the other a sun casting a
glance on the side of a pillar, and the beams reflecting, with this
motto, *Splendente Refulget*; in which devices there seems an
agreement, the elder brother to allude to his own nature and
the younger to his fortune.' Montgomery was a favourite of
James, who had recently given him the earldom, and it was to
the two brothers that Heminge and Condell were to dedicate
the Shakespeare Folio ten years later. Apparently Shakespeare
devised the allegory for Rutland, and Burbage, an amateur
painter, executed it, for on 31 March his steward entered in his
account book: 'To Mr Shakspeare in gold about my Lordes
impreso, 48s.; to Richard Burbage for paynting and making
yt, in gold 48s.'

   A fortnight before the tilt Shakespeare had bought a London
house, paying for it more than twice the price he had paid for
New Place sixteen years before. This was the gatehouse of the
old Blackfriars priory, which Henry Walker, a member of the
Minstrels' Company of London, had bought for £100 in 1604,
and of which the Catholic John Fortescue had been tenant at
the time of Gunpowder Plot. No doubt Shakespeare bought the
house primarily as an investment, his only property in London,
but as it was only a few yards from the Blackfriars theatre it
looks as though he may have thought of living there for a
time, now that the City was free from plague. It was a compli-
cated transaction. On 10 March the property was sold for £140
to 'William Shakespeare of Stratford Vpon Avon, gentleman,
William Johnson, citizein and Vintener of London, John
Jackson and John Hemmyng of London, gentlemen'. The
three friends whom Shakespeare associated with himself were
trustees, who would hold the property after his death so that it
would not automatically go to his wife, as London property, or
at least a third of it, customarily did. Anne, who would be a
wealthy and therefore desirable widow, might marry again and
carry the house into the hands of another husband, but Shakespeare intended leaving all the property that would have gone
to Hamnet to Susanna's long-expected and longed-for son, as

head or representative of the family that he had founded. On the following day he mortgaged the house to Walker for £60, presumably as security against payment of the balance of the purchase money, and signed the mortgage, as he had signed the conveyance, with Johnson and Jackson. William Johnson was landlord of the Mermaid, and John Jackson one of the 'sirenaical gentlemen' who frequented his tavern, related by marriage to the Blackfriars brewer Elias James, whose epitaph Shakespeare is said to have written on his death in 1610.

Having bought a London house, Shakespeare would stay to see to any necessary repairs, probably living in it for a time while he put the finishing touches to *Henry VIII* with Fletcher, and directed its rehearsal at the Globe. Although there is no external evidence to prove that Fletcher had a hand in the play, we know that the two men were collaborating at this time, and the verse of Fletcher cannot be mistaken for that of Shakespeare. Here are introductory speeches by Buckingham, Wolsey, and Queen Katharine:

> Every man,
> After the hideous storm that follow'd, was
> A thing inspired, and not consulting broke
> Into a general prophecy: That this tempest,
> Dashing the garment of this peace, aboded
> The sudden breach on't.

> If I am
> Traduced by ignorant tongues, which neither know
> My faculties nor person, yet will be
> The chronicles of my doing, let me say
> 'Tis but the fate of place, and the rough brake
> That virtue must go through.

> This makes bold mouths:
> Tongues spit their duties out, and cold hearts freeze
> Allegiance in them; their curses now
> Live where their prayers did; and it's come to pass
> This tractable obedience is a slave
> To each incensed will.

And here are their farewells to life and happiness:

> A most unnatural and faithless service!
> Heaven has an end in all: yet, you that hear me,
> This from a dying man receive as certain:
> Where you are liberal of your loves and counsels
> Be sure you be not loose.
>   I have ventured,
> Like little wanton boys that swim on bladders,
> This many summers in a sea of glory,
> But far beyond my depth: my high-blown pride
> At length broke under me, and now has left me,
> Weary and old with service, to the mercy
> Of a rude stream that must for ever hide me.
>
> And, sure, those men are happy that shall have 'em.
> The last is, for my men; they are the poorest,
> But poverty could never draw 'em from me;
> That they may have their wages duly paid 'em,
> And something over to remember me by.

'The genius of Shakespeare comes in and goes out with Katharine', wrote Johnson; but in fact Katharine, as well as Buckingham and Wolsey, comes in with the genius of Shakespeare and goes out with the talent of Fletcher; comes in with the taut, masculine, varied verse of the one, and goes out with the languishing, flaccid and monotonous verse of the other; monotonous because it is always the same: a series of metrically regular lines followed by a redundant syllable and a pause: *hear me, left me, hide me, from me, have 'em, paid 'em*. Yet it was Fletcher's sweet sentiment that appealed to the seventeenth century and even to Johnson, and even today any popularity that *Henry VIII* may be said to retain lies in Fletcher's pageantry and the protracted farewells of Henry's victims.

Presumably Shakespeare was at Greenwich on 8 June, when James summoned his company to entertain the Savoyard ambassador with a performance of *Cardenio*, by which time *Henry VIII* was ready for production, and he may also have been in the Globe on that disastrous afternoon of 29 June.

Jonson was there, which suggests that it may have been the
first performance, for he wrote:

> the Globe, the glory of the Bank:
> Which, though it were the fort of the whole parish,
> Flanked with a ditch, and forced out of a marish,
> I saw with two poor chambers taken in,
> And razed; ere thought could urge this might have been!

The chambers were guns fired to announce the entry of King
Henry in the fourth scene of the first act – *Drum and Trumpet,
Chambers dischargd*, ran the stage-direction – but some of the
wadding set fire to the reeds with which the galleries were
thatched, and then, according to a contemporary rhymester:

> Out runne the knightes, out runne the lordes,
>   And there was great adoe;
> Some lost their hattes, and some their swordes;
>   Then out runne Burbidge too;
> The reprobates, though druncke on Munday,
> Prayd for the Foole and Henry Condye.
>   Oh sorrow, pittifull sorrow, and yett all this is true.
>
> The perrywigges and drumme-heades frye,
>   Like to a butter firkin;
> A wofull burneing did betide
>   To many a good buffe jerkin.
> Then with swolne eyes, like druncken Flemminges,
> Distressed stood old stuttering Heminges.
>   Oh sorrow, pittifull sorrow, and yett all this is true.

'All is True' was an alternative title for *Henry VIII*, and was
used by Sir Henry Wotton, who also called it 'a new play', in
his description of the disaster: how the wadding 'kindled in-
wardly, and ran round like a train, consuming within less than
an hour the whole house to the very grounds. This was the
fatal period of that virtuous fabric, wherein yet nothing did
perish but wood and straw, and a few forsaken cloaks; only
one man had his breeches set on fire, that would perhaps have
broiled him, if he had not by the benefit of a provident wit put
it out with bottle ale.' 'Nothing did perish but wood and straw,

and a few forsaken cloaks'! The precious play-books were saved, without which we should never have had half of the plays of Shakespeare, and *Twelfth Night, Macbeth, Antony and Cleopatra*, and *The Tempest* would be no more than names. The first thought of distressed and stuttering Heminge must have been for their stock, and no doubt it was he, helped perhaps by Shakespeare himself, who rescued the manuscripts that were soon to be given to the world in the Folio.

Within a year a new Globe had risen from the ashes of the old, tiled this time instead of thatched, and said to be the fairest playhouse that ever was in England, far finer than before. The first estimate of cost was about £800, of which the Burbage brothers would have to pay half, and the other housekeepers, of whom there were now seven, the remainder. Shakespeare, therefore, was called upon to pay some £60, but the estimate was much too small, for eventually the cost proved to be £1,700, and rather than pay £120 towards the rebuilding he may have transferred his interest to a more active member of the company. Indeed, it is possible that the burning of the Globe decided him to retire from the theatre altogether, that in addition to disposing of his interest in the Globe he also sold his share in the Blackfriars and in the fellowship itself, that he let his gatehouse to a new tenant, John Robinson, and returned to Stratford for good.

CHAPTER 10

1613–16

STRATFORD

*

SHAKESPEARE'S departure from London would be hastened
by the news from Stratford. Susanna had been accused of in-
continency and adultery by young John Lane of Bridge Street,
who had said in the hearing of Robert Whatcott, Shakespeare's
friend, that she 'had the running of the reins and had been
naught with Rafe Smith at John Palmer's'. Rafe Smith was a
married man of thirty-five – Susanna was thirty – and John
Palmer a gentleman of Compton. Neither Susanna's husband
nor her father was the sort of man to overlook such an insult,
nor was Susanna herself one to allow her reputation to be
treated lightly, and in July she brought an action for slander in
the Consistory Court at Worcester, where Whatcott appeared
on her behalf. Lane, however, did not appear, and Susanna's
character was cleared by his excommunication. He was a Catholic, and a few years later led an attack on the new Puritan vicar,
for which exploit he was presented by the churchwardens as a
drunkard.

It seems probable that while Shakespeare was in London he
had agreed to collaborate with Fletcher in another play, a
dramatization of Chaucer's *Knight's Tale*, the romance of Palamon and Arcite, and that in the summer of 1613 he wrote most
of the first act of *The Two Noble Kinsmen*, and parts of acts three
and five, leaving the gaps to be filled in by Fletcher, to whom he
sent his script. He would want to see what Fletcher had made
of his work and no doubt went up to London for the first
performance at the Blackfriars theatre that winter. He cannot
have been pleased with what he saw and heard. The Arcite that
he had created spoke like this:

> I am in labour
> To push your name, your ancient love, our kindred
> Out of my memory; and i' the self-same place
> To seat something I would confound: so hoist we
> The sails that must these vessels port ev'n where
> The heavenly Limiter pleases!

Fletcher's Arcite like this:

> The worst is death; I will not leave the kingdom:
> I know my own is but a heap of ruins,
> And no redress there; if I go, he has her.
> I am resolv'd: another shape shall make me,
> Or end my fortunes; either way I'm happy.

And then Fletcher had invented a nasty little sub-plot about a gaoler's daughter who went mad for love of Palamon. Shakespeare was a tolerant man, but he could not allow it to be thought that he was in any way responsible for such unpleasant nonsense, and it was the last time that he collaborated with Fletcher or with anyone else. When the play was published twenty years later, it was as

Presented at the Blackfriers by the Kings Maiesties servants, with great applause: Written by the memorable Worthies of their time: Mr John Fletcher and Mr. William Shakespeare. Gent.

The applause would be mainly for the gaoler's daughter and Fletcher's Palamon and Arcite.

The King's Men were fortunate in having the use of the Blackfriars theatre while the Globe was being rebuilt, and also in having a new play which Shakespeare probably saw there a few days before or after the first performance of *The Two Noble Kinsmen*. This was John Webster's masterpiece, *The Duchess of Malfi*, after Shakespeare's, greatest of all Jacobean tragedies. But in addition to its merit as a work of art it is important as the only play that gives the parts taken by the principal actors at the first performance. Burbage played Ferdinand, Lowin the villainous Bosola, Condell the Cardinal, Ostler, who died in the following year, Delio, while John Underwood and Nicholas

Tooley doubled parts and the boy Richard Sharp played the Duchess. Heminge had given up acting to become their business manager, and there is no mention of Shakespeare. Perhaps the Christmas of 1613 was the first that he had spent at home with his family since he left Stratford to seek his fortune in Armada year.

His new-found leisure would give him time to catch up with his reading. There was Philemon Holland's translation of the Latin *Britannia* of William Camden, the antiquarian of the Herald's College who had defended the grant of arms to John Shakespeare and paid a tribute to the poet in his *Remains*, a shortened English version of *Britannia*:

If I would come to our time, what a world could I present to you out of Sir Philip Sidney, Ed. Spencer, Samuel Daniel, Hugh Holland, Ben Johnson, Th. Campion, Mich. Drayton, George Chapman, John Marston, William Shakespeare, and other most pregnant wits of these our times, whom succeeding ages may justly admire.

Hugh Holland was a Cambridge don who was himself to add a tribute to Shakespeare as the 'Poets' King' in a halting sonnet prefixed to the Folio. It was in the *Remains* that Shakespeare had found material for *King Lear* and *Coriolanus*, and a suggested derivation of his name: 'from that which they commonly carried, as . . . Fortescue, that is Strong-shield, and in some such respect, Breake-speare, Shake-Speare, Shotbolt'. Less flattering was John Speed's allusion in his recent *History of Great Britain* to the falsifying poet and stage-player who had transformed the martyred Oldcastle into that ruffianly robber Falstaff. He had probably read Bacon's survey of modern knowledge, *The Advancement of Learning*, but a new volume of his *Essays* had just appeared, to be chewed and digested, unlike the *Crudities* of his Mermaid Tavern crony, Thomas Coryat, a light-hearted account of a walking-tour in Europe, which was only to be tasted. Dekker's *Gull's Hornbook* would remind him of the life of the London theatre, for among other matter were ironical instructions as to how a gallant should behave himself in a playhouse: coming in late, carrying a stool on to the stage, making as much noise as possible, laughing in the middle of a tragedy, and finding fault with play and players alike. Another book of the theatre was Heywood's *Apology for Actors*, with its tribute to dead players, Tarlton and Singer, and Shakespeare's former fellows, Pope, Phillips, and Sly, and its censure of recent satirical plays that inveighed against the government and the peculiar humours of living men. Heywood added an *Epistle* in which he protested against William Jaggard's reissue of *The Passionate Pilgrim* in a form even more impudent than the original edition, for not only did he once again ascribe all the poems in the miscellany to Shakespeare, but he had added two recently published poems of Heywood as well. This looked, wrote Heywood, as though he had stolen them from Shakespeare, who, 'to do himself right', had published them in his own name. With characteristic modesty he added that his work was quite unworthy of Shakespeare, who 'I know much offended with M. Jaggard that (altogether unknown to him) presumed to make so bold with his name'. There were altogether too many presumptuous publishers making bold with his name.

There was poetry in plenty to engage him, for in addition to that of the pregnant wits saluted by Camden – Daniel, Jonson, Campion, Chapman, and Drayton, the first part of whose interminable *Polyolbion* had just come out – there was the passionate and questing poetry of Donne, revolutionary both in manner and in content, calling all in doubt and questioning the simple, ordered universe of the Middle Ages. What Shakespeare thought of his work we do not know, though we may guess that he admired the poetry, which in some ways resembled his own late verse, while disapproving of the philosophy. It made disturbing reading for his conservative mind, and he may have turned for comfort to the splendid and confident prose of the Authorized Version of the Bible.

Then, if there was music at New Place, as we may be sure there was, again there was new work in plenty. His friend Thomas Morley was dead, but the veteran William Byrd was still alive, and had just collaborated with John Bull and the youngest member of that golden age, Orlando Gibbons, in the publication of *Parthenia*, a collection of music for the virginal, possibly the first to be printed in England. Then there were Thomas Campion's *Books of Ayres*, the madrigals of Thomas Weelkes and John Wilbye, and the songs of the lutenists, John Dowland, Philip Rosseter, and Robert Johnson, who had written the music for *The Tempest*. We can imagine the evening music at New Place on Shakespeare's fiftieth birthday in April 1614: the Halls and Harts as guests, and perhaps the Greenes and young Thomas Quiney, Judith at the virginal and Shakespeare with his lute singing Johnson's settings of Ariel's songs.

But there was work to be done as well as leisure to be filled with reading, music, and the conversation of friends. Although he had written his last play, some of his work called for revision, in particular the early *All's Well that Ends Well* with which he had fiddled some ten years before, and it seems probable that he rewrote parts of this in 1614. The Countess's speech, in the 'Venus and Adonis' stanza, must have been written at about the time of Hamnet's death, which marked the end of his lyrical period:

> Even so it was with me when I was young:
>> If ever we are nature's, these are ours; this thorn
> Doth to our rose of youth rightly belong;
>> Our blood to us, this to our blood is born;
> It is the show and seal of nature's truth,
> Where love's strong passion is impress'd in youth.

Here is the rewriting in his latest style, when the sinewy verse moves with the freedom of prose:

>> And his honour,
> Clock to itself, knew the true minute when
> Exception bid him speak, and at this time
> His tongue obey'd his hand: who were below him
> He used as creatures of another place.

Perhaps he never finished the play to his satisfaction, but he added full directions similar to those in *The Tempest* for the benefit of the King's Men who would have to produce it without his help.

He would, however, go up to London in the spring for the opening of the new Globe, probably with a performance of one of his own plays. There was, he would find, another rebuilding on Bankside. Henslowe, as interested in bears, bulls, and dogs as he was in players, was converting the old Beargarden into an arena that would accommodate all four species, having made a contract with a carpenter to build a

place or Plaichouse fitt & convenient in all thinges, bothe for players to playe in, and for the game of Beares and Bulls to be bayted in the same, and also a fitt and convenient Tyre house and a stage to be carryed and taken awaie, and to stande vppon tressels.

The 'Heavens', of course, had to be supported without posts on the removable stage which they sheltered, but in all other ways the building was to resemble the Swan, and was to be called the Hope.

The new Beargarden-theatre was only half finished when Shakespeare returned to New Place for his birthday and what was to prove a disturbing summer. On 9 July, almost exactly a year after the burning of the Globe, Stratford was ravaged by another great fire, which within a few hours gutted fifty-four houses as well as numerous barns and stables, burned a great store of corn, hay, and timber, and did damage amounting to £8,000. New Place escaped, but Shakespeare had had his fair share of fires. On the following day his friend John Combe died, leaving most of his estate to his nephew Thomas, younger brother of William Combe of College House, £10 to Francis Collins, the Warwick lawyer who had drawn up his will, and £5 to 'Master William Shakespeare'. He also directed that 'a convenient tomb of the value of three score pounds' should be set over him when he was buried beside the altar in the church, and it was almost certainly Shakespeare who recommended the Bankside stonemason and sculptor, Gerard Johnson, promising the executors to commission him to do the work when next he went to London. A month later old Abraham Sturley died, and was buried at Stratford two days after Shakespeare's aunt, Margaret Cornwall, was buried at Snitterfield. She was his mother's sister, who, after the death of her first husband, Alexander Webbe, had married Edward Cornwall, who thus became master of the house where John Shakespeare had lived as a boy before he left the farm for Stratford in the middle of the previous century.

Shortly after the fire, probably on the occasion of the official sermon given on Election Day in September, the Shakespeares entertained the visiting preacher at New Place, the Corporation contributing a quart of sack and a quart of claret, value twenty pence, towards the hospitality.

It was now that the enclosure controversy broke out again. This time, however, it was occasioned not by an attempt of the lord of the manor to enclose common pasture on the Bankcroft, but by the proposal of a group of landlords to enclose the open fields at Welcombe. The conservative Corporation took alarm, strenuously opposed the promoters, who were led by the cousins Arthur Mainwaring and William Replingham, and ordered Thomas Greene as Town Clerk to prepare a list of freeholders. This, dated 5 September 1614, began:

Mr Shakspeare. 4 yardland. Noe common nor ground beyond Gospell Bushe, noe grownd in Sandfield, nor none in Sloe Hill Field beyond Bishopton, nor none in the enclosure beyond Bishopton.

The scheme did not affect Shakespeare's Old Stratford estate, but it would affect the profit from his tithe investment in the neighbouring Welcombe fields, adversely if arable land were converted into pasture, as seems to have been the intention, though favourably if it led to heavier crops through better methods of arable farming. His 'cousin' Thomas Greene, holder of part of the batch of the same tithes, would be similarly affected, and in October Replingham, presumably to try to prevent their active opposition, signed an agreement to compensate them for any loss. Greene was in London negotiating unsuccessfully with Mainwaring and Replingham, and drafting a letter to the Privy Council, when on 17 November he made a note in his diary:

At my Cosen Shakspeare commyng yesterday to towne I went to see

him howe he did. He told me that they assured him they ment to
inclose noe further then to Gospell Bushe . . . and that they meane in
Aprill to servey the Land & then to gyve satisfaccion & not before.

It is possible that Shakespeare was not in the best of health, for
his son-in-law, Dr Hall, accompanied him, and Greene added:
'He and Mr Hall say they think there will be nothyng done at
all.'

There were a number of reasons that might have brought
Shakespeare up to London: to consult Greene about the enclosure, to inquire about the title deeds of his Blackfriars house, to
order John Combe's monument from Gerard Johnson, to visit
his old friends at the Globe, and to see Jonson's latest comedy
at the newly opened Hope theatre. This was *Bartholomew Fair*, a
roaring, rollicking anti-Puritan play in the Induction to which
Jonson referred impolitely to Henslowe's Beargarden-theatre
as a place 'as dirty as Smithfield, and as stinking every whit', had
a hit at those members of his audience who still thought *The
Spanish Tragedy* and *Titus Andronicus* the best plays yet, and
ironically apologized for his realism, for his lack of 'a servant-
monster' and a 'nest of antiques', such as were supplied by
'those that beget tales, tempests, and such like drolleries'. So
much for the author of *The Winter's Tale* and *The Tempest*. Shakespeare would not mind, nor would his son in law, for he would
not be there. Dr Hall had not come to London to see a play, certainly not to see an anti-Puritan satire. Nor would he be likely
to join Shakespeare and Jonson at the Mermaid. The two
dramatists had much to talk about, particularly Jonson, who
would be full of his plan to publish a collected edition of his
works, an unprecedented proposal, for plays were generally
still dismissed as ephemeral trifles, only a fraction of those
written getting into print, and nobody yet had had the audacity
to publish a collection in folio and call them his 'Works'. Although Shakespeare was careless about the way in which his
plays were published, Jonson's project must have set him
thinking along similar lines; after all, half of his work was still
in manuscript, he had the time to revise and prepare it for the
press, and the chances are that he borrowed a few of his old

manuscripts from Heminge and returned with them to Stratford. It was work for the winter.

He was probably back by the beginning of December, as was Greene, who found that the survey had already been made and that young William Combe, a large landowner in Welcombe, now supported the enclosure. On the 9th the leading members of the Corporation called at College House and tried to persuade him 'to forbear further proceedings tending to enclosure', but Combe answered arrogantly that it was Mainwaring's undertaking rather than his own, that he would do nothing to stay it, and that as soon as the frost was over he would begin to make hedges and ditches. On the following day Greene looked for Replingham at the Bear and at New Place, but missed him, and when he found him 'he was not to be spoken with'. Apparently Greene was genuinely anxious to prevent the enclosure, apart from the official attitude he had to take as Town Clerk, for when he heard a rumour that the scheme was at an end he made a note that he was all the more suspicious, 'for those might be words to make us careless'. Shakespeare's attitude is more difficult to define, but after a Council meeting on the 23rd, letters were written to Mainwaring and him, and Greene wrote personally 'to my Cosen Shakespeare', enclosing 'a note of the inconveniences that would grow by the enclosure'. This suggests that the official letters were identical, and that Shakespeare supported, or at least did not actively oppose, Mainwaring, though it may be that the Corporation and Greene were asking for a positive declaration from him and some sort of action against the scheme. On the whole it seems probable that he disapproved. His conservative instincts would tend to make him sympathize with the equally conservative Corporation, and the man who wrote *King Lear*, unless he was a consummate humbug, could scarcely approve of a policy that threatened to throw men out of work and add to the 700 poor within the borough. Then, from a purely selfish point of view, he seems to have had nothing to gain from enclosure, and Replingham's word was no absolute guarantee against loss. His position was the same as Greene's, and Greene was opposed to the project.

On the other hand, it must be remembered in favour of the enclosers that, however selfish their motives, they were the party of progress, and that all the surviving records of the controversy are those of their opponents.

Meanwhile the frost had broken, Combe had sent his men to dig a great ditch and bank, which by the beginning of January was nearly 300 yards long, and when the Corporation told him that some of their leading members would throw it down he replied, 'O would they durst, the Puritan knaves!' The aldermen were cautious, on Greene's advice sending on their spades before, proceeding 'in such private manner as that none might see them go', and then 'in the gentlest manner they could, endeavoured to hinder the malefactors from their unlawful digging'. Combe found this toast-and-butter, aldermanly opposition merely amusing, but more difficult to deal with were the women and children who swarmed over the land, destroying his hedges and ditches, and he tried to bribe Greene to make a truce, at the same time threatening 'that within this twelvemonth all the fields should be laid down greensward if they did not agree'. Six hundred strips of arable, he said, would be converted to pasture. But Combe had overshot himself. The Corporation decided to petition the Lord Chief Justice, and at the Warwick Assizes in March Sir Edward Coke ruled that no enclosure should be made either by Combe or by anyone else until good cause should be shown.

So matters stood when Shakespeare celebrated his fifty-first birthday in April 1615, shortly after which he may have gone to London on business concerning his Blackfriars house. When he bought it from Henry Walker he had not received the title deeds, which were held by Mathias Bacon from whom Walker himself had bought it in 1604. They formed part of the deeds of the whole of the old Lodging of the Prior of Blackfriars, which had been split up into a number of houses, but according to the terms under which Bacon had inherited the property he was not allowed to surrender them. Shakespeare, therefore, on 26 April joined with the other owners in a friendly Bill of Complaint by which Bacon received authority from the Court of Chancery to surrender the deeds. It was a cumbersome proceeding, but characteristic of Shakespeare's businesslike conduct; all the properties that he had bought were now indisputably his.

He was now free to get on with his work, which, however, was probably little more than a re-reading of his plays – some of which, *Henry VI* and *The Two Gentlemen of Verona*, for example, he must almost have forgotten – making the minimum of alterations and smiling at his youthful excesses, at the conceits in *King John*, the bawdiness in *Romeo and Juliet*, the puns in *Richard II*, and the exuberant lyricism of his early verse. The enclosure was still a subject for gossip, and in September Greene made a note of a conversation between his 'cousin' and his brother John: 'W Shakspeares tellyng J Greene that I was not able to beare the encloseinge of Welcombe.' In his haste Greene sometimes wrote 'I' for 'he', and it may be that he did so here, for the memorandum would have more point if it were Shakespeare himself who objected to the enclosure. In any event, it was Greene's last reference to his cousin.

Soon after this, preparations must have been begun for the wedding of Judith and Thomas Quiney, who was already negotiating the exchange of his little tavern, 'Atwood's' in High Street, for the more commodious 'Cage' on the other side, at the corner of Bridge Street. The match would please Shakespeare, for Thomas was a son of his old friend Richard Quiney, though he may have felt some misgiving about the discrepancy in age, Judith being nearly thirty-one and Thomas only twenty-six, almost as big a difference as that between himself and Anne. The wedding was probably planned for the latter half of January, and in anticipation of the event Shakespeare made his will, calling in Francis Collins, the Warwick lawyer who had acted for John Combe, to prepare a draft. It began with the date, January, and the usual formulas about health and religious belief:

In the name of god Amen I William Shackspeare of Stratford vpon Avon in the countie of Warr gent in perfect health & memorie god be praysed doe make & Ordayne this my last will & testament in manner & forme followeing. That is to saye ffirst I Comend my Soule into the handes of god my Creator, hoping & assuredlie beleeving through thonelie merittes of Jesus Christe my Saviour to be made partaker of lyfe ever-lastinge, And my bodye to the Earth whereof yt ys made.

There is no need to doubt that he was in perfect health, for he was not the sort of man to defer the making of his will until he was on his deathbed, and since his retirement his worldly activities had been largely a preparation for this: the sale of his shares in the Globe, the Blackfriars theatre, and the King's company, his investment in the Blackfriars gatehouse, the securing of his titles to his property, and the agreement with Replingham safeguarding the income from his tithes. It was not for himself that he was doing this, but for his posterity, for the founding of a family had become almost an obsession, and what would have gone to Hamnet was to go to Susanna and her eldest, and yet unborn, son.

The draft was ready for signing after the wedding, but for some reason or other, perhaps the illness of either Judith or Thomas, it had to be postponed. Unfortunately the season when marriages were prohibited without special licence began on 28 January and lasted until 6 April, and it looks as though Thomas, rather than wait for nearly three months or pay for the expensive licence, decided to take the risk of discovery by the Bishop of Worcester, and on 10 February 1616 the marriage was celebrated in the parish church – 'Tho Queeny tow Judith Shakspere' – presumably by the easy-going vicar John Rogers. A local informer, however, one William Nixon, reported the irregularity, and the young couple were summoned to Worcester; they did not go, nor did they appear after a second summons, and as a result, not only had they to pay the licence fee and a fine of 7s., but they were excommunicated as well. It was an inauspicious start to their married life, a humiliation that Shakespeare would not appreciate, and Thomas must have gone down in his estimation for his mismanagement of the affair.

The will remained unsigned, probably because Shakespeare went up to London shortly after the wedding. For the last ten years Ben Jonson had supplied the principal entertainment at the Revels with his masques – his latest one, *The Golden Age Restored*, had proved so popular that it was twice performed in January – and his position at Court had just been officially recognized by the King, who granted him a pension of a hundred marks a year, so making him in all but name the first Poet Laureate of England. Shakespeare would wish to celebrate the occasion with his old friend and the other poets of the Mermaid fraternity, Drayton, Donne, Fletcher, and Beaumont among others, particularly as the folio edition of Jonson's works was also on the point of publication. Perhaps they over-celebrated, for forty-six years later the Vicar of Stratford, John Ward, noted in his diary: 'Shakespear, Drayton, and Ben Jhonson, had a merry meeting, and itt seems drank too hard, for Shakespear died of a feavour there contracted.' Ward was probably right, for he had his information from Judith, then an old lady of seventy-seven, and if anybody knew what happened to her father at this critical period of her wedding it was she. Perhaps the same fate overtook Beaumont, for he died, aged only thirty-two, at the beginning of March, and if Shakespeare rode the ninety miles from London to Stratford at about the same time he may have been a very sick man when he reached New Place and the ministrations of John Hall.

On 25 March he called in Collins again and revised his will, the main alterations referring to Judith and her husband, which necessitated the rewriting of the first page. When it was finished he signed each of the three sheets: 'William Shakspere', 'Willm̃ Shakspere', and finally, 'By me William Shakspeare'. The witnesses were Francis Collins, Juline Shaw, John Robinson,* Hamnet Sadler, and Robert Whatcott; the executors John and Susanna Hall; the overseers 'Thomas Russell Esquier & ffrauncis Collins gent'.

Minor bequests were: to the poor of Stratford £10, to Thomas Combe his sword, to Thomas Russell £5, to Francis Collins £13 6s. 8d., to his godson William Walker 20s.; to

* Probably the John Robinson baptized at Stratford in 1589, and just possibly the tenant of Shakespeare's Blackfriars house.

Hamnet Sadler, William Reynolds, Anthony Nash, John Nash, and his 'ffellowes John Hemynge Richard Burbage & Henry Cundell 26s. 8d. A peece to buy them Ringes'. The last three were all who remained of the original fellowship of the Lord Chamberlain's company formed twenty-two years before, the men to whom he must have assigned the work that he himself would never finish, the preparation of his plays for publication in folio; and seven years later, when Burbage too was dead, the survivors described in their preface how they had 'scarce receiued from him a blot in his papers'.

The only mention of his wife is an addition made at the time of revision: 'Item I gyve vnto my wief my second best bed with the furniture', that is, the hangings. There is nothing surprising about this; Anne was legally entitled to live at New Place and to a life interest in one third of her husband's estate, excluding the Blackfriars house, so that there was no need to make special provision for her. But apparently the bed had a sentimental value, and she asked for it when the revision was made. Moreover, the will is a very matter-of-fact document without any terms of affection; it is 'my sister Joan', and 'my daughter Susanna', not 'my dear sister', 'my beloved daughter', and in the same way there is no term of endearment for his wife.

To his sister, Joan Hart, he left £20, the Henley Street house for life, and all his 'wearing Apparrell'; it would come in useful for her growing sons, to whom he also left £5 apiece.

To Judith he gave £100 as her marriage portion, another £50 in consideration of her surrendering to Susanna her rights in the Chapel Lane cottage, and the interest on a further £150 until her husband had settled land on her of an equal value, when it was to be paid to him. She was also to have his 'broad silver gilt bole'.

His granddaughter Elizabeth Hall was to have all his plate with the exception of Judith's bowl.

All the rest of his 'goodes chattels Leases plate Jewels & householde stuffe whatsoever' went to Susanna and John Hall. Then, the vital item: he left all his real estate, all his houses and land, to Susanna, or rather entailed them upon Susanna and her sons, failing whom Elizabeth and her sons, failing whom Judith and her sons, 'and for defalt of such issue to the Right heires of me the saied William Shackspere for ever'. And so 'the newe place wherein I nowe dwell', the two Henley Street houses, the Blackfriars house, the Old Stratford estate, and all his 'barnes stables Orchardes gardens landes tenements & hereditamentes' went to Susanna, and were to be handed on from eldest son to eldest son in perpetuity. It was a vain provision, and Shakespeare's ambition to establish a family foundered. Susanna had no more children, Judith's three sons all died young, Elizabeth, though twice married, was childless, and when she died in 1670 the line of Shakespeare was extinct.

Shakespeare lived for another month after signing his will on 25 March. In the middle of April his brother-in-law William Hart died. A week later, in spite of all the skill and ministrations of his son-in-law, the poet too was gone. He died on 23 April, possibly his fifty-second birthday, and on the 25th was buried within the chancel of the decaying church of the Holy Trinity.

THE SHAKESPEARE FAMILY

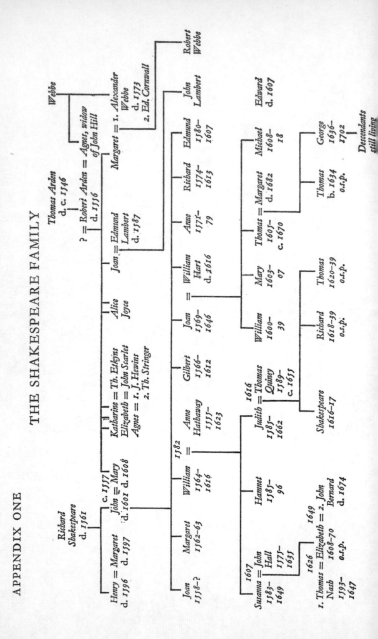

APPENDIX TWO

INTER-RELATIONSHIP OF THE FAMILIES OF

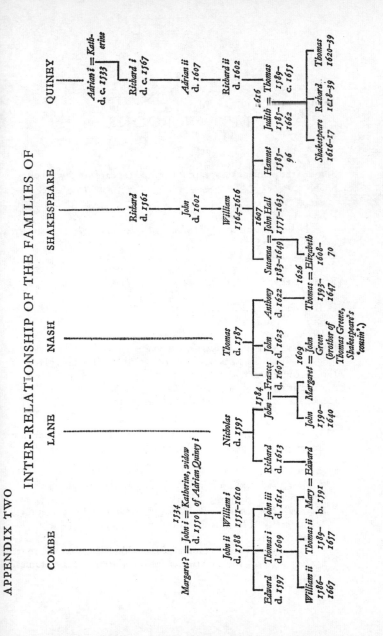

LIST OF BOOKS

*

Some of the principal biographies of Shakespeare are given below:

Nicholas Rowe, *Some Account of the Life of Mr William Shakespear*, 1709.

Edmond Malone, *The Life of William Shakspeare*, 1821.

J. O. Halliwell-Phillipps, *Outlines of the Life of Shakespeare*, 2 volumes, 1887.

Georg Brandes, *William Shakespeare*, 2 volumes, 1897.

Sidney Lee, *A Life of William Shakespeare*, 1898.

Frank Harris, *The Man Shakespeare and his Tragic Life Story*, 1909.

Joseph Quincy Adams, *A Life of William Shakespeare*, 1923.

E. K. Chambers, *William Shakespeare: A Study of Facts and Problems*, 2 volumes, 1930.

J. Dover Wilson, *The Essential Shakespeare*, 1932.

Peter Alexander, *Shakespeare's Life and Art*, 1938.

Edgar I. Fripp, *Shakespeare, Man and Artist*, 2 volumes, 1938.

Ivor Brown, *Shakespeare*, 1949.

Marchette Chute, *Shakespeare of London*, 1949.

Hesketh Pearson, *A Life of Shakespeare*, 1949.

A. L. Rowse, *William Shakespeare*, 1953

This is a list of some of the most important books to which any modern biographer must be indebted:

Baldwin, T. W.
  William Shakspere's Petty School, University of Illinois Press, Urbana, 1943.
  William Shakspere's Small Latine & Lesse Greeke, 2 volumes, University of Illinois Press, Urbana, 1944.
Chambers, E. K.
  The Elizabethan Stage, 4 volumes, Clarendon Press, Oxford, 1923.
  William Shakespeare: A Study of Facts and Problems, 2 volumes, Clarendon Press, Oxford, 1930.

288

Fripp, E. I.
Master Richard Quyny, Oxford University Press, 1924.
Shakespeare's Stratford, Oxford University Press, 1928.
Shakespeare, Man and Artist, 2 volumes, Oxford University Press, 1938.
Hotson, J. L.
Shakespeare versus Shallow, Nonesuch Press, London, 1931.
I, William Shakespeare, Jonathan Cape, London, 1937.
Shakespeare's Sonnets Dated, and Other Essays, Rupert Hart-Davis, London, 1949.
The First Night of 'Twelfth Night', Rupert Hart-Davis, London, 1954.
Shakespeare's Wooden O, Rupert Hart-Davis, London, 1959.
Shakespeare Survey: An Annual Survey of Shakespearian Study & Production, edited by Allardyce Nicoll, Cambridge University Press, 1948 onwards.
Shakespeare Quarterly: the organ of the Shakespeare Association of America, edited by J. G. McManaway, New York, 1949 onwards.

INDEX

*

Some other books published by
Penguins are described on
the following pages

SHAKESPEARE'S TRAGEDIES

AN ANTHOLOGY OF MODERN CRITICISM

Edited by Laurence D. Lerner

Shakespeare's tragedies have always been fertile acres for comment and criticism. The same dramas which inspired a Keats to write poetry appealed to A. C. Bradley – or to Ernest Jones, the psycho-analyst – as studies of character; and where the New Criticism has been principally interested in language and imagery, other critics in America have seen the plays as superb examples of plot and structure. Most of Aristotle's elements of tragedy have found their backers, and – as the editor points out in his introduction – these varying approaches to Shakespeare are by no means incompatible.

In this volume Laurence Lerner has assembled the best examples of the modern schools of criticism and arranged them according to the plays they deal with. With its 'Suggestions for further reading' and the general sections on tragedy, this is a book which will stimulate the serious reader and do much to illuminate Shakespearean drama.

THE AGE OF SHAKESPEARE

Edited by Boris Ford

The series of which this volume forms part is not a *Bradshaw* or a *Whitaker's Almanack* of information; nor has it been designed on the lines of the standard Histories of Literature. It is intended for those many thousands of general readers who accept with genuine respect what is known as our 'literary heritage', but who might none the less hesitate to describe intimately the work of such writers as Pope, George Eliot, Langland, Marvell, Yeats, Tourneur, Hopkins, Crabbe, or D. H. Lawrence, or to fit them into any larger pattern of growth and development. It is with such readers in mind that this guide to the history and traditions of our literature, this contour-map to the literary scene, has been planned. It attempts to draw up an ordered account of literature that is concerned, first and foremost, with value for the present, and this as a direct encouragement to people to read for themselves.

This volume covers the period of Shakespeare's own lifetime. It contains a long general survey of the English literary renaissance, and also an account of the social context of literature in the period. Then there follow a number of essays which consider in detail the work and importance of individual dramatists and poets and prose-writers, but above all the dramatists, for this was their age: five of the essays are devoted to Shakespeare's plays alone. Finally, this volume contains an appendix giving short author-biographies and, in each case, standard editions of authors' works, critical commentaries, and lists of books for further study and reference.